SEDONA
Realm of the Vortex

A Photographic Exploration

Scott Shaw

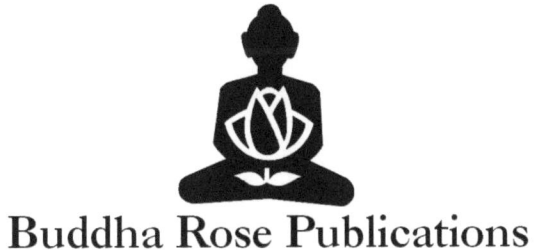

Buddha Rose Publications

Sedona: Realm of the Vortex
Copyright © 2012 by Scott Shaw
www.scottshaw.com
All Rights Reserved

No part of this book may be reproduced in any manner without the expressed written permission of the author or the publishing company.

First Edition 2012

ISBN: 1-877792-66-7
ISBN 13: 978-1-877792-66-3

Printed in the United States of America

10 9 8 7 6 5 4 3 2 1

Sedona
Realm of the Vortex

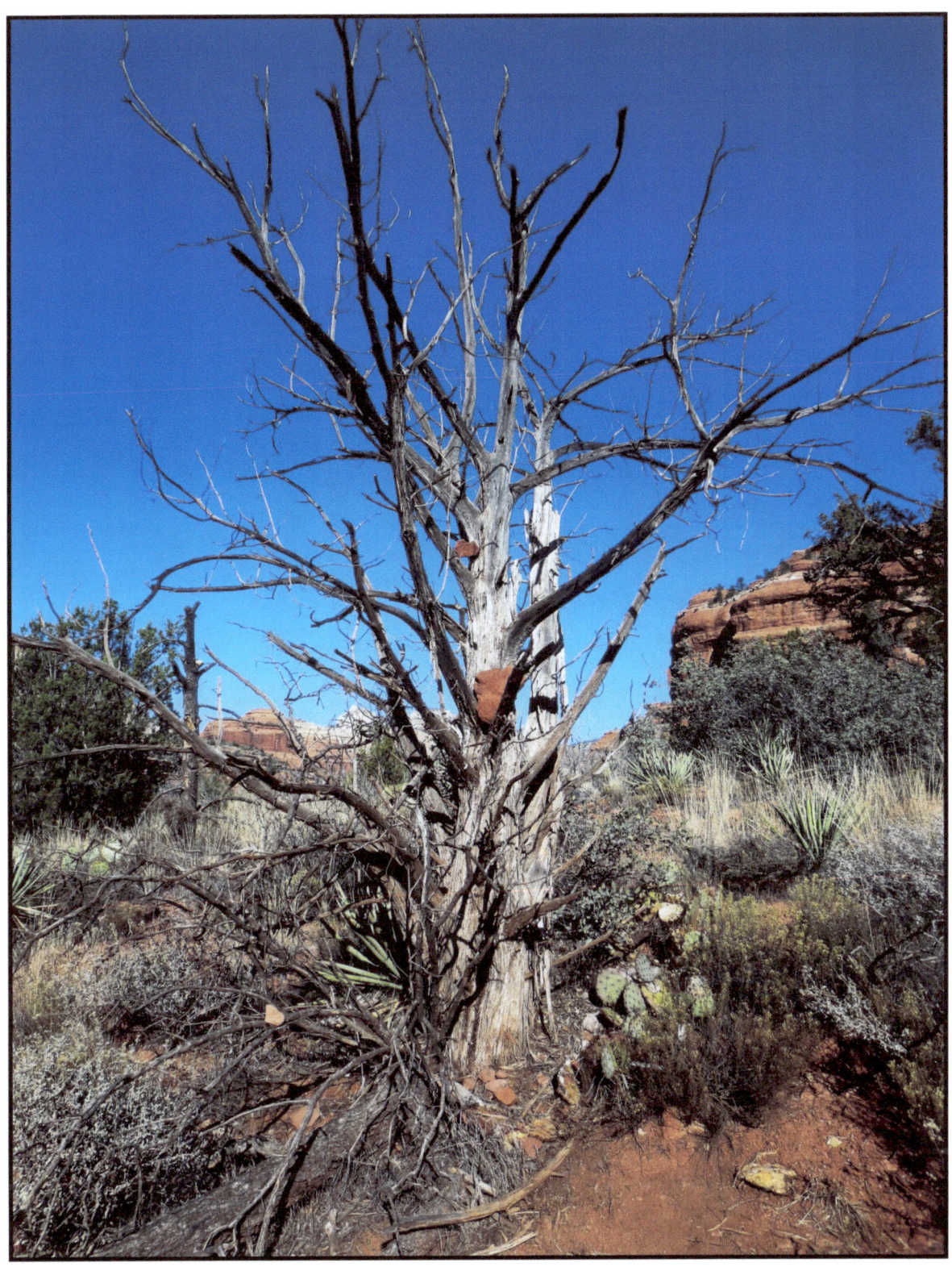

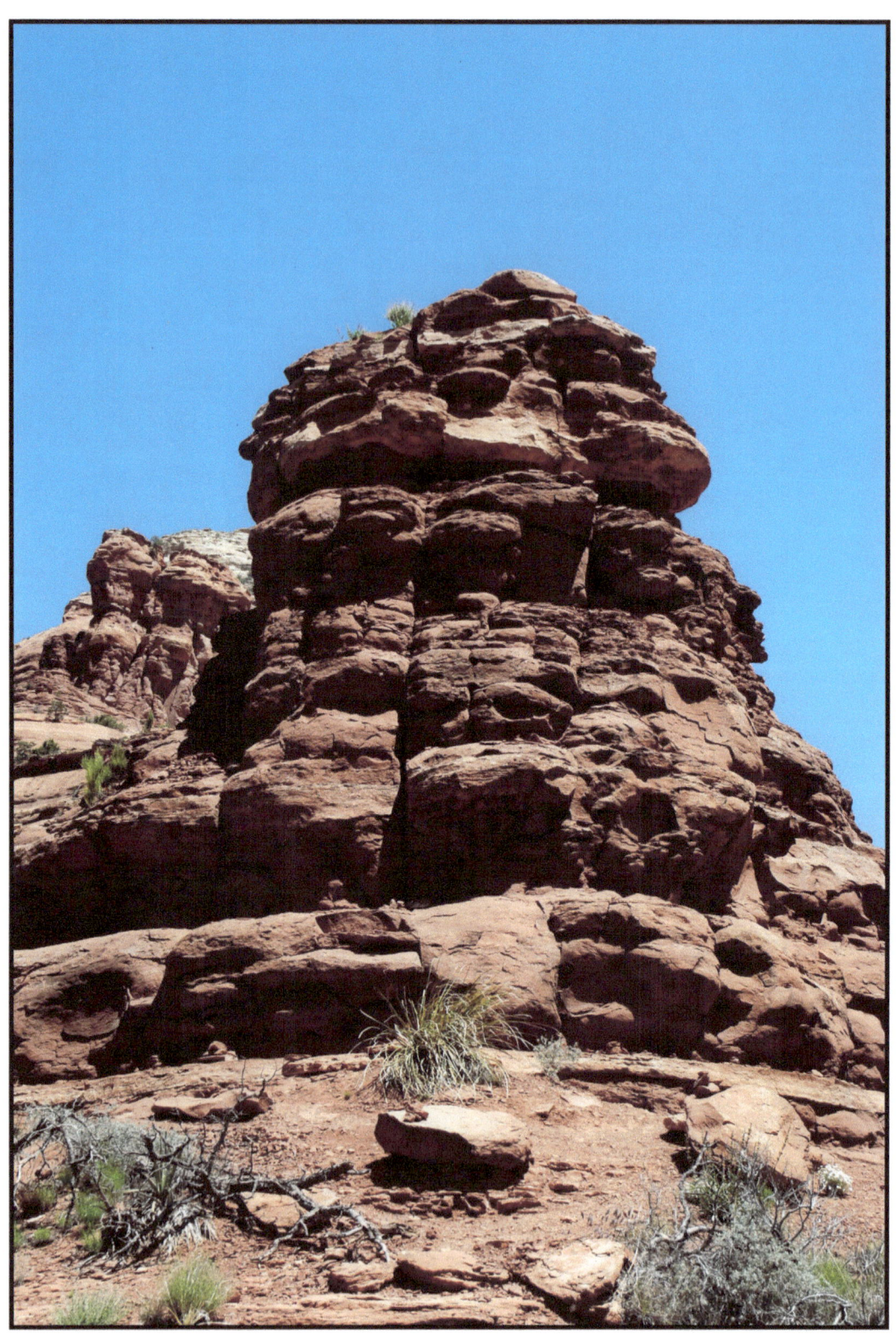

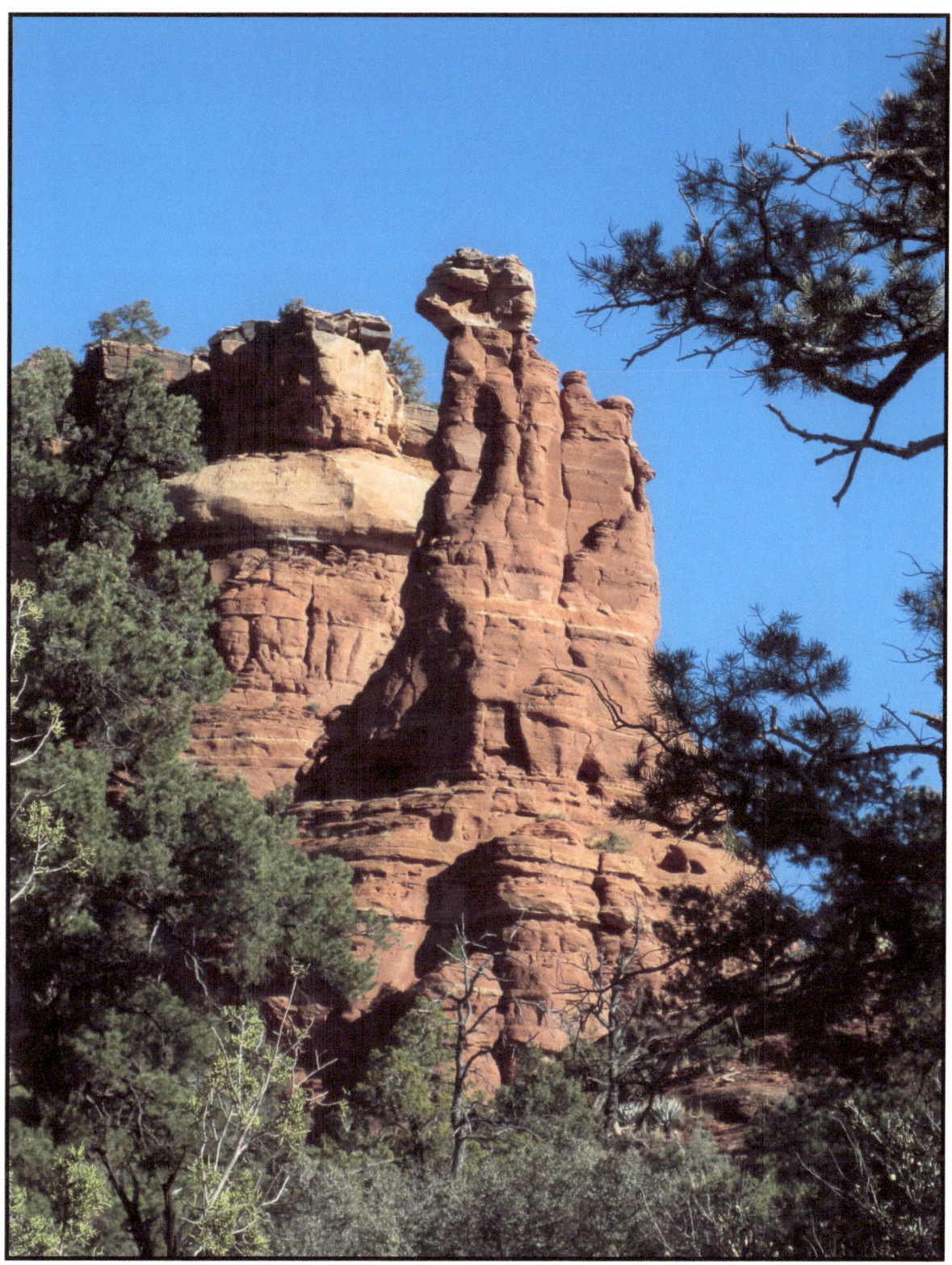

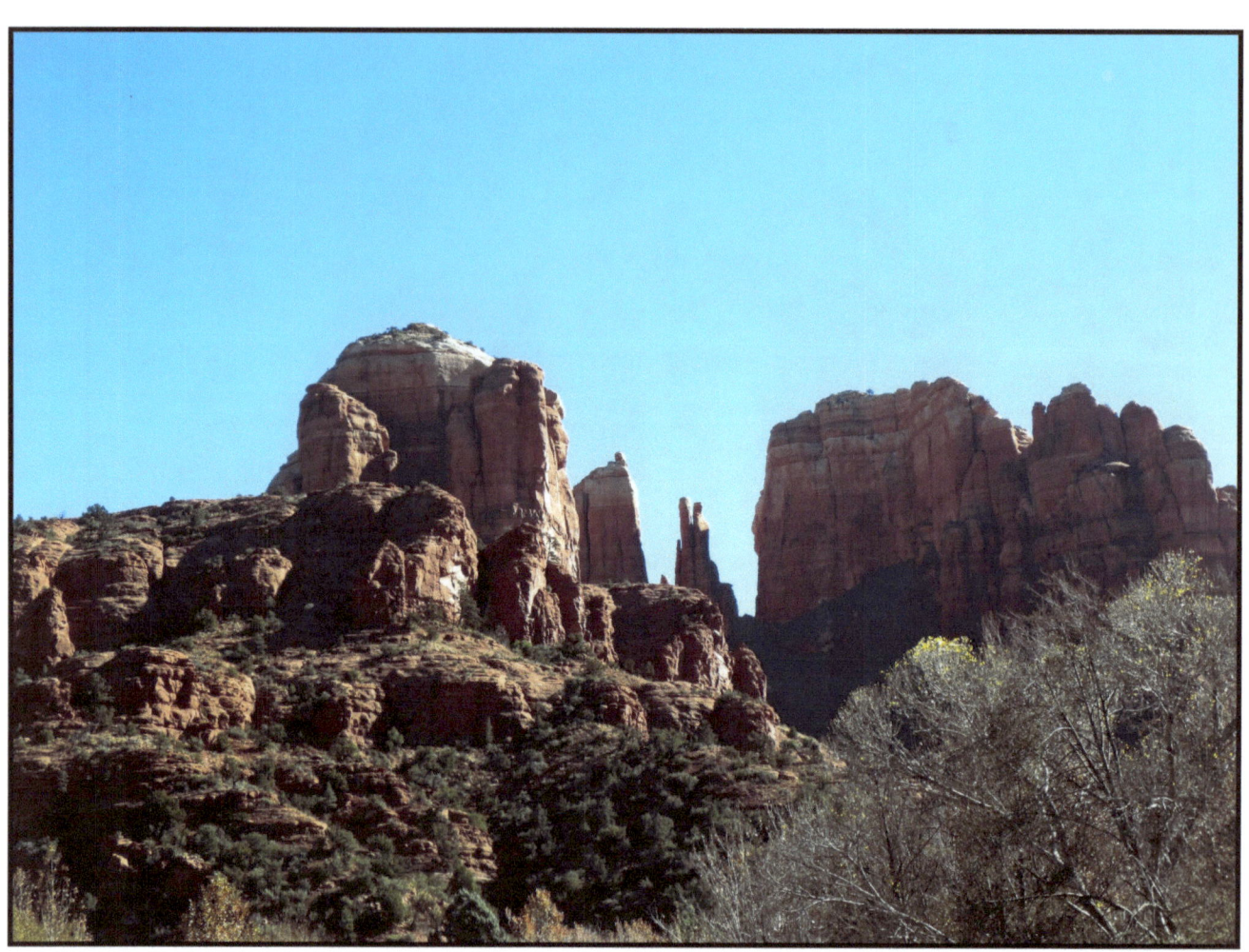

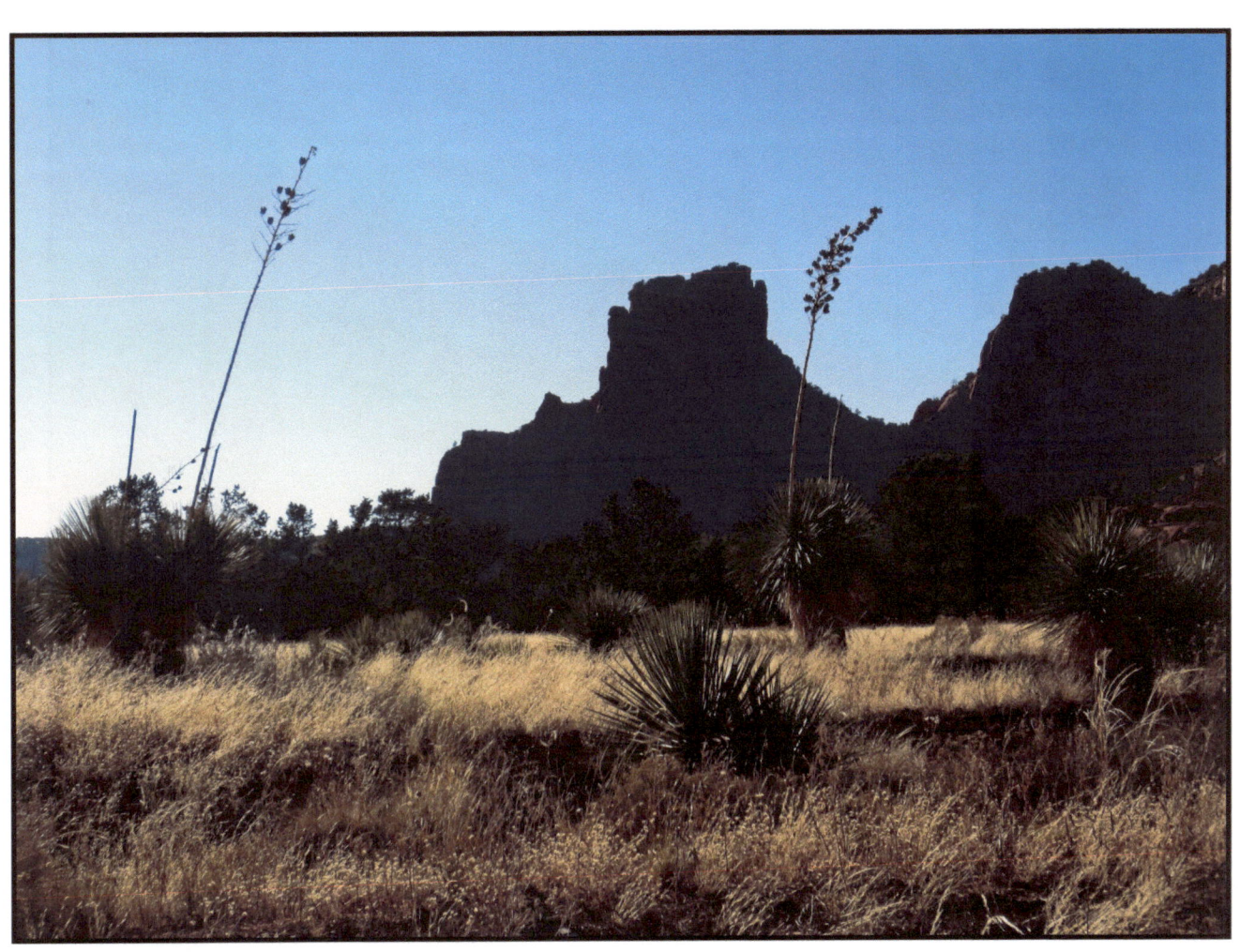

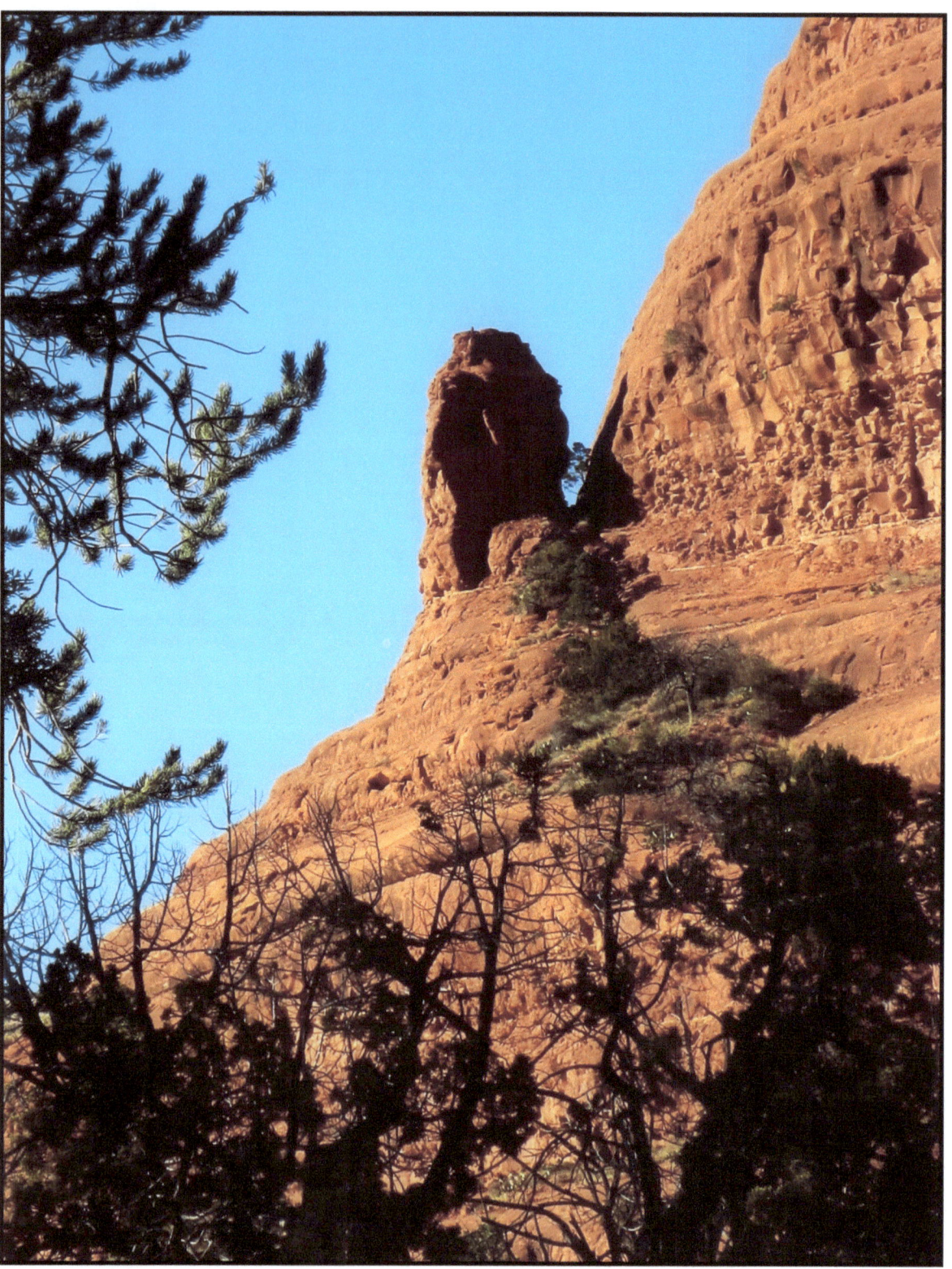

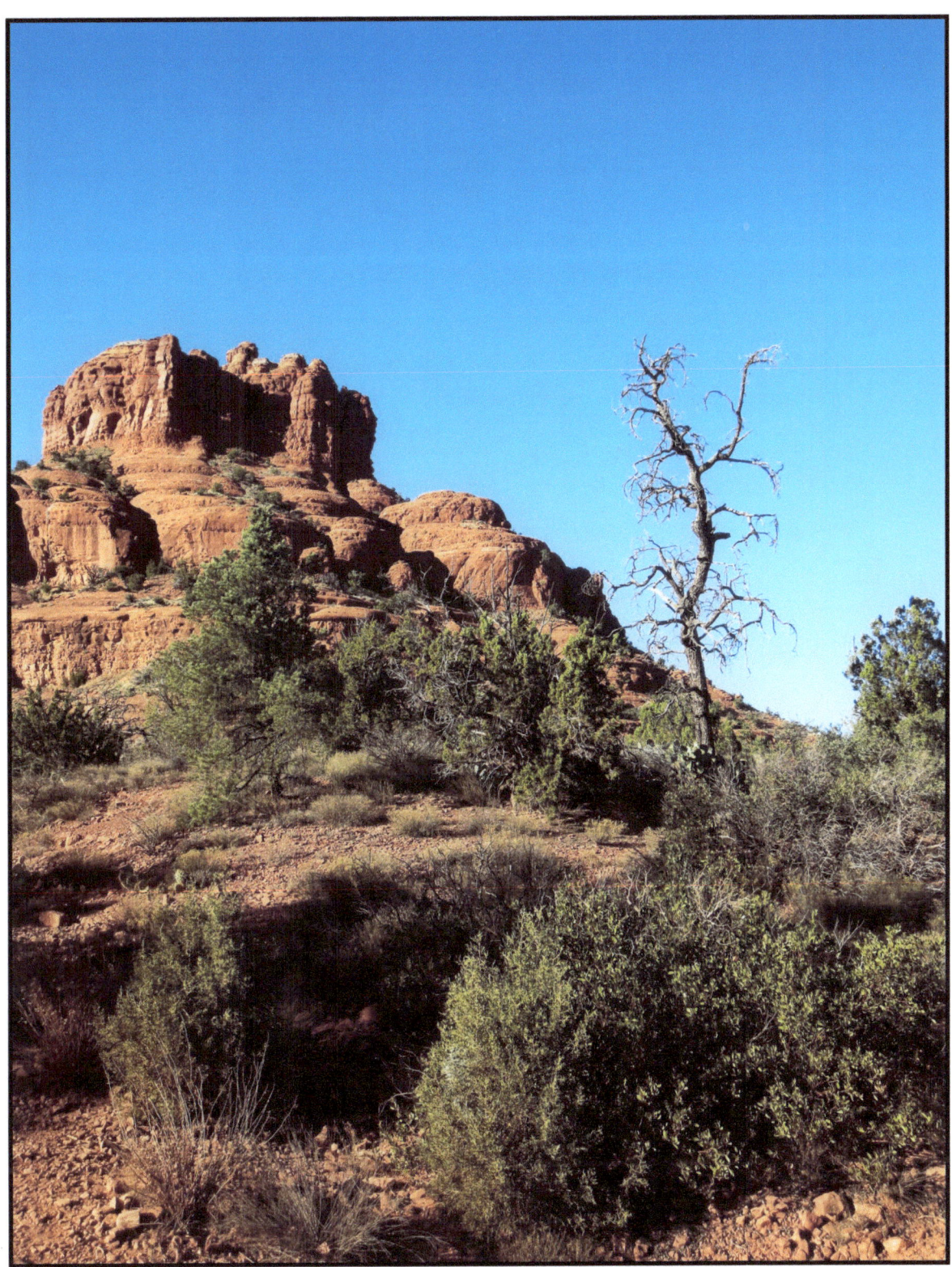

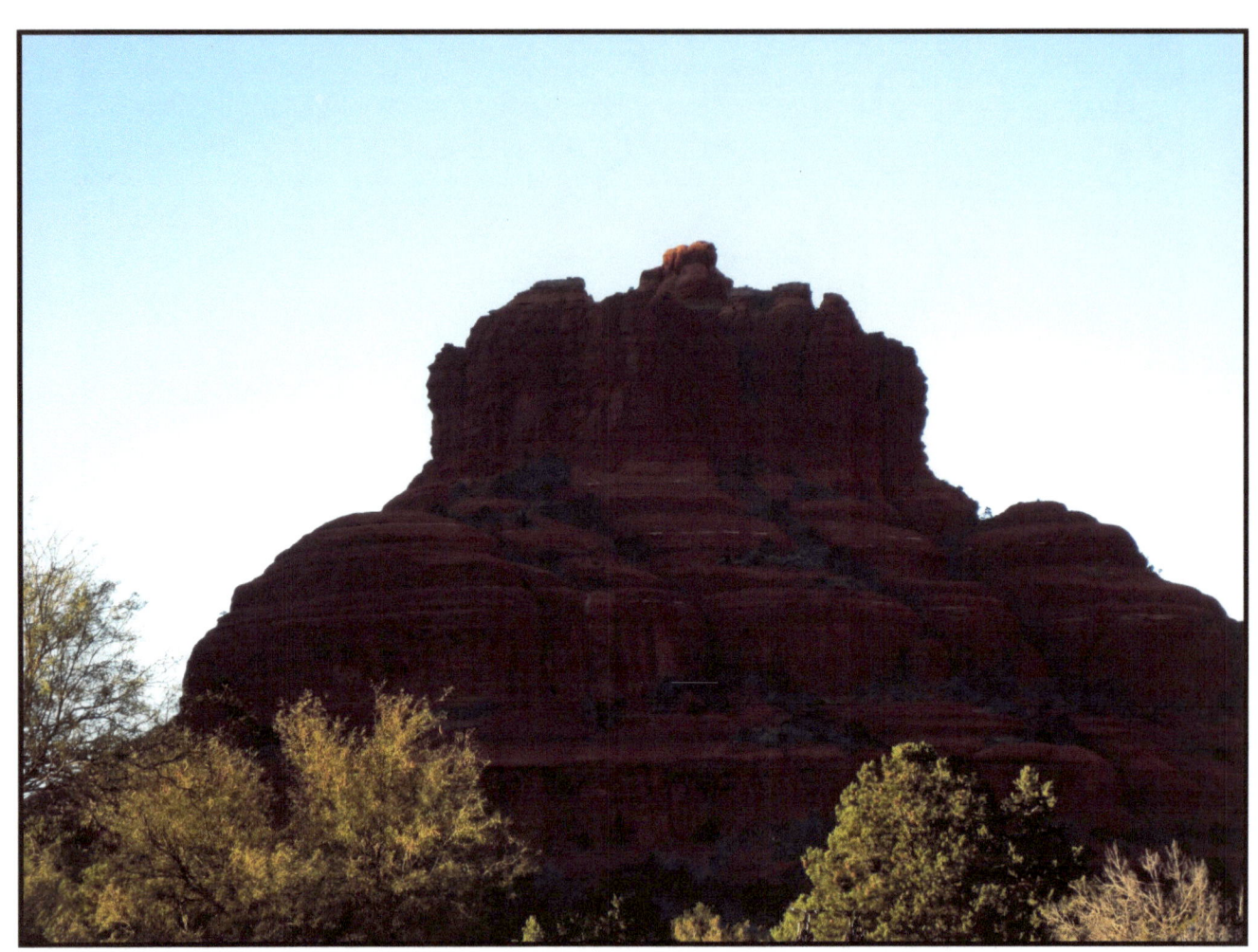

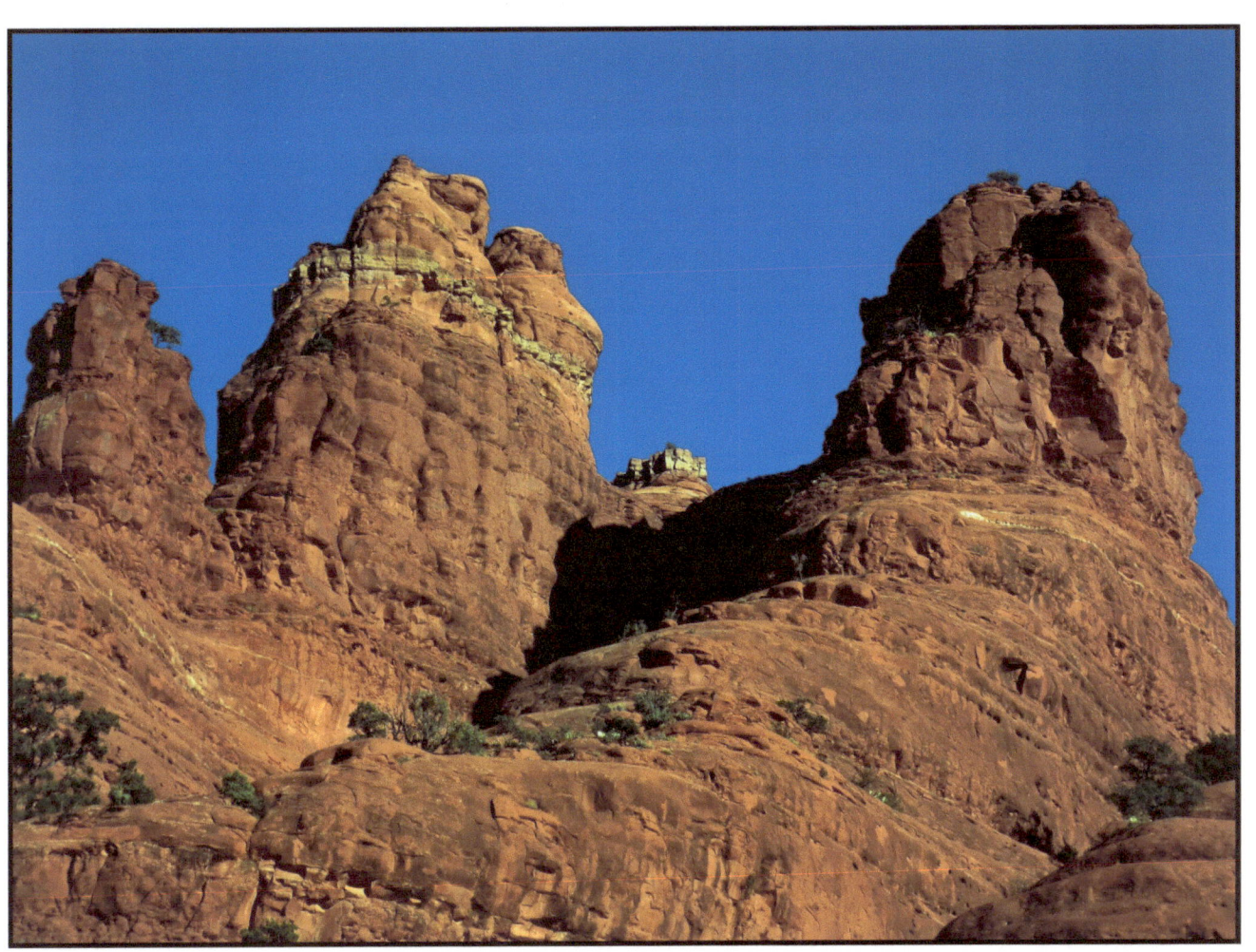

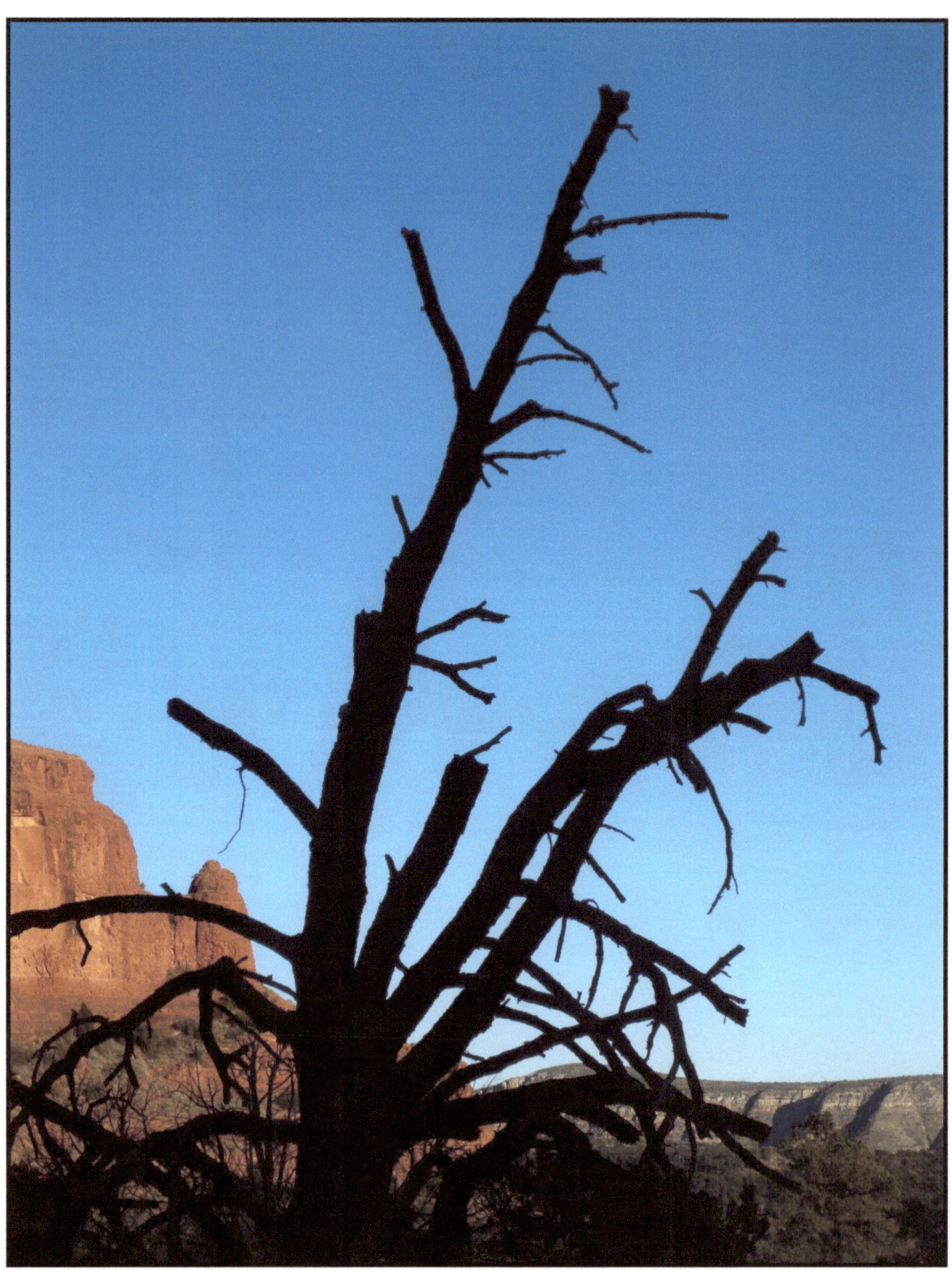

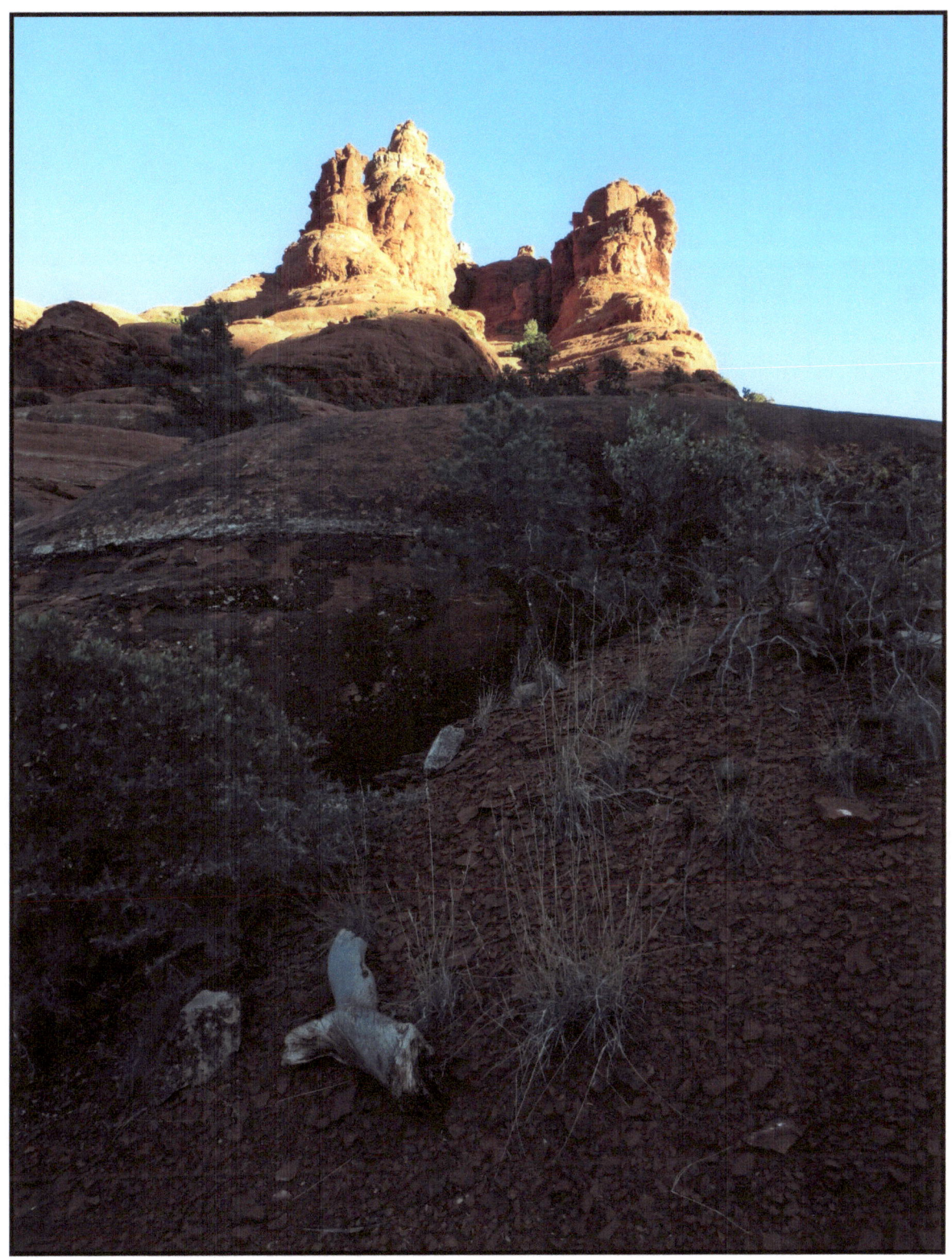

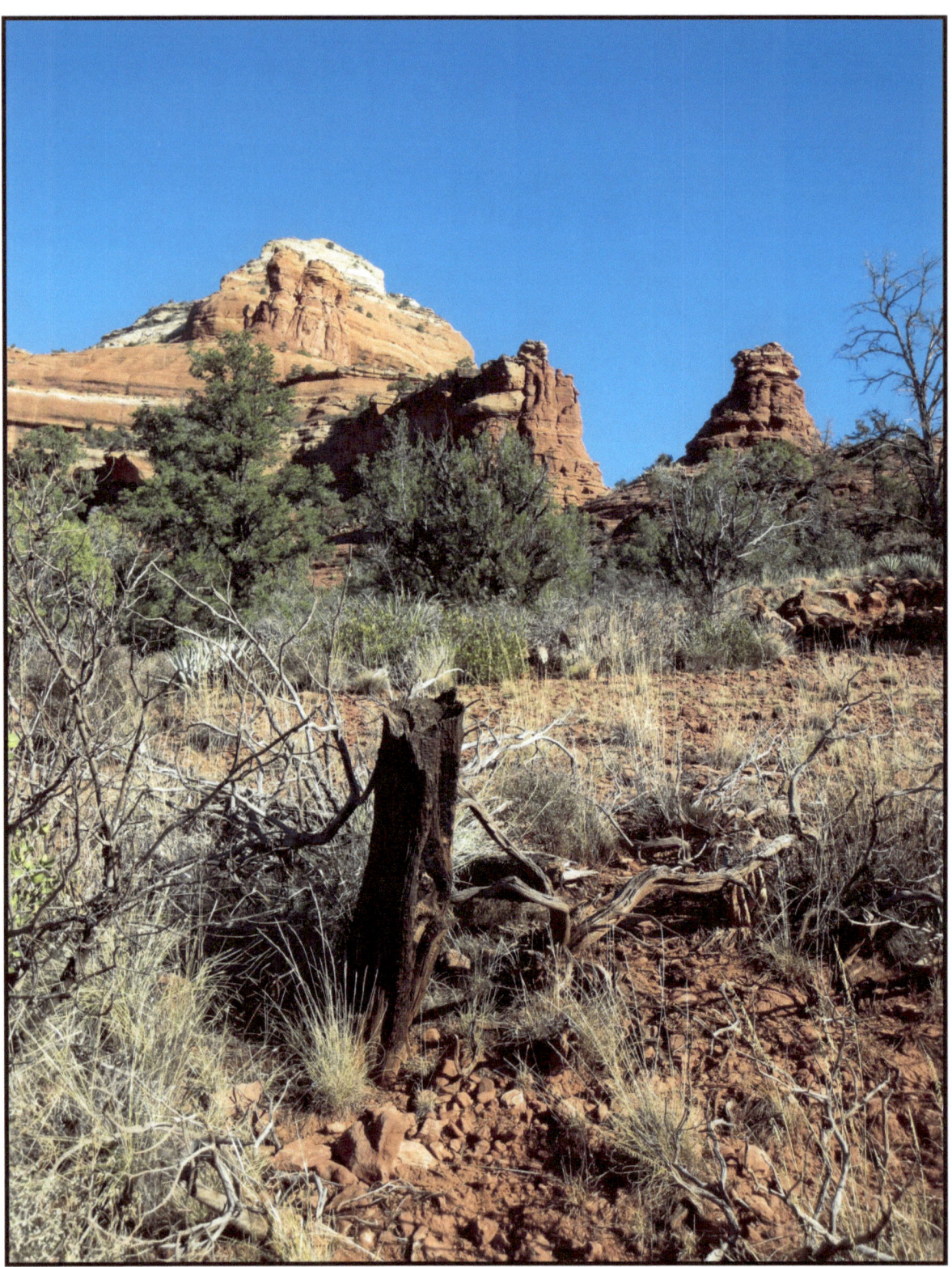

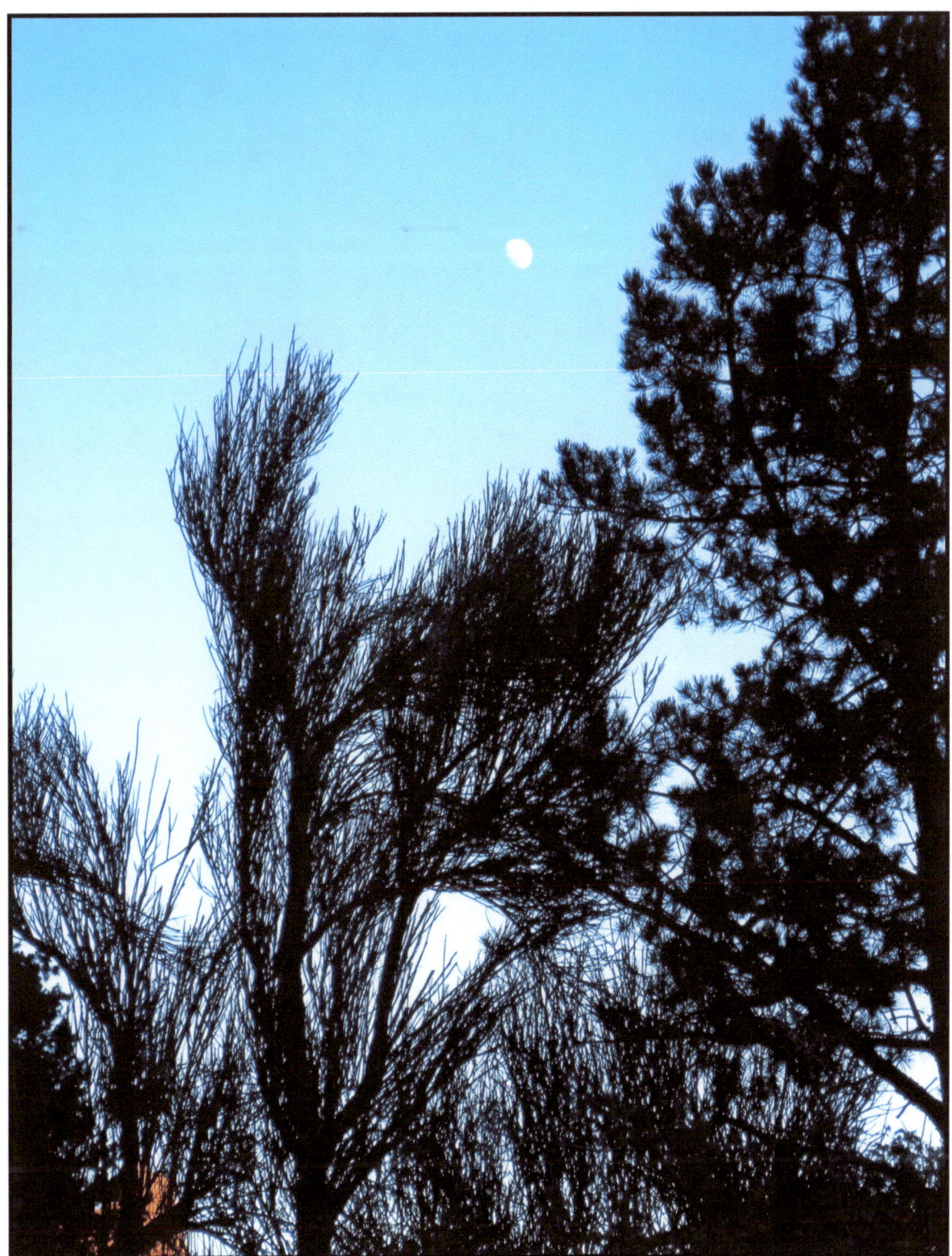

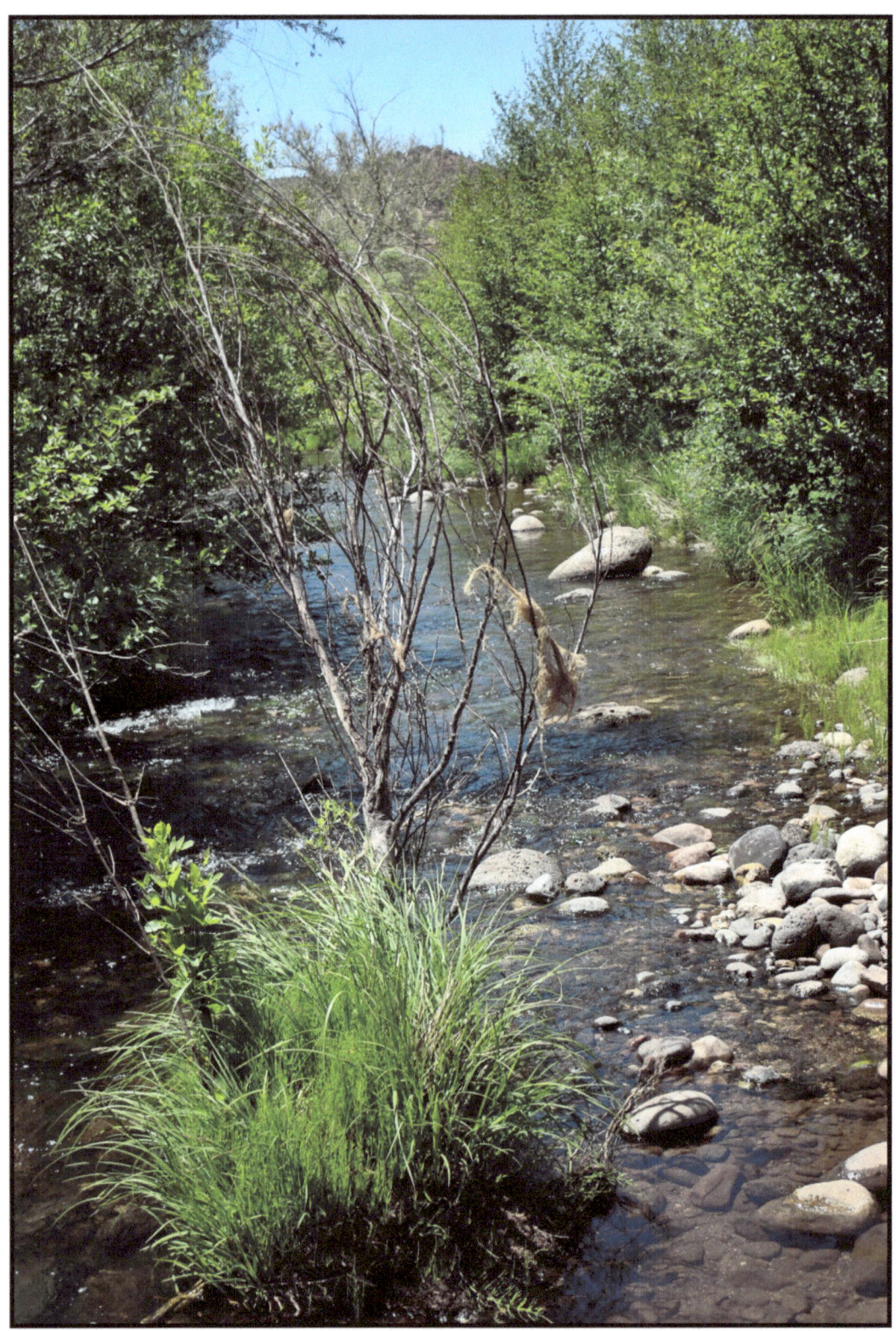

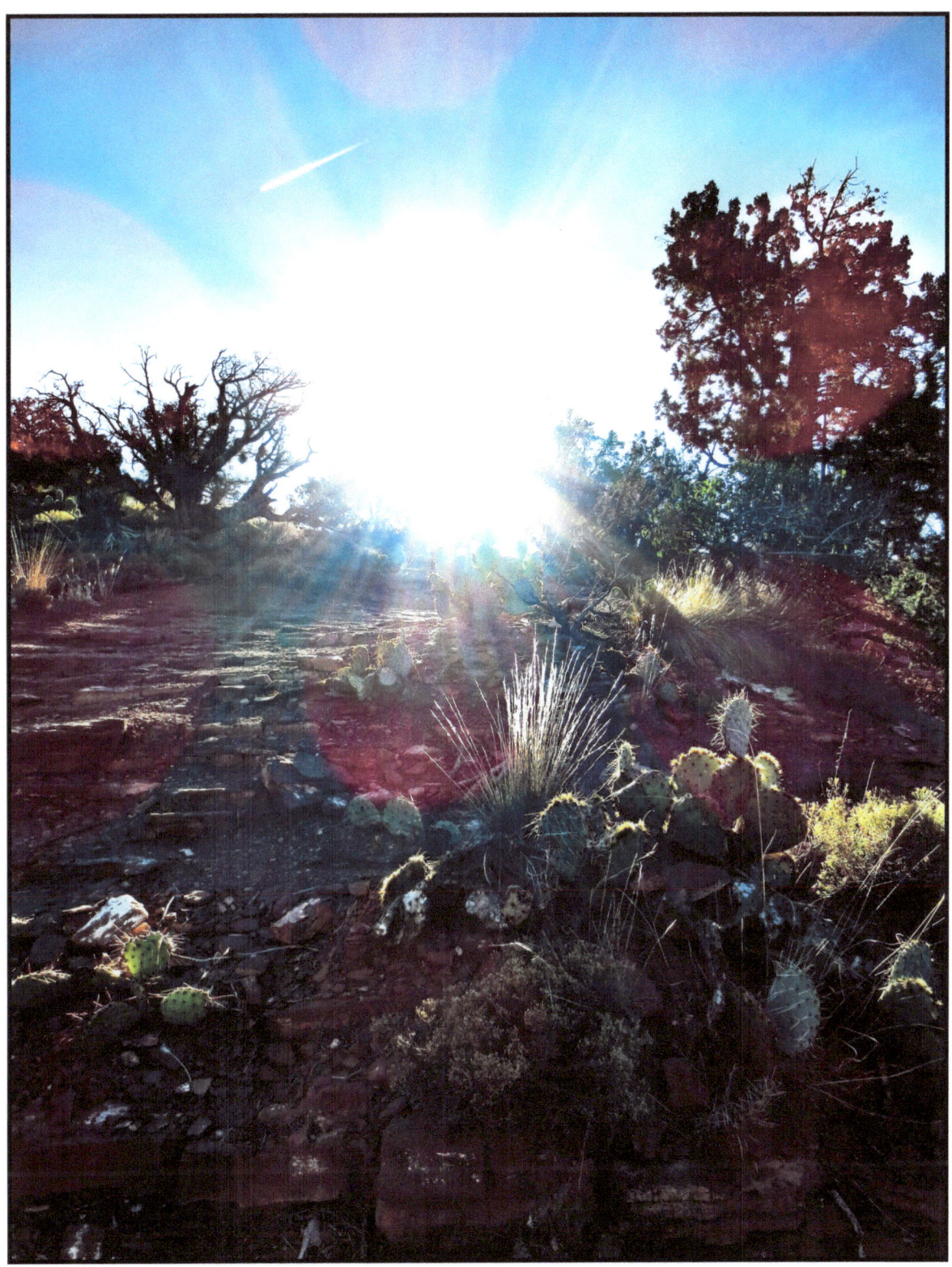

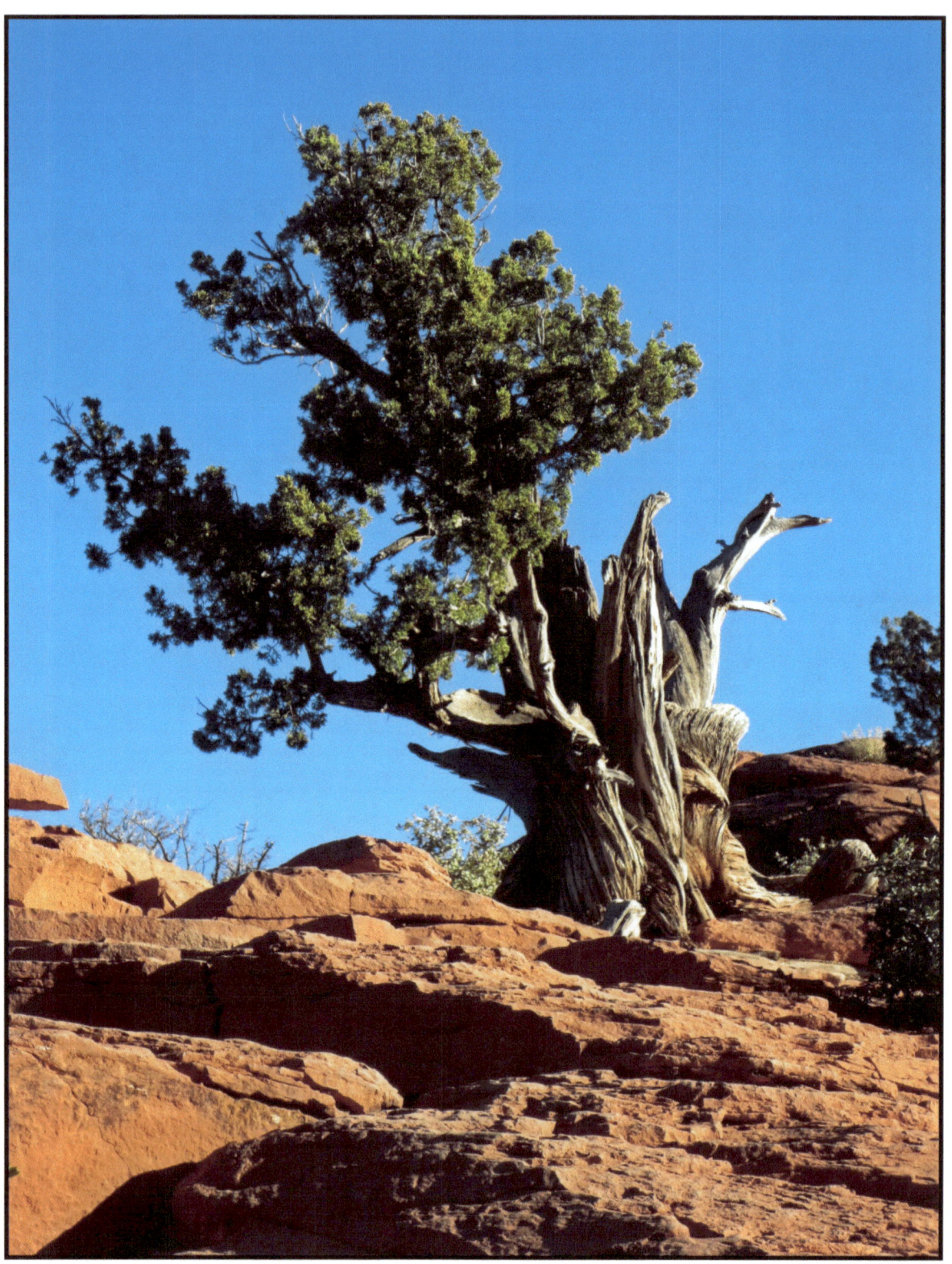

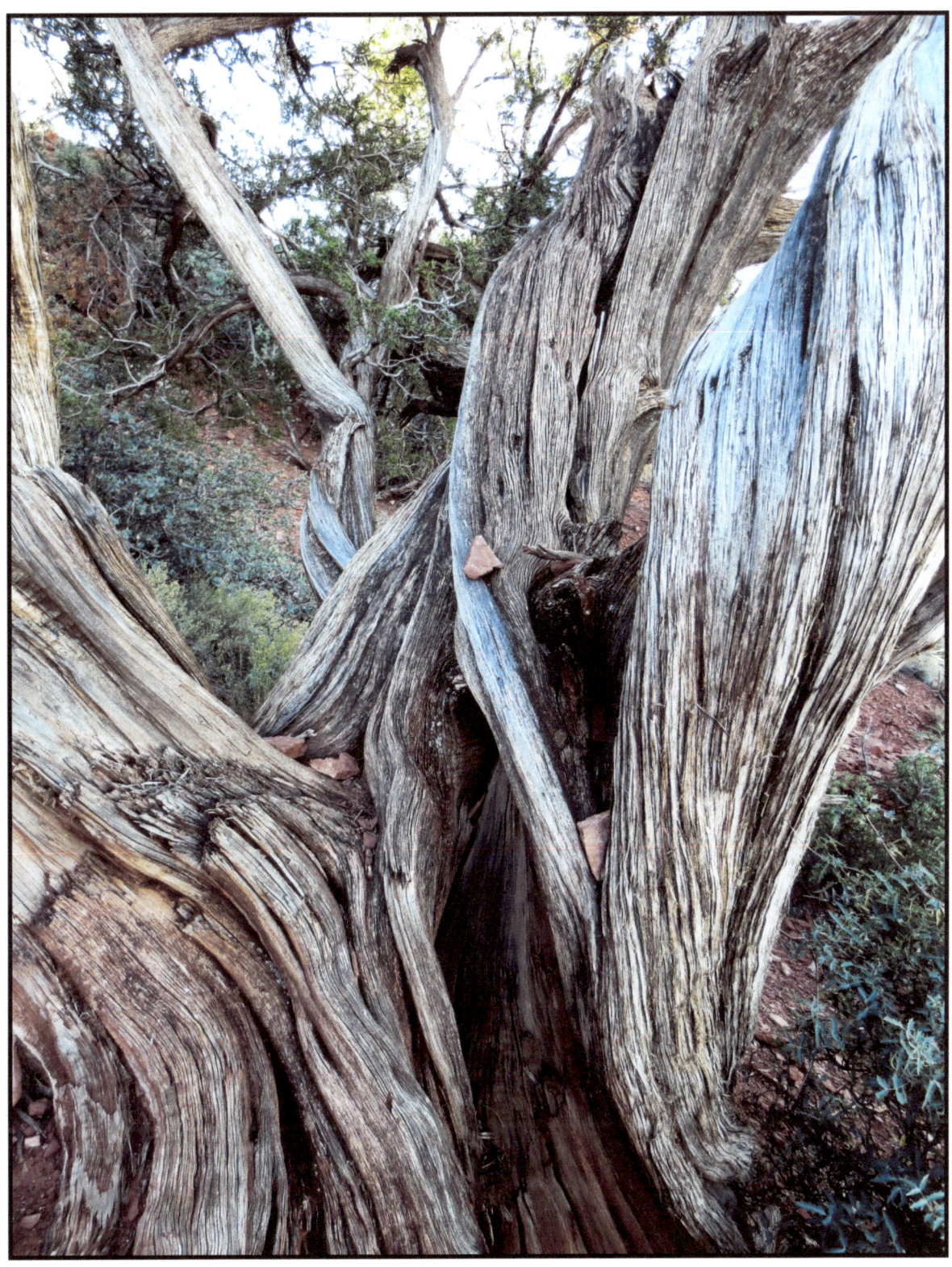

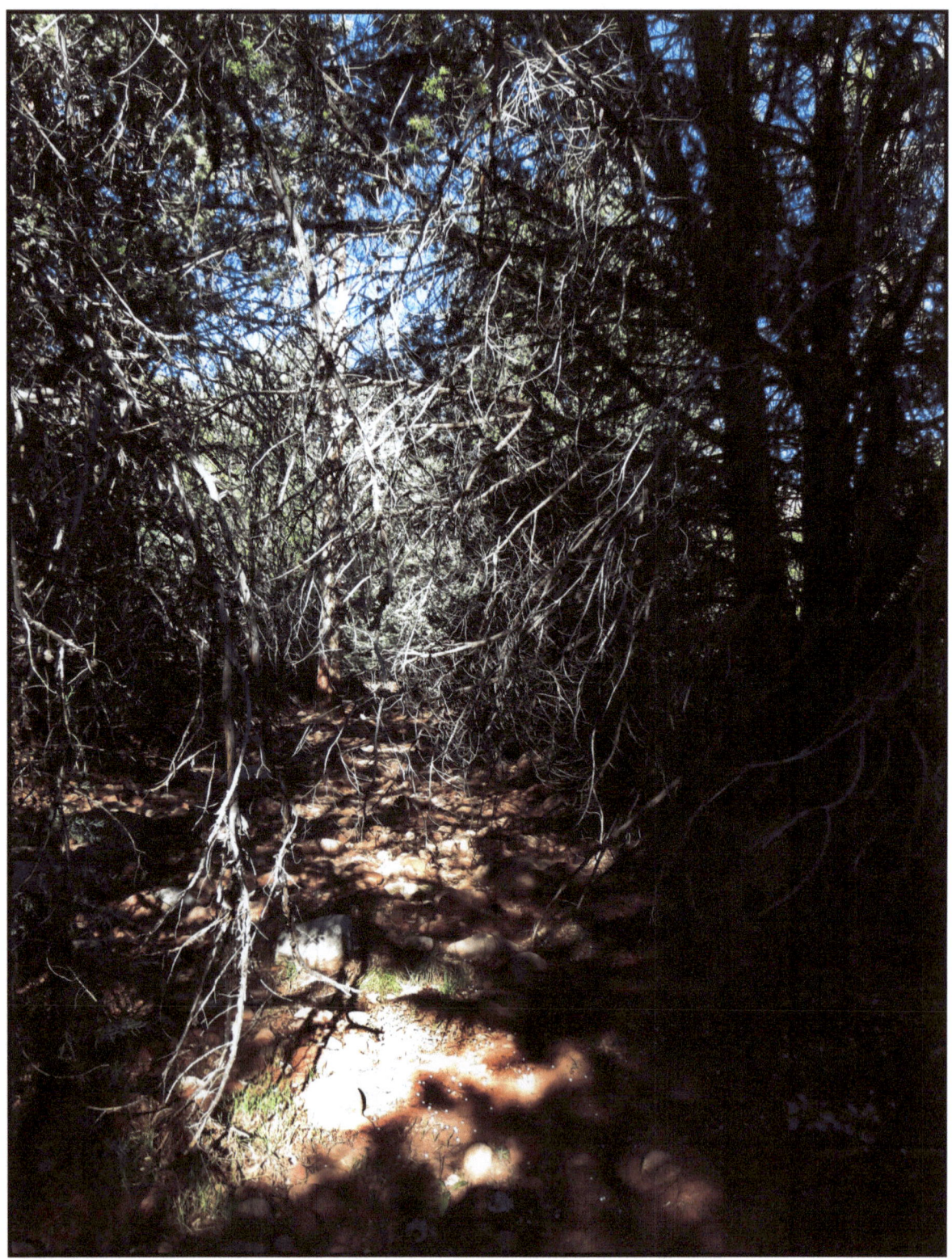

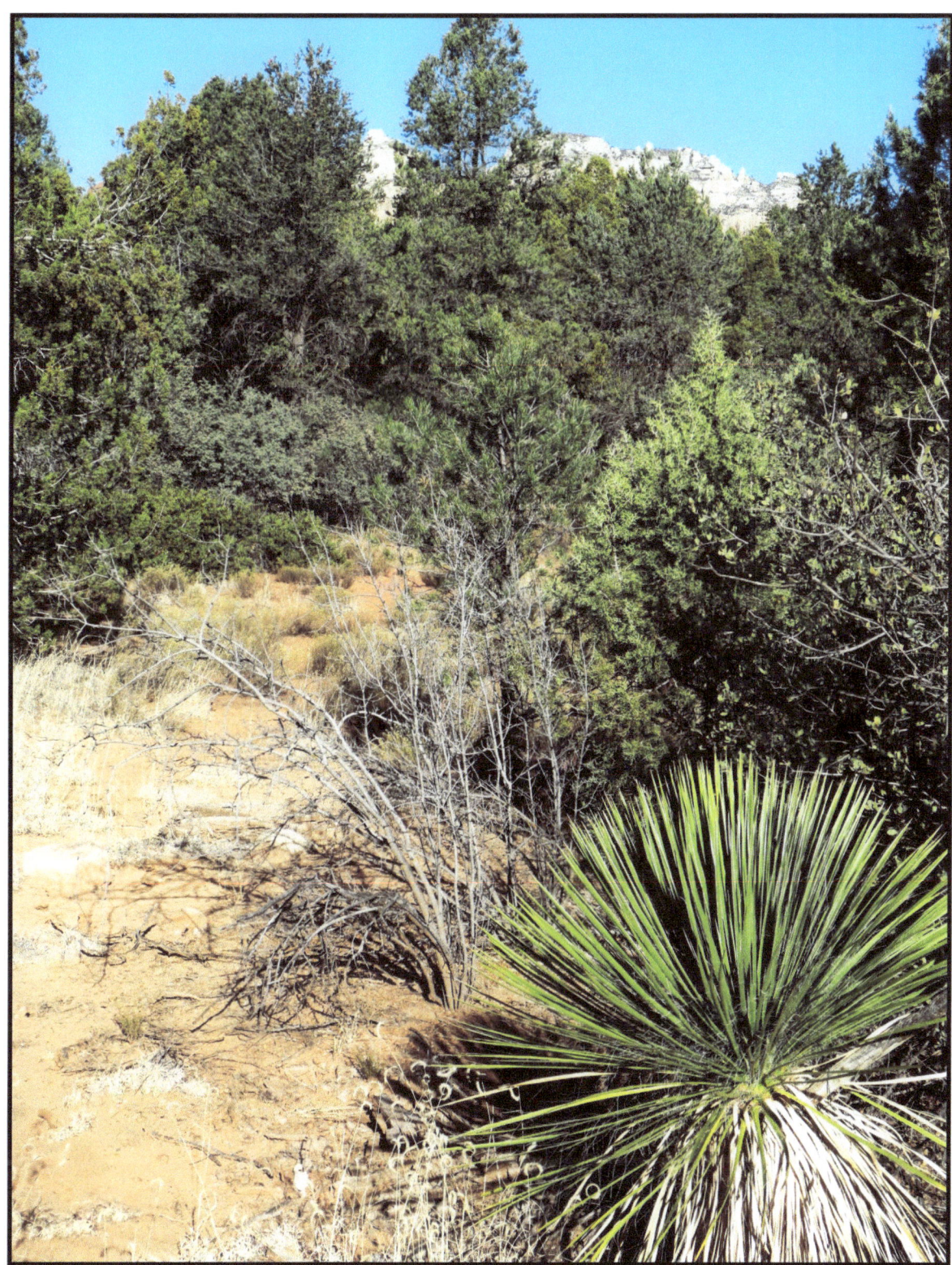

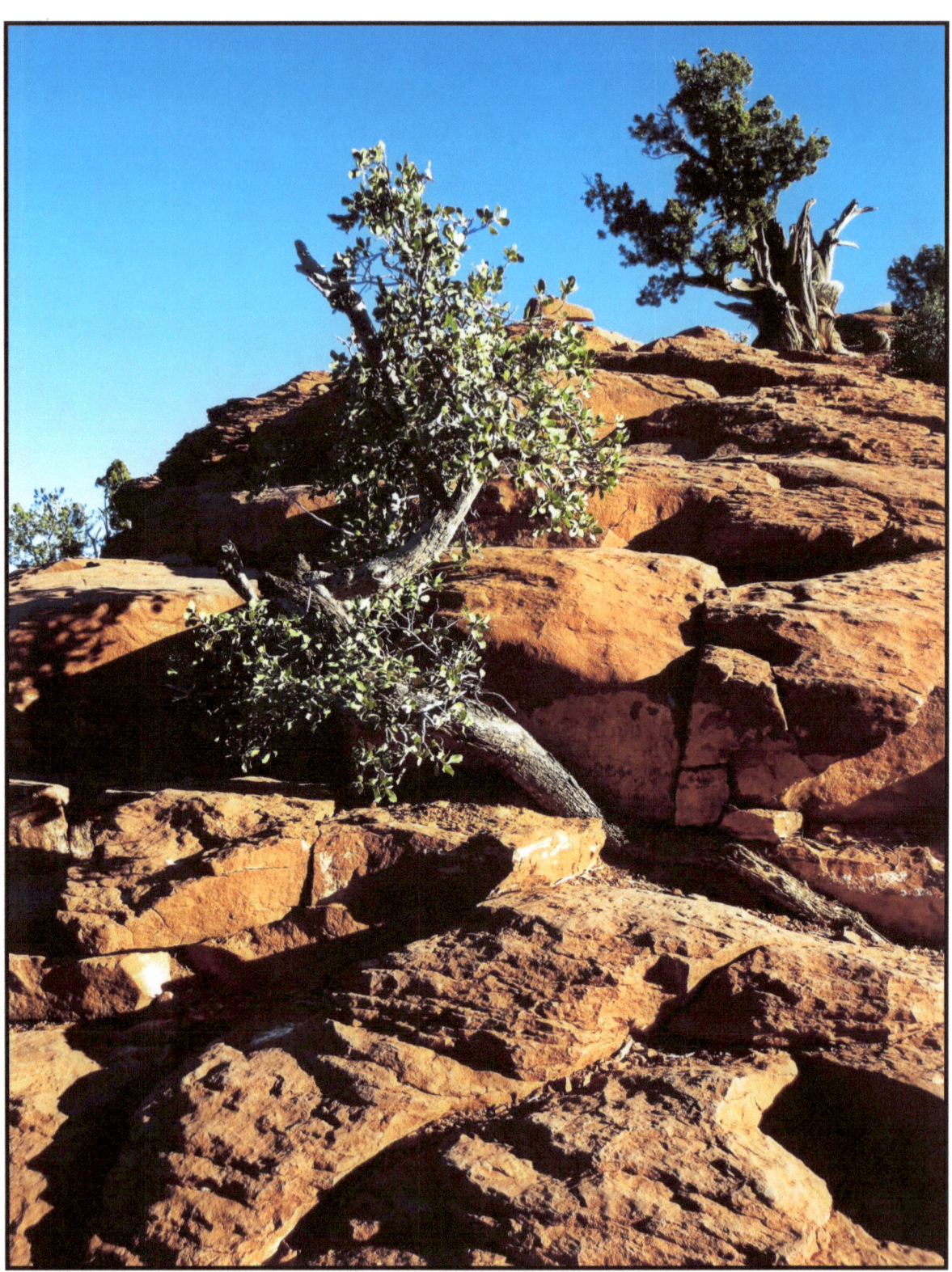

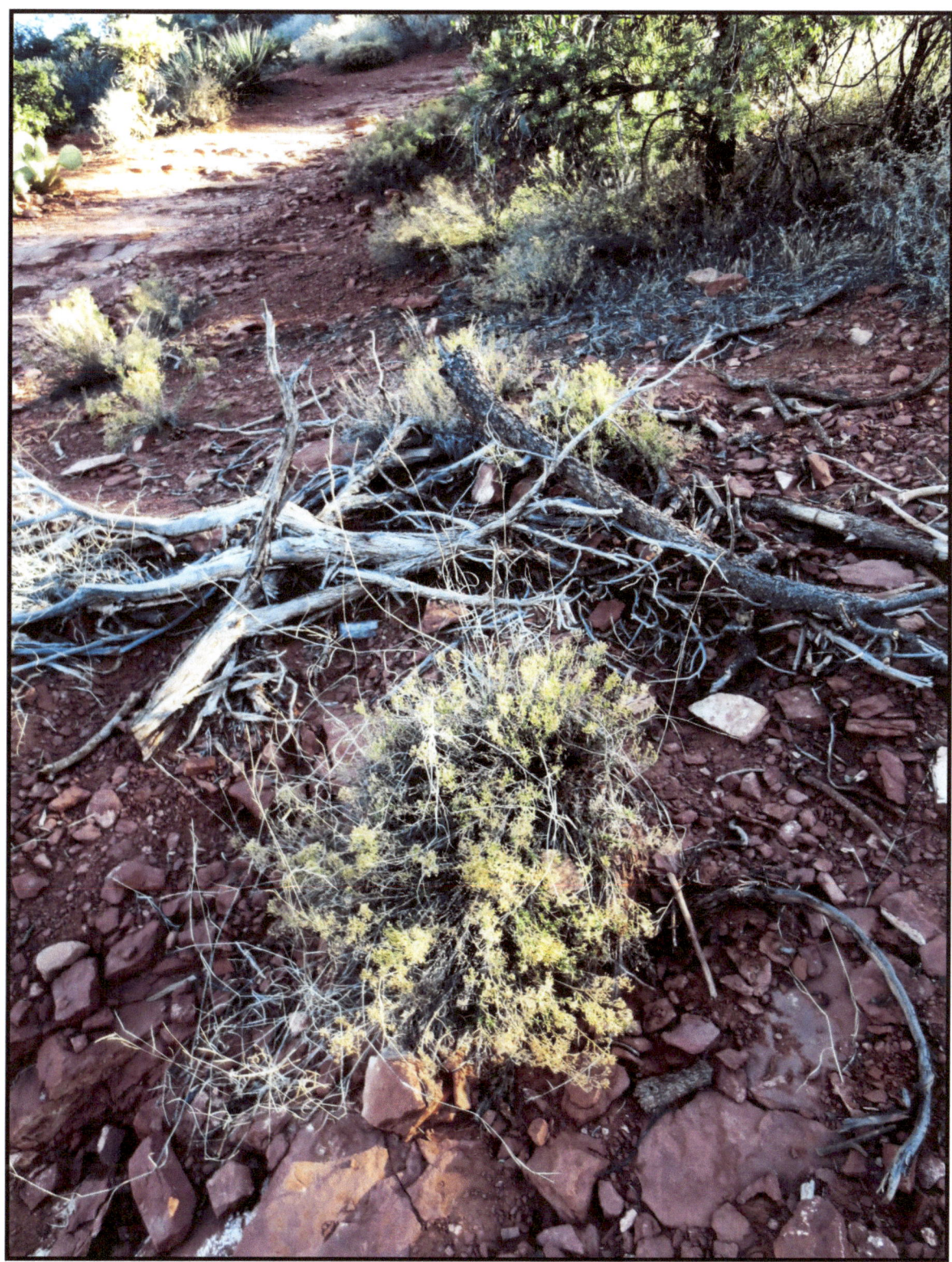

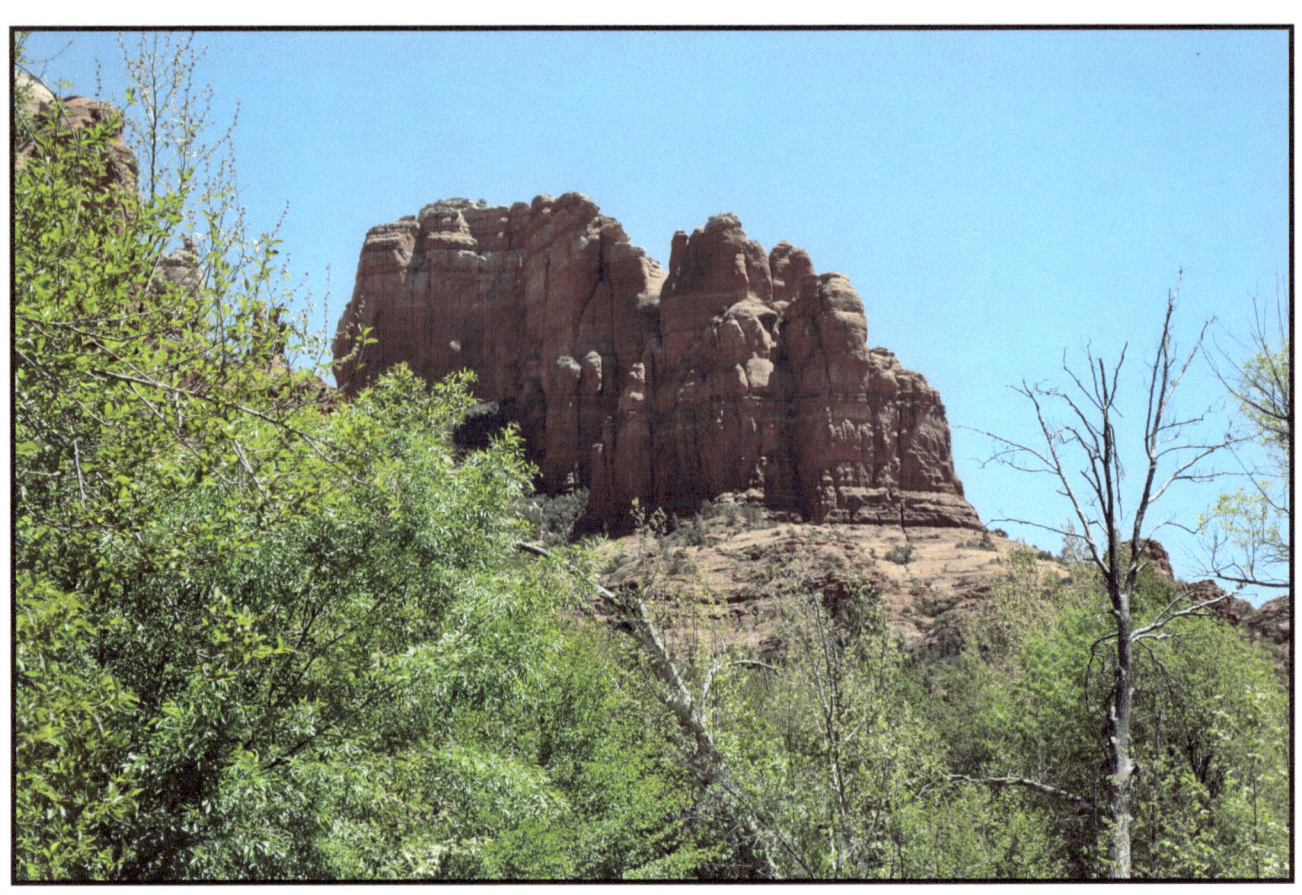

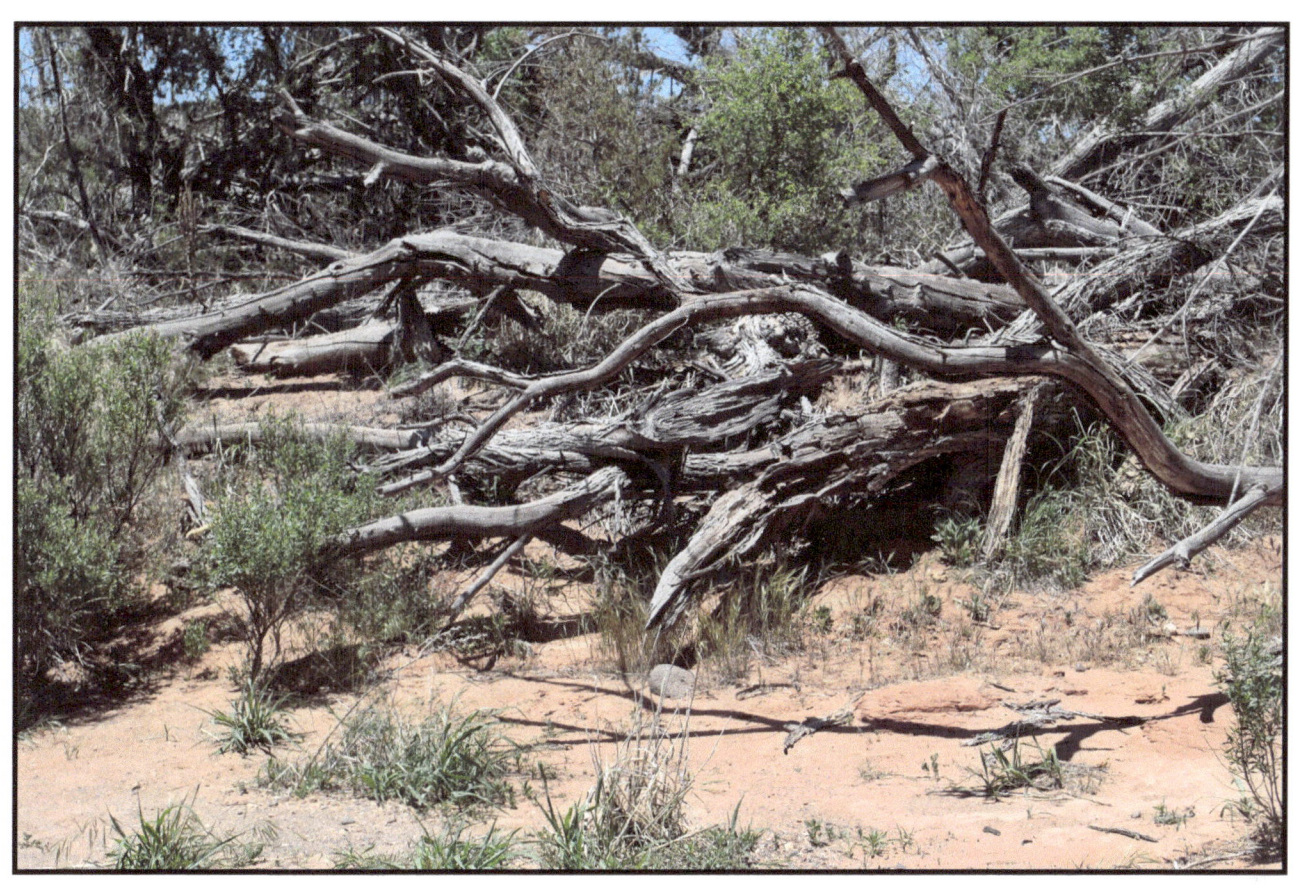

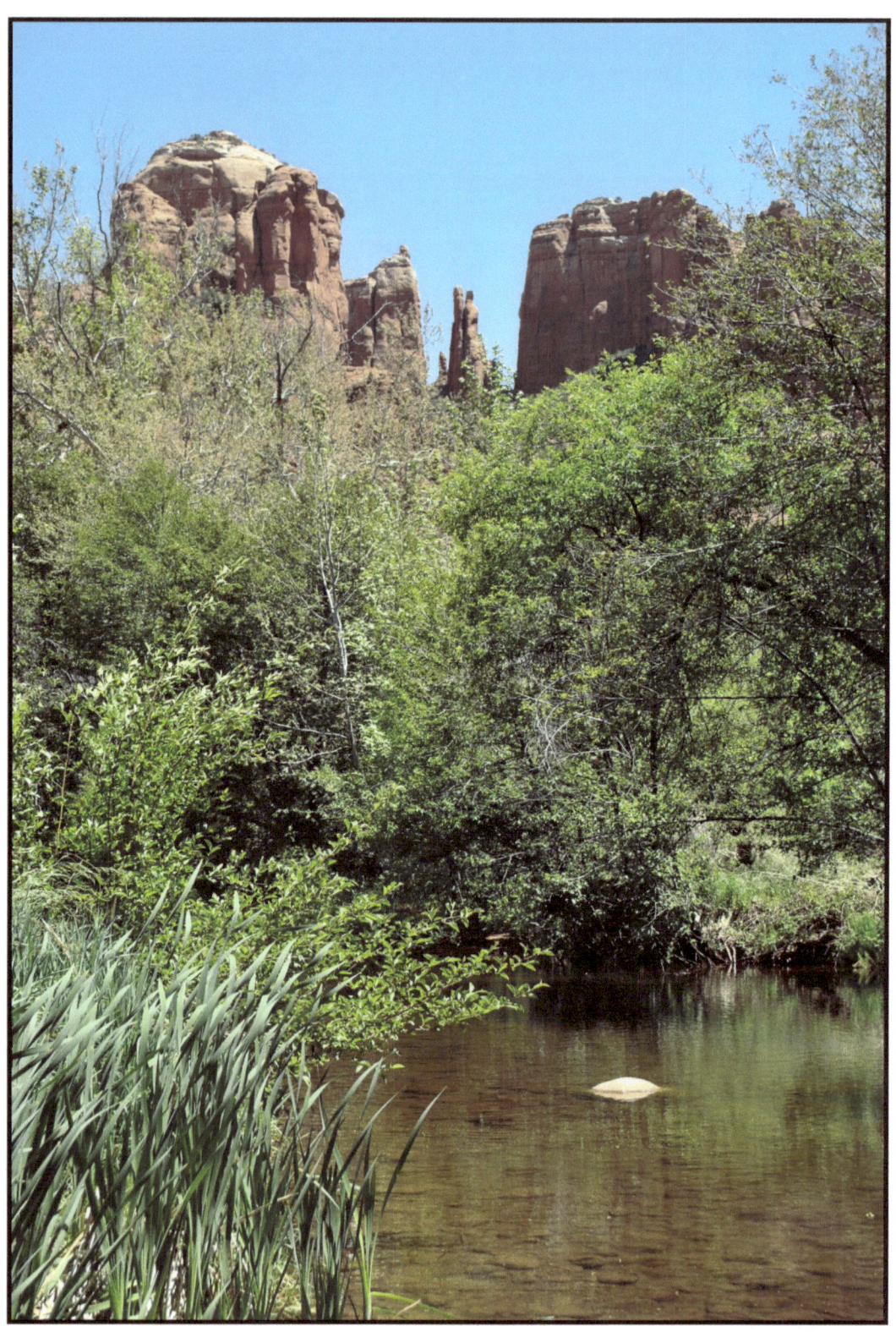

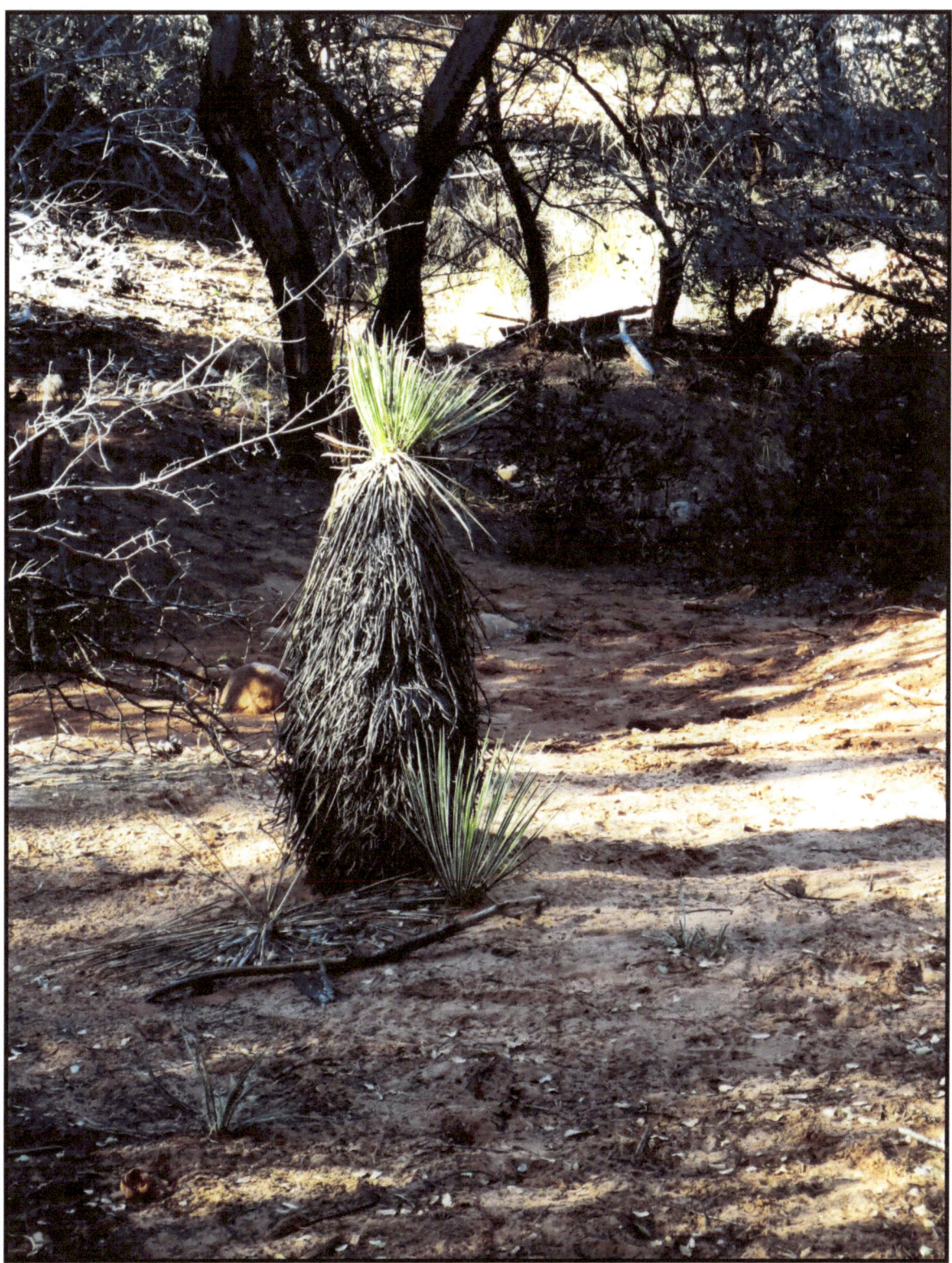

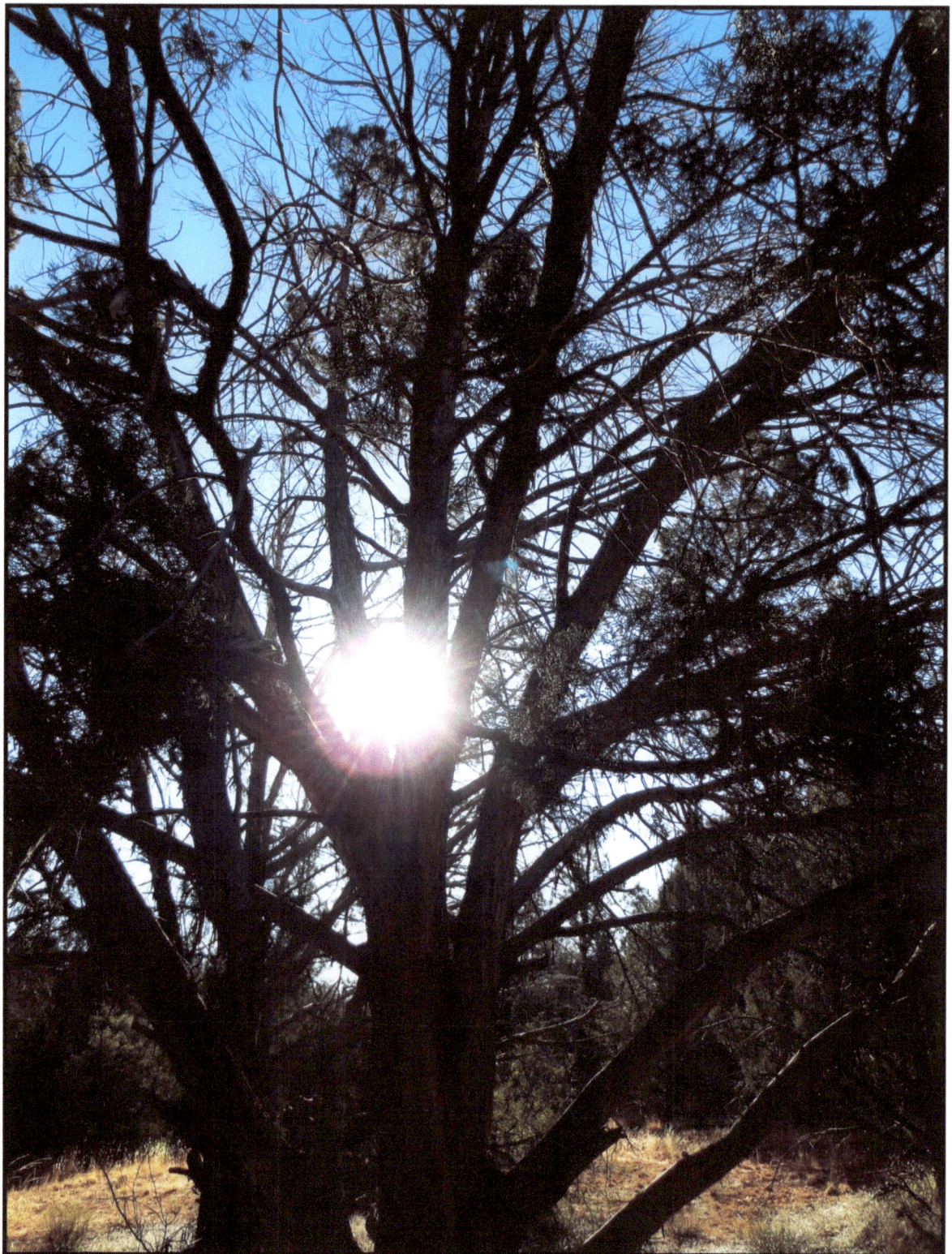

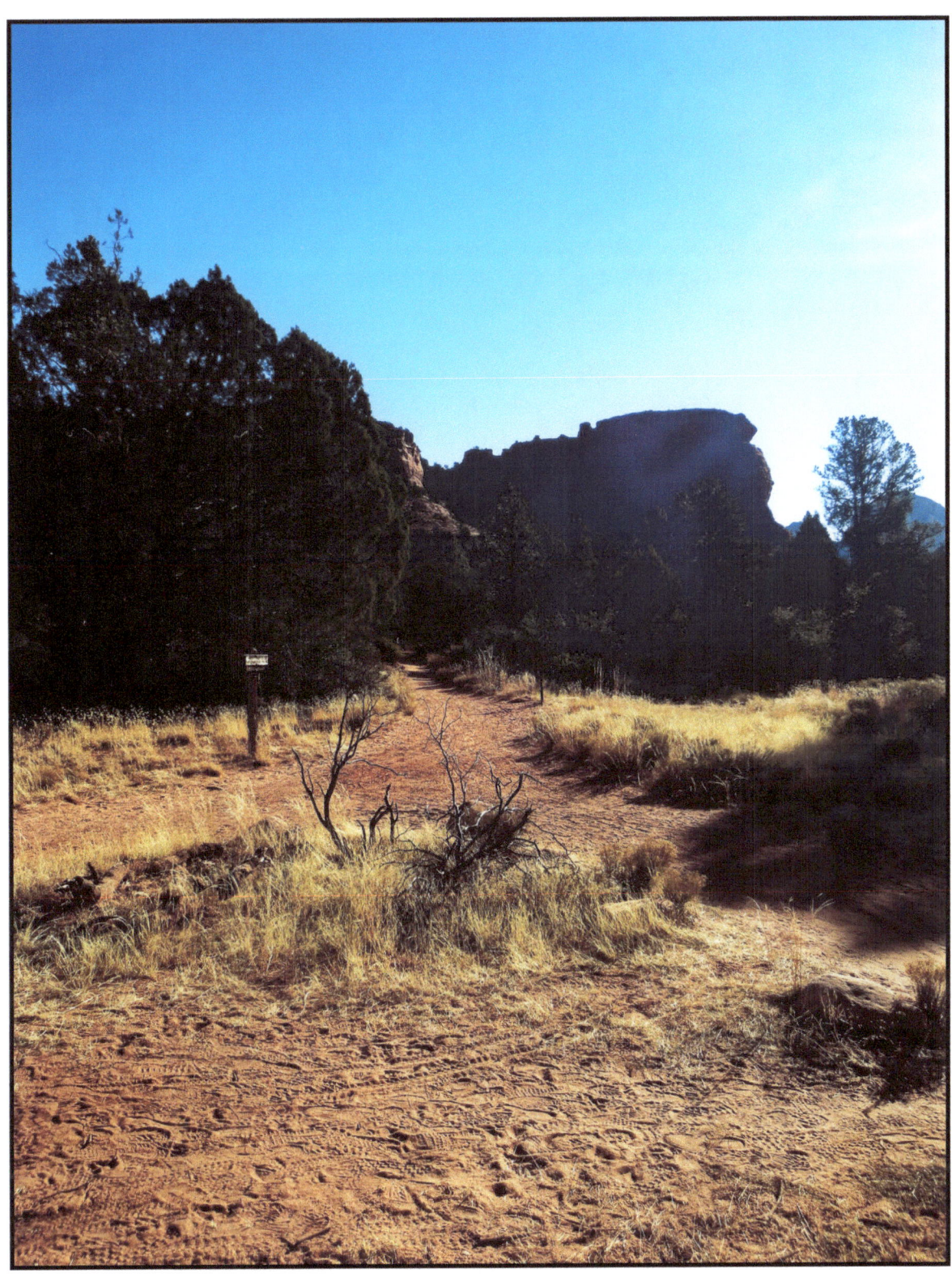

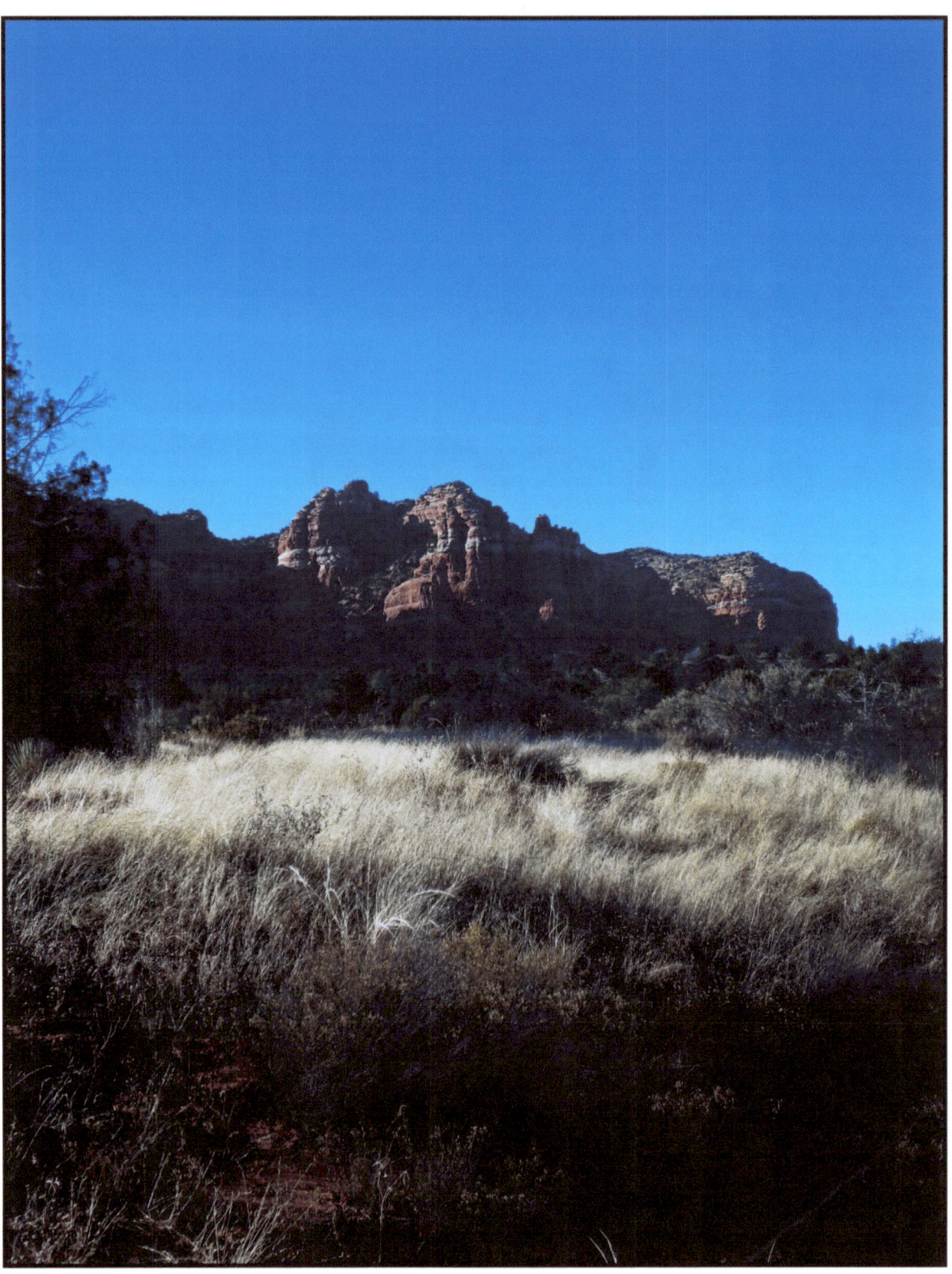

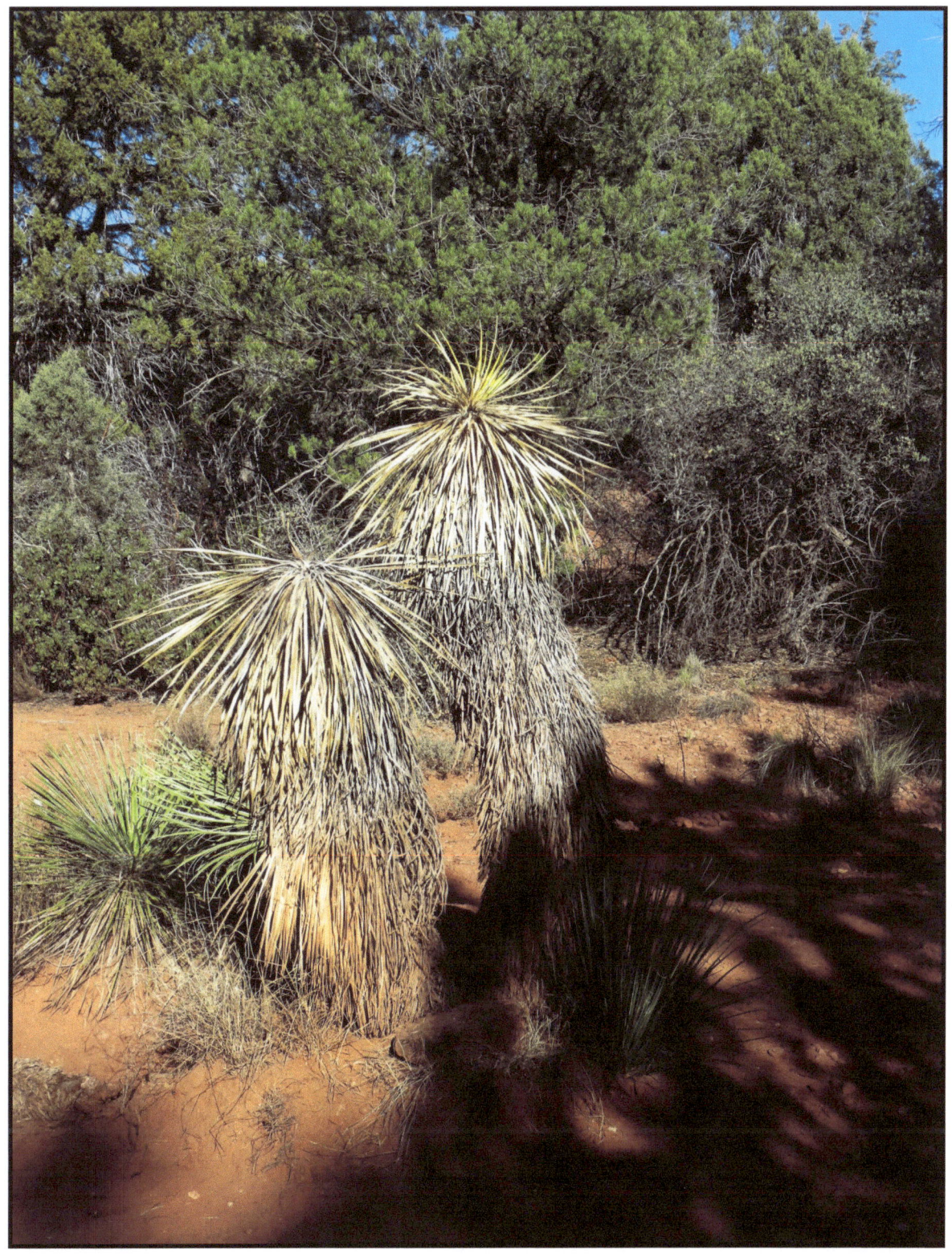

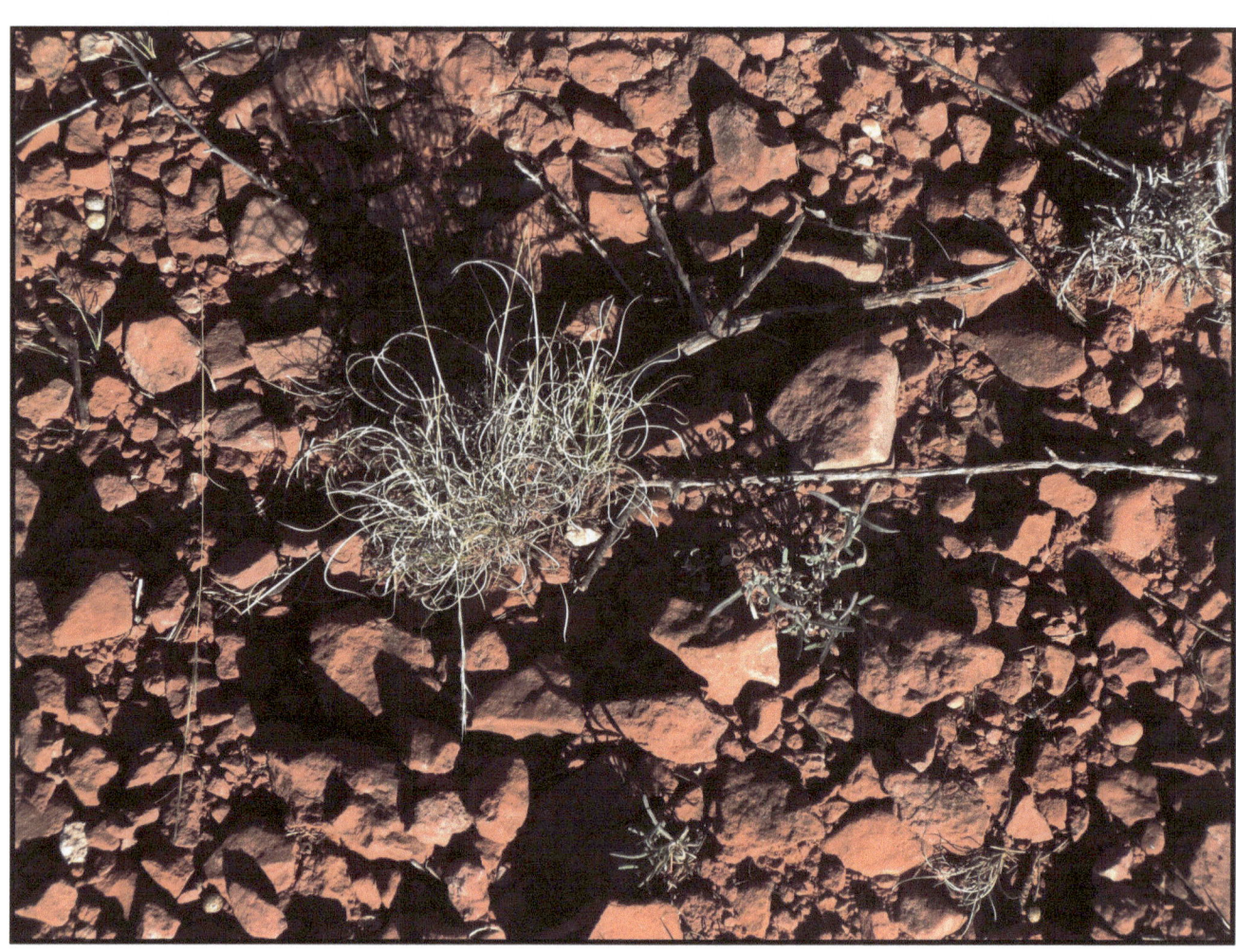

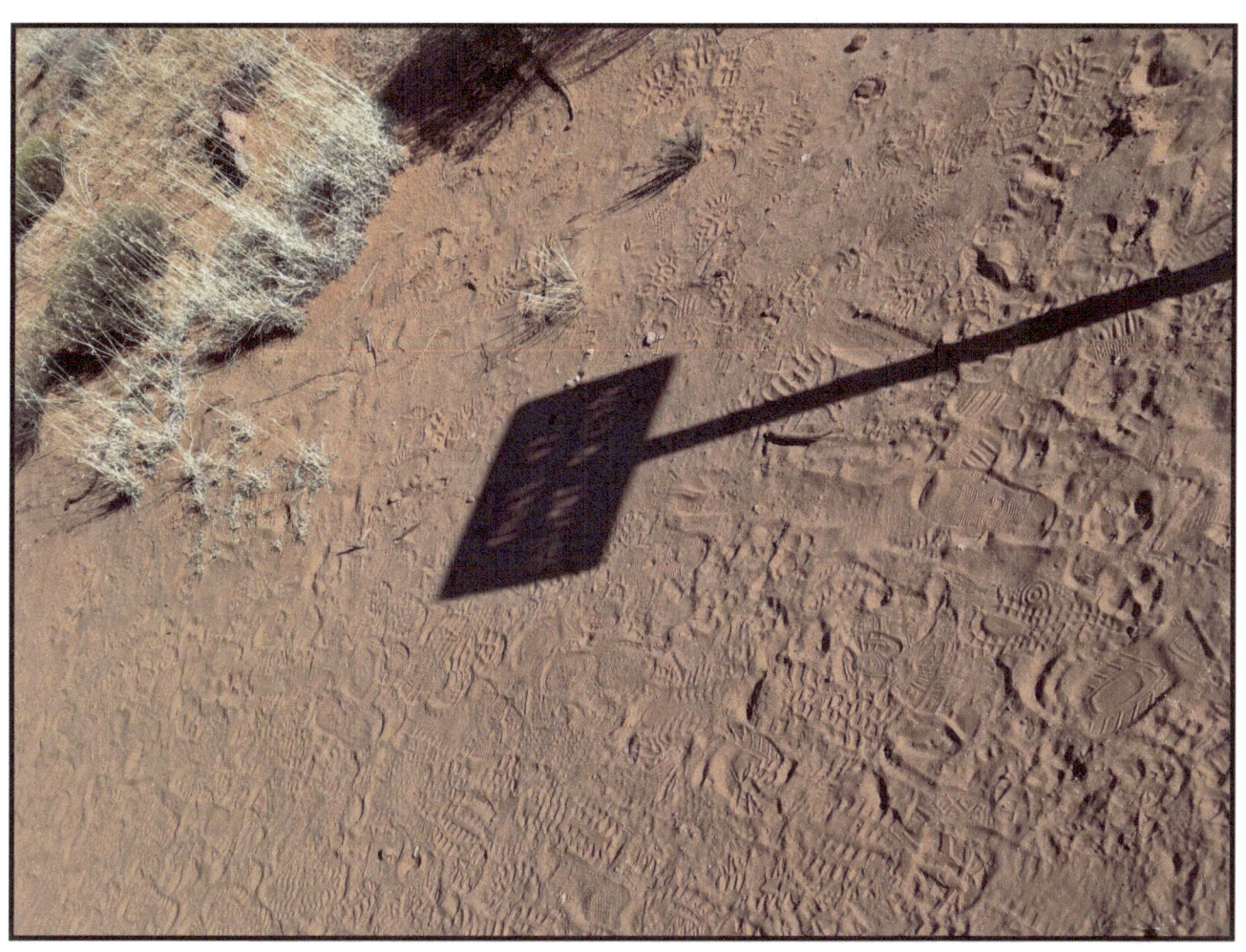

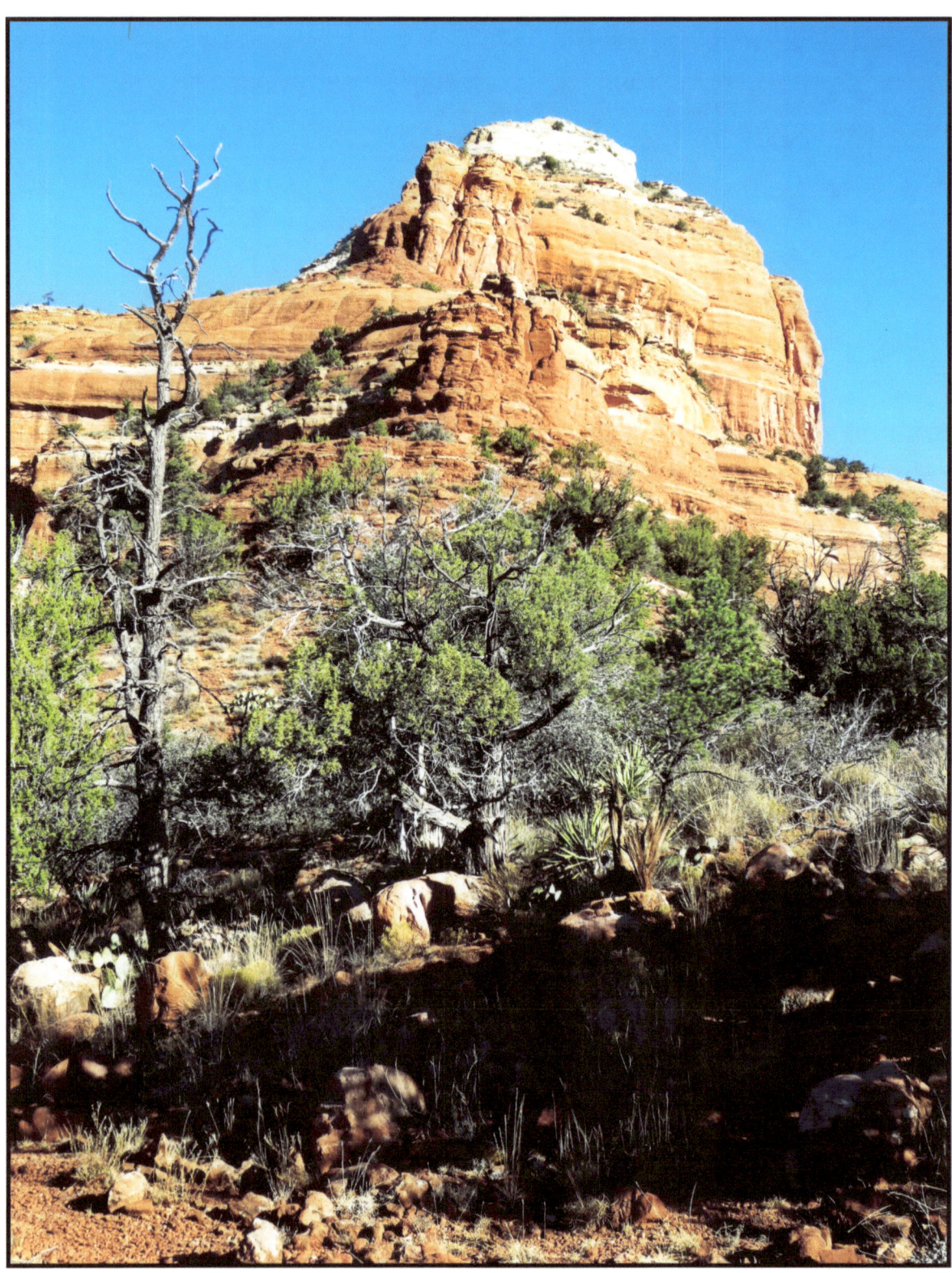

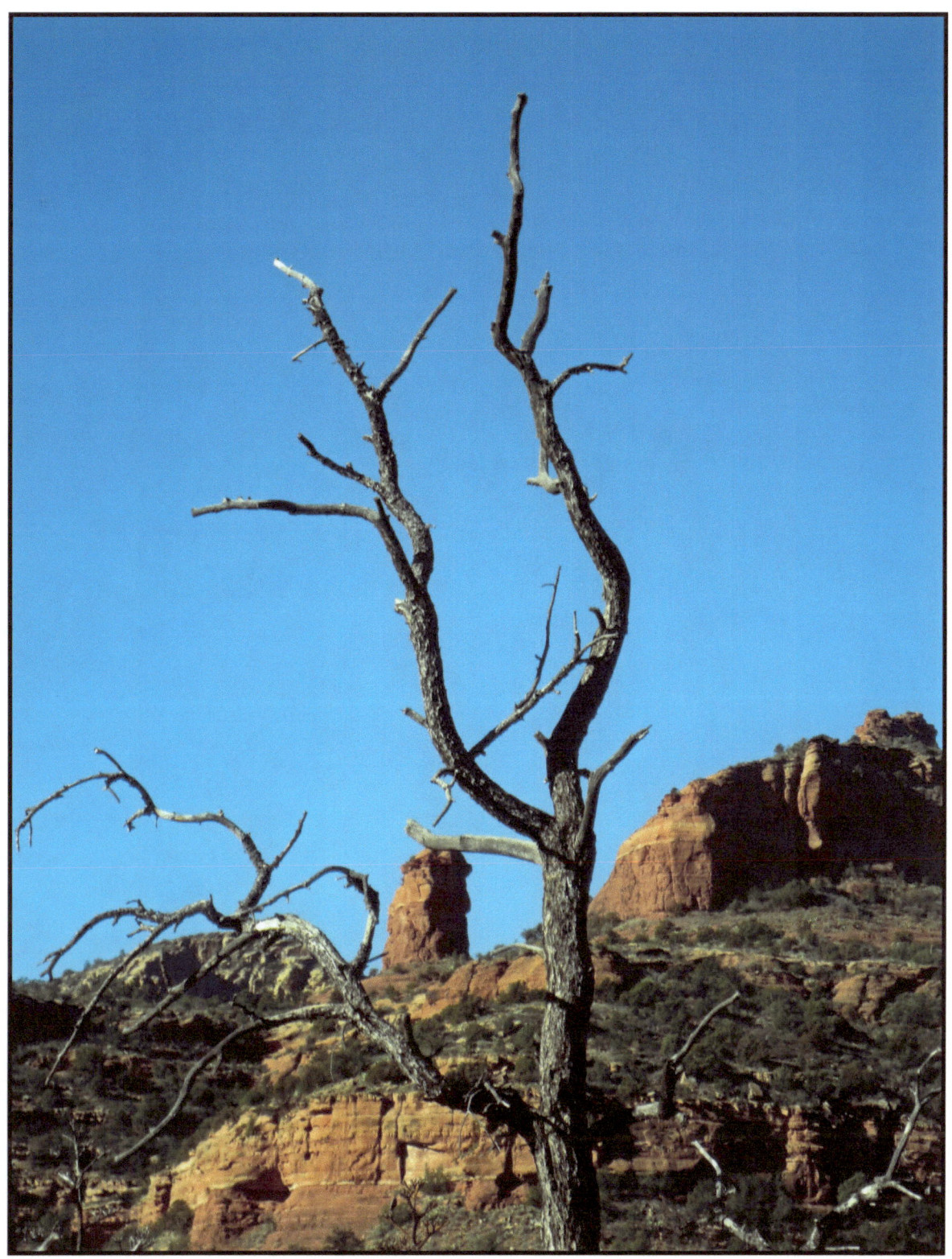

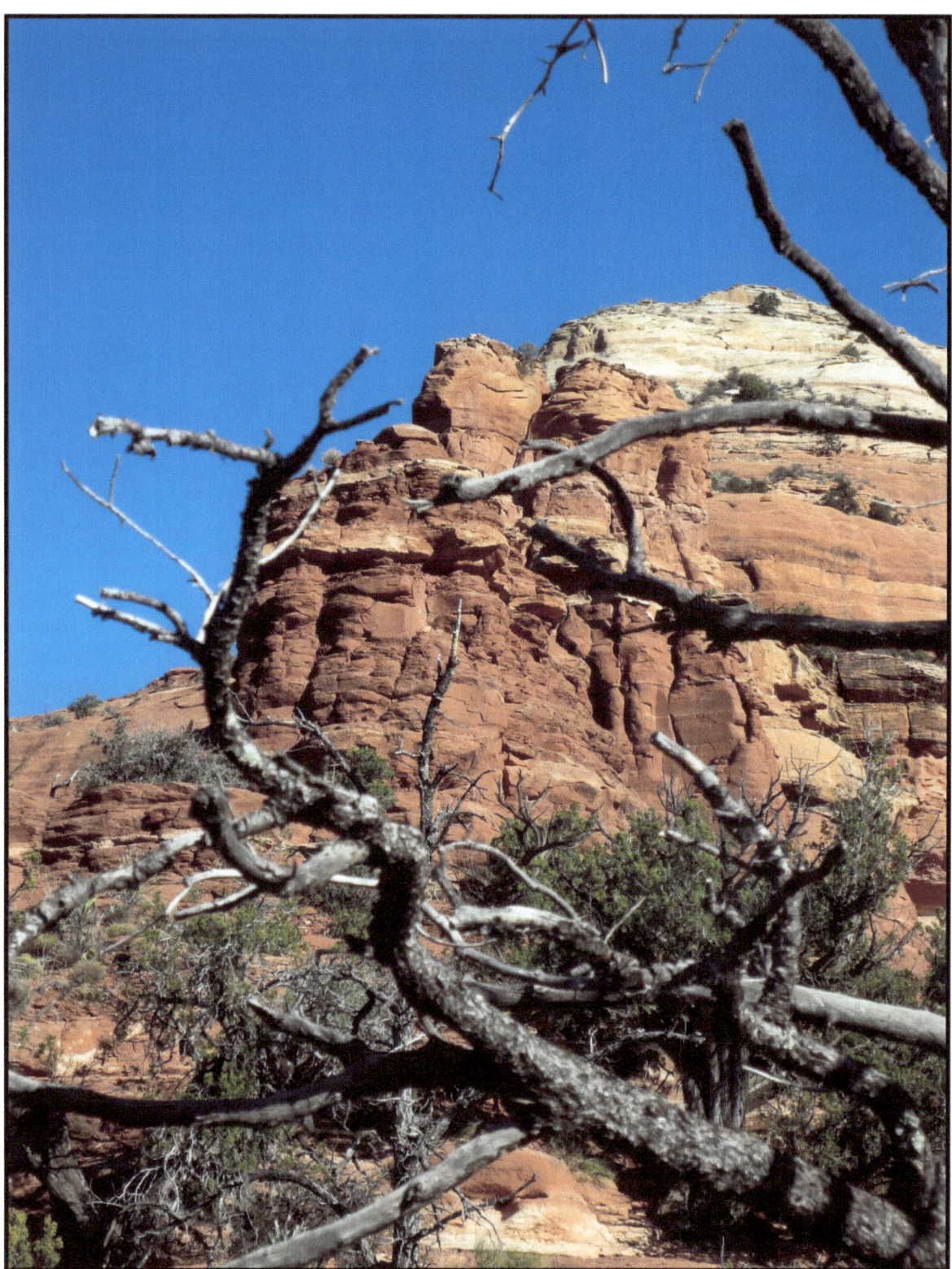

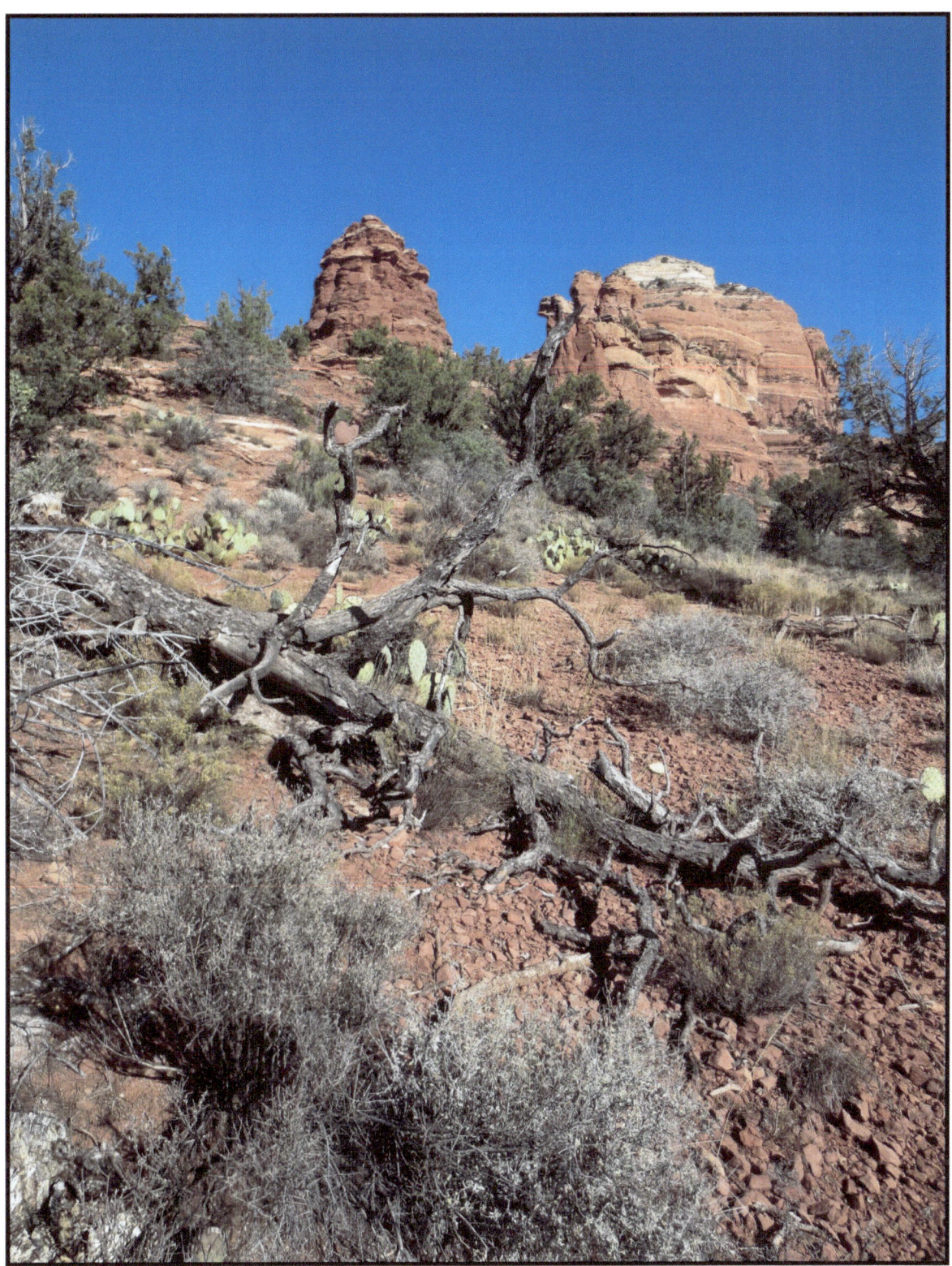

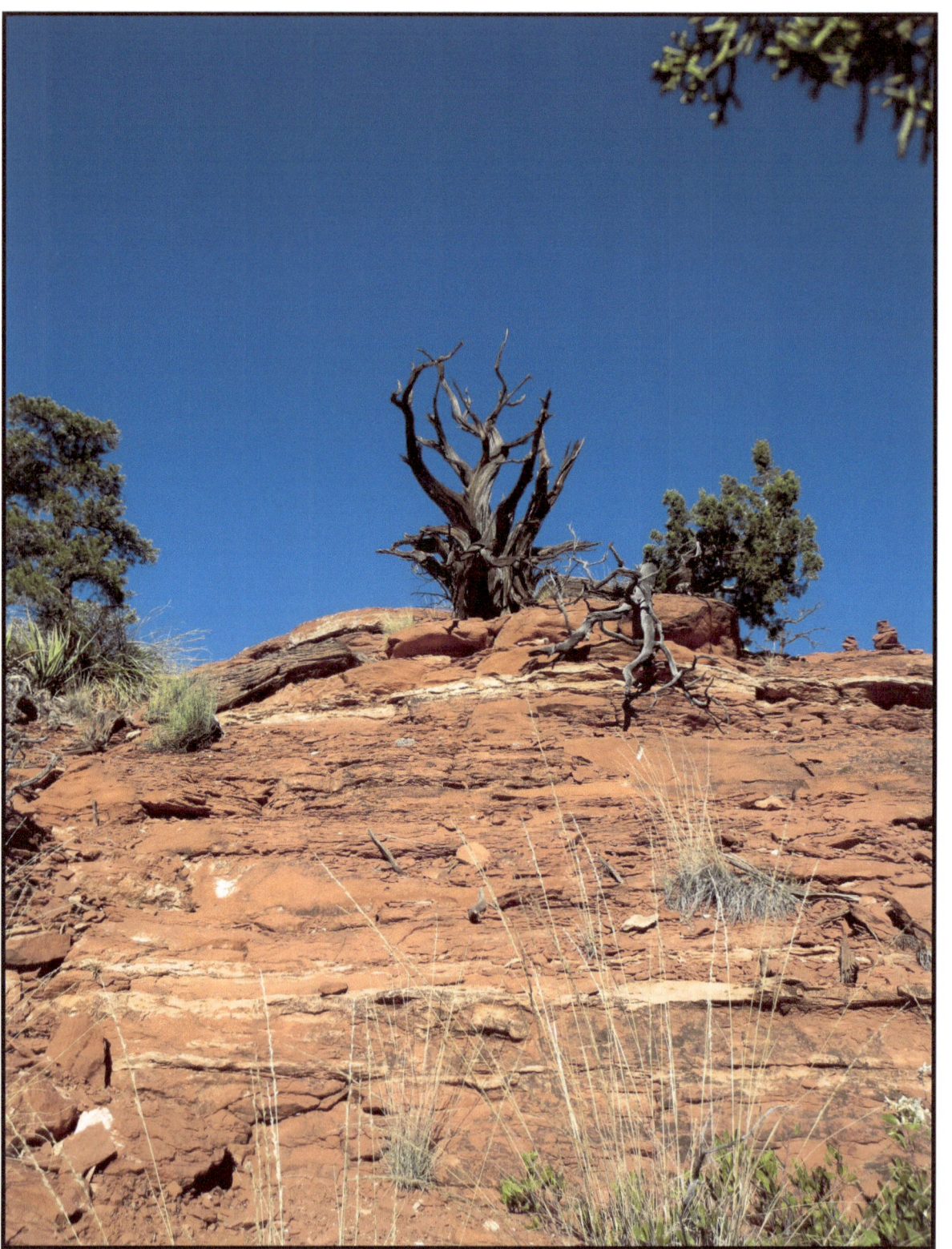

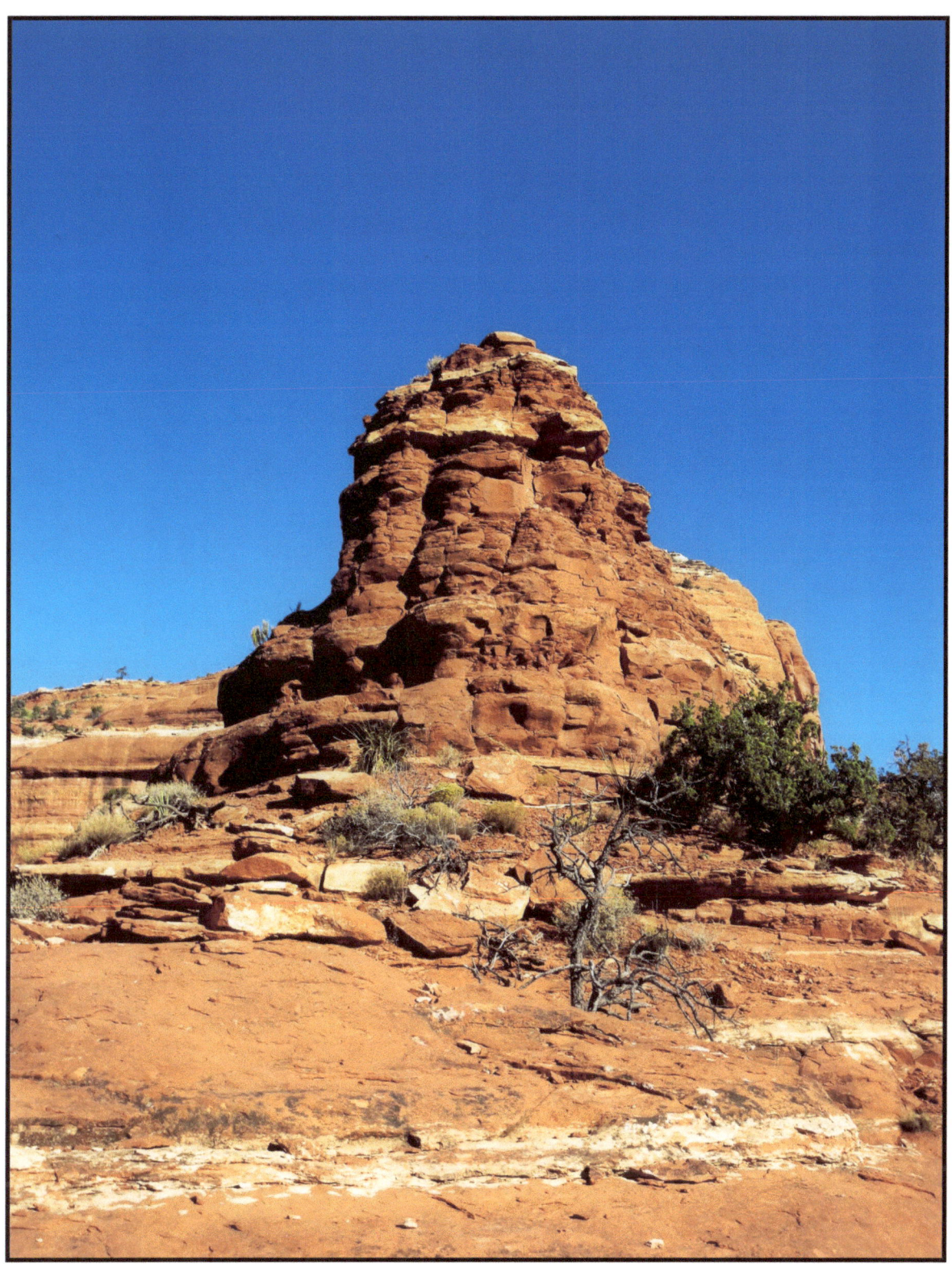

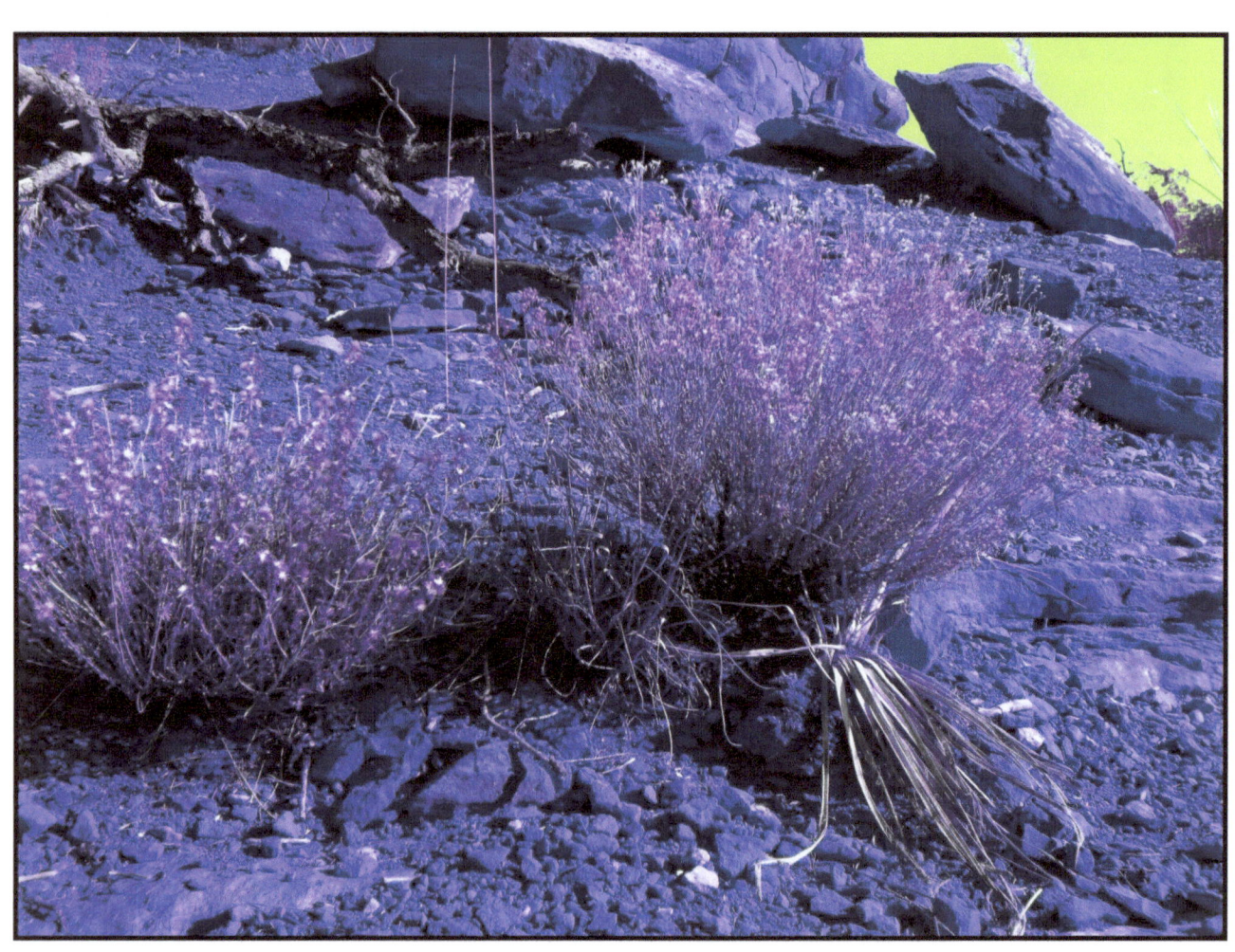

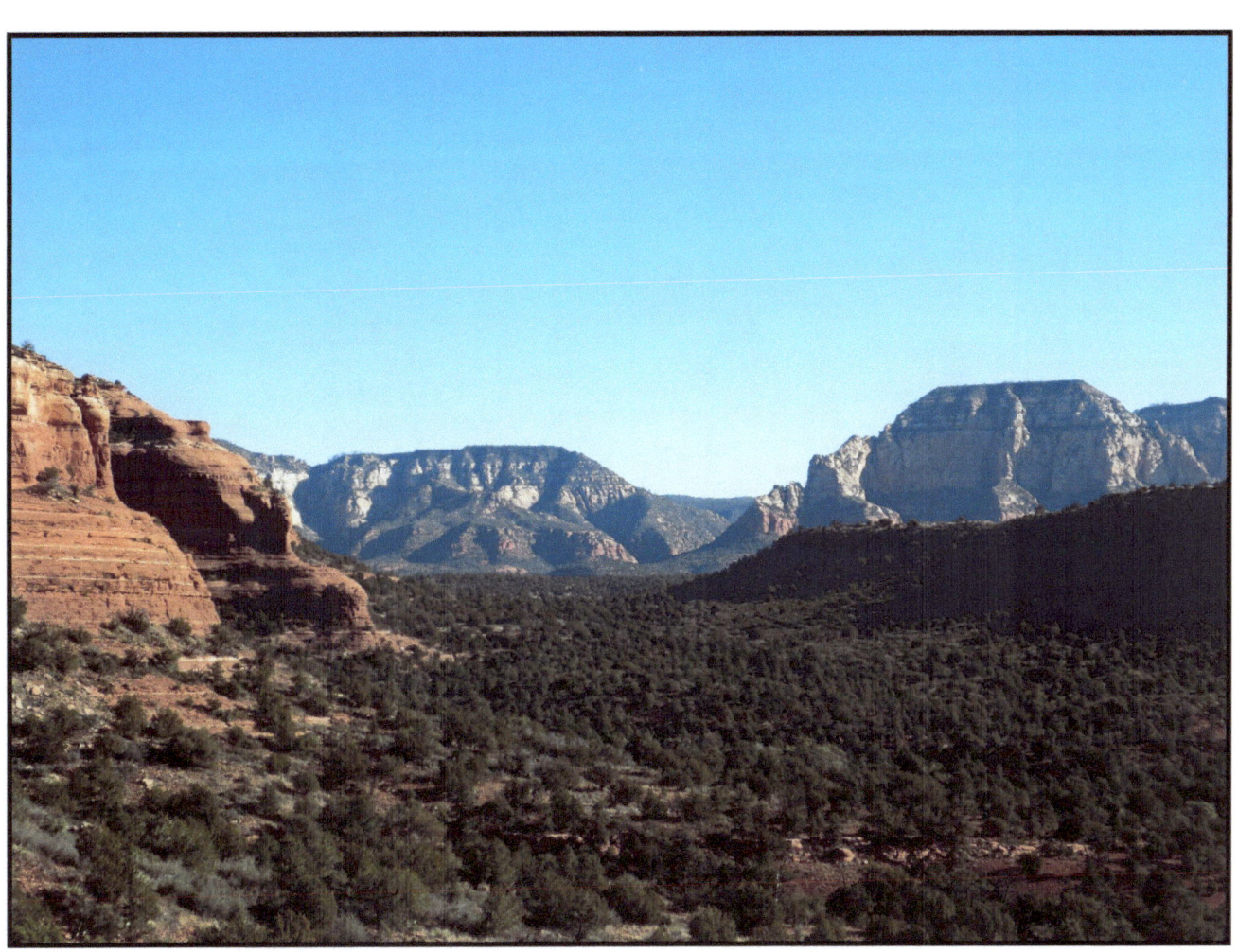

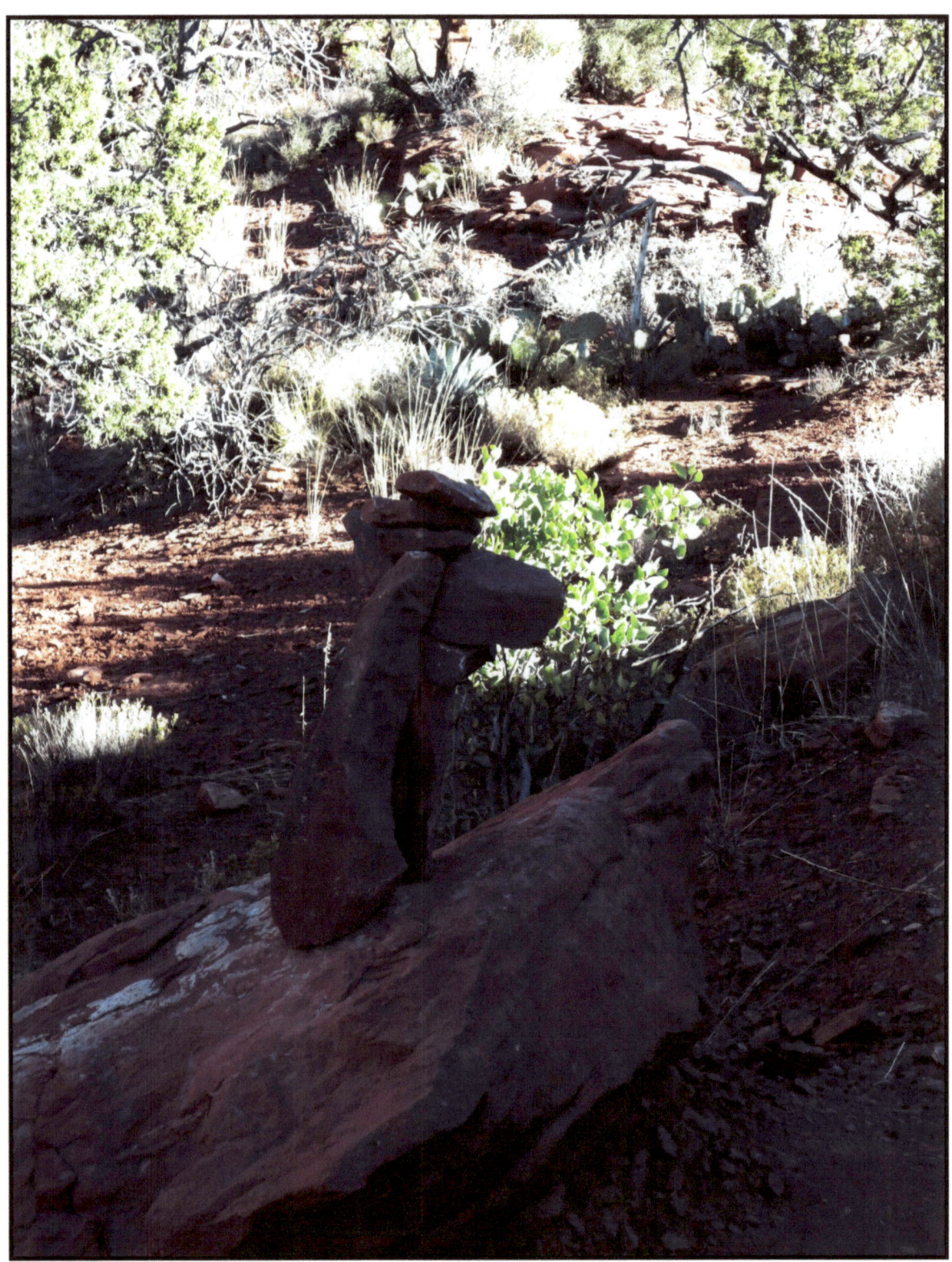

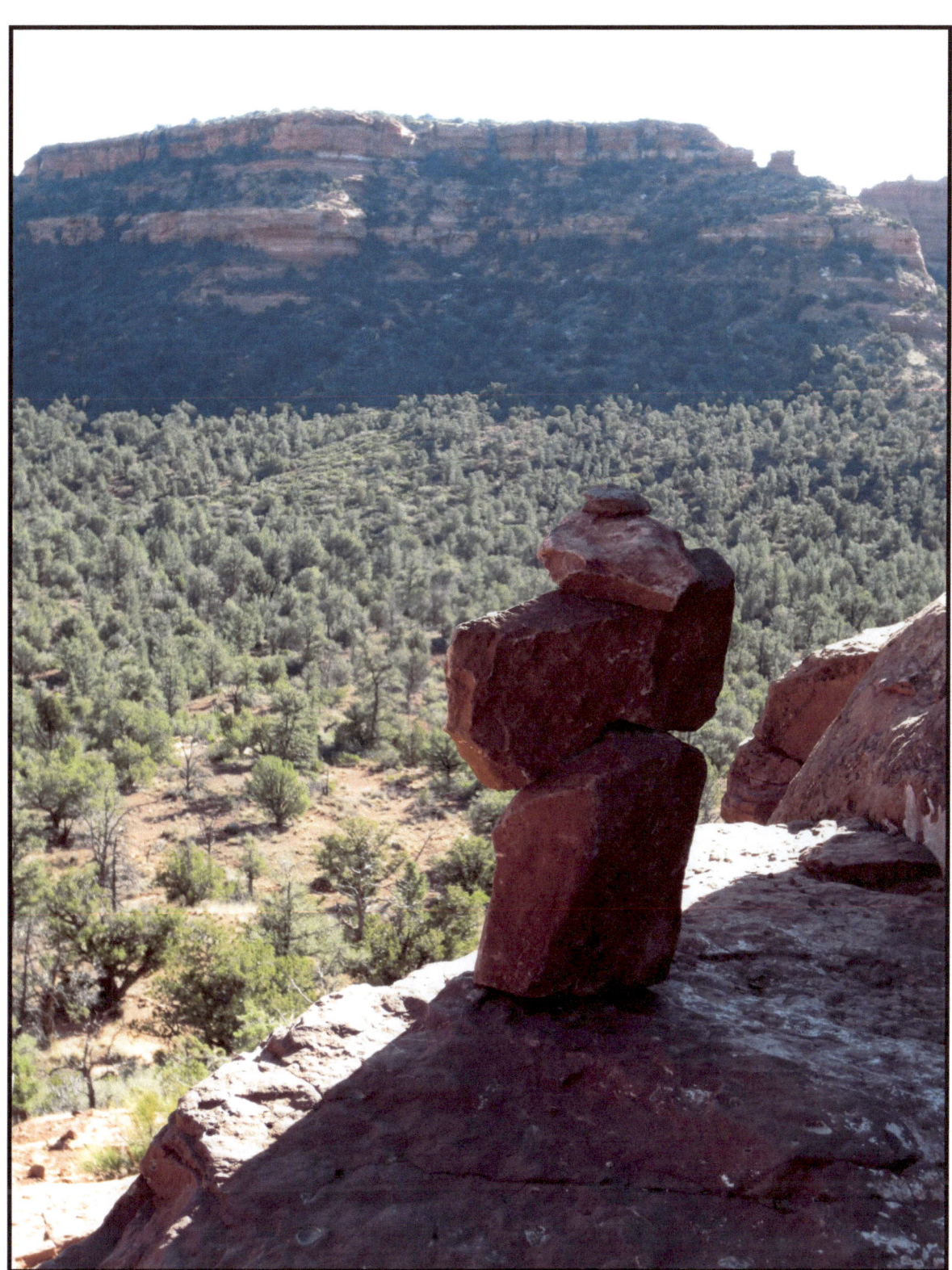

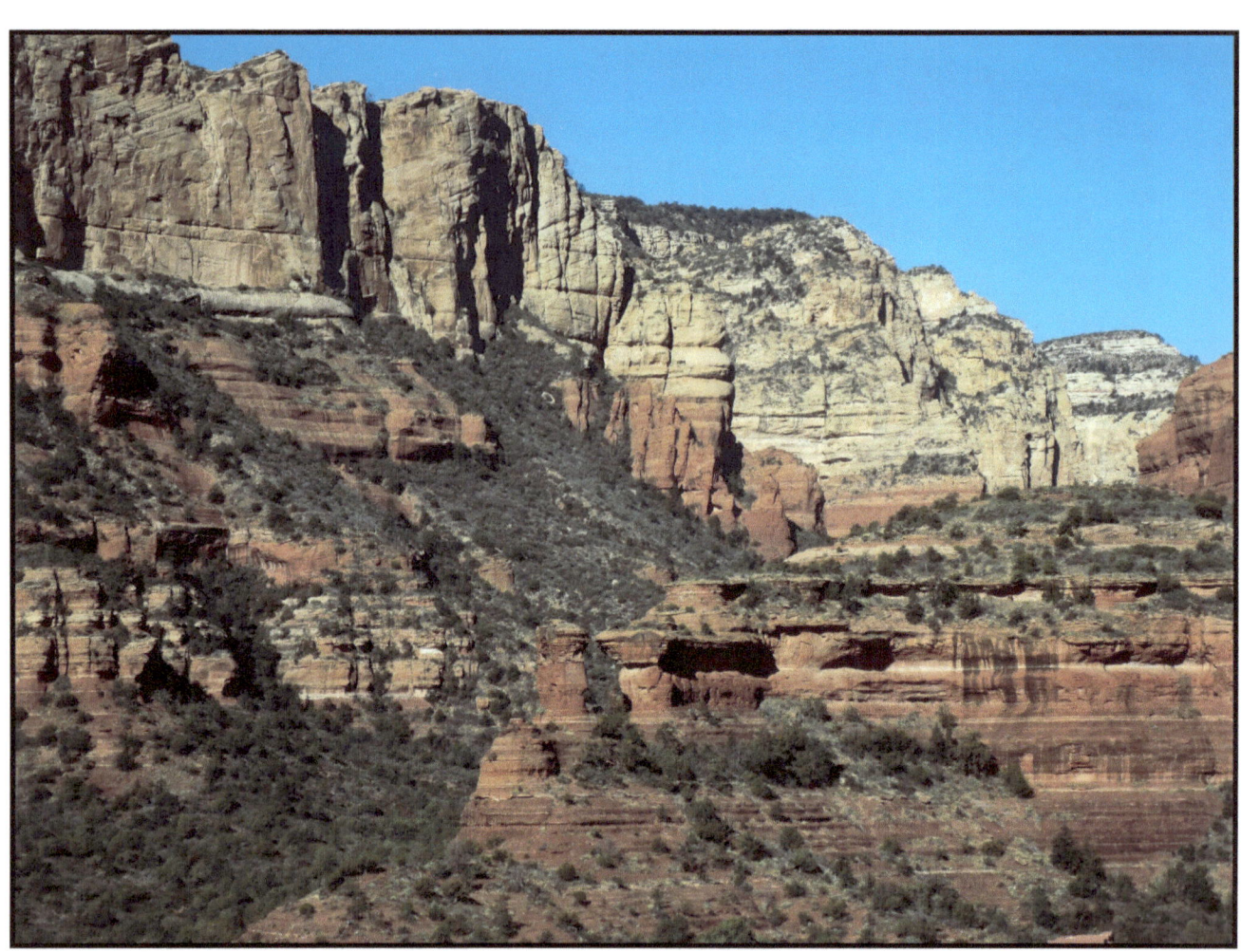

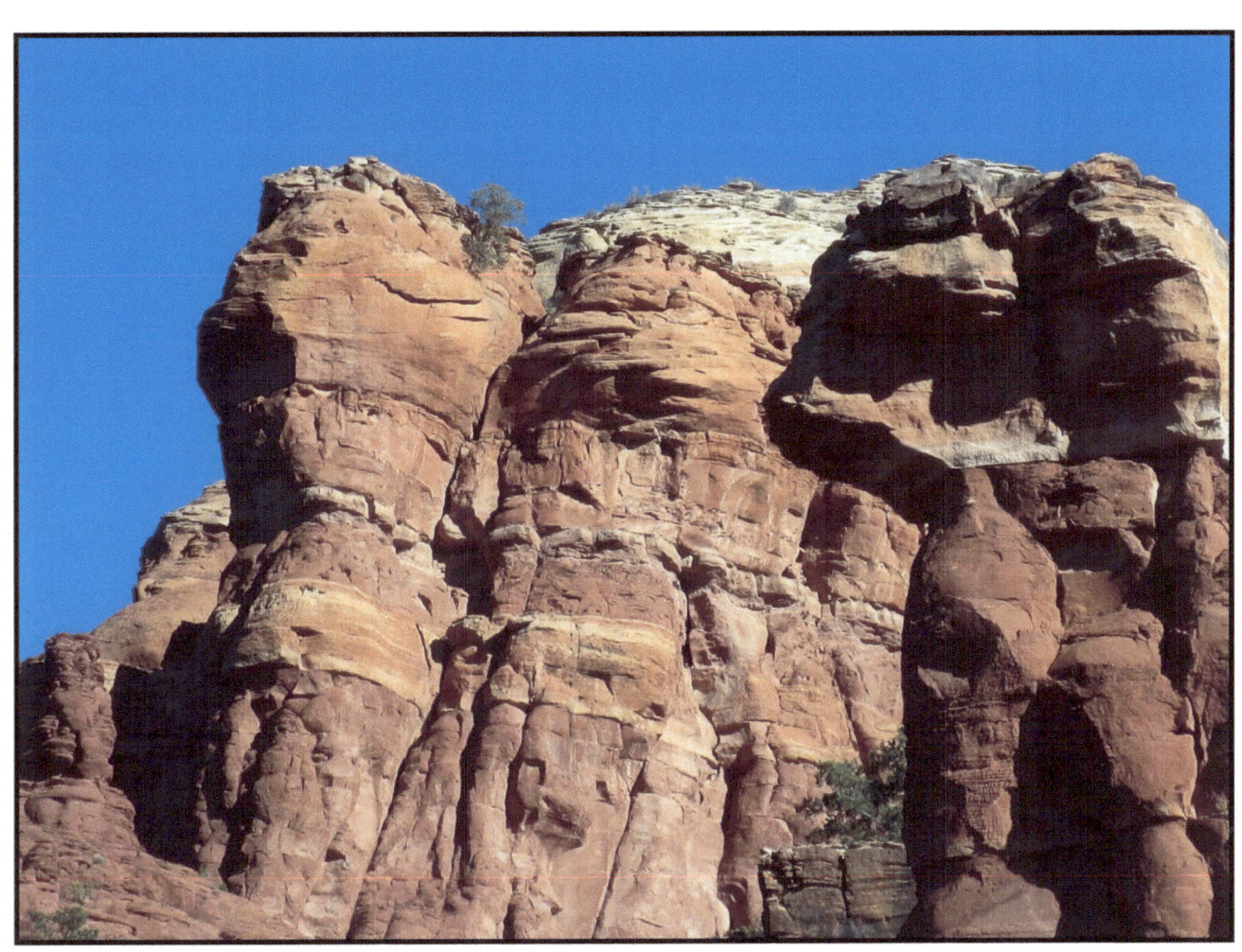

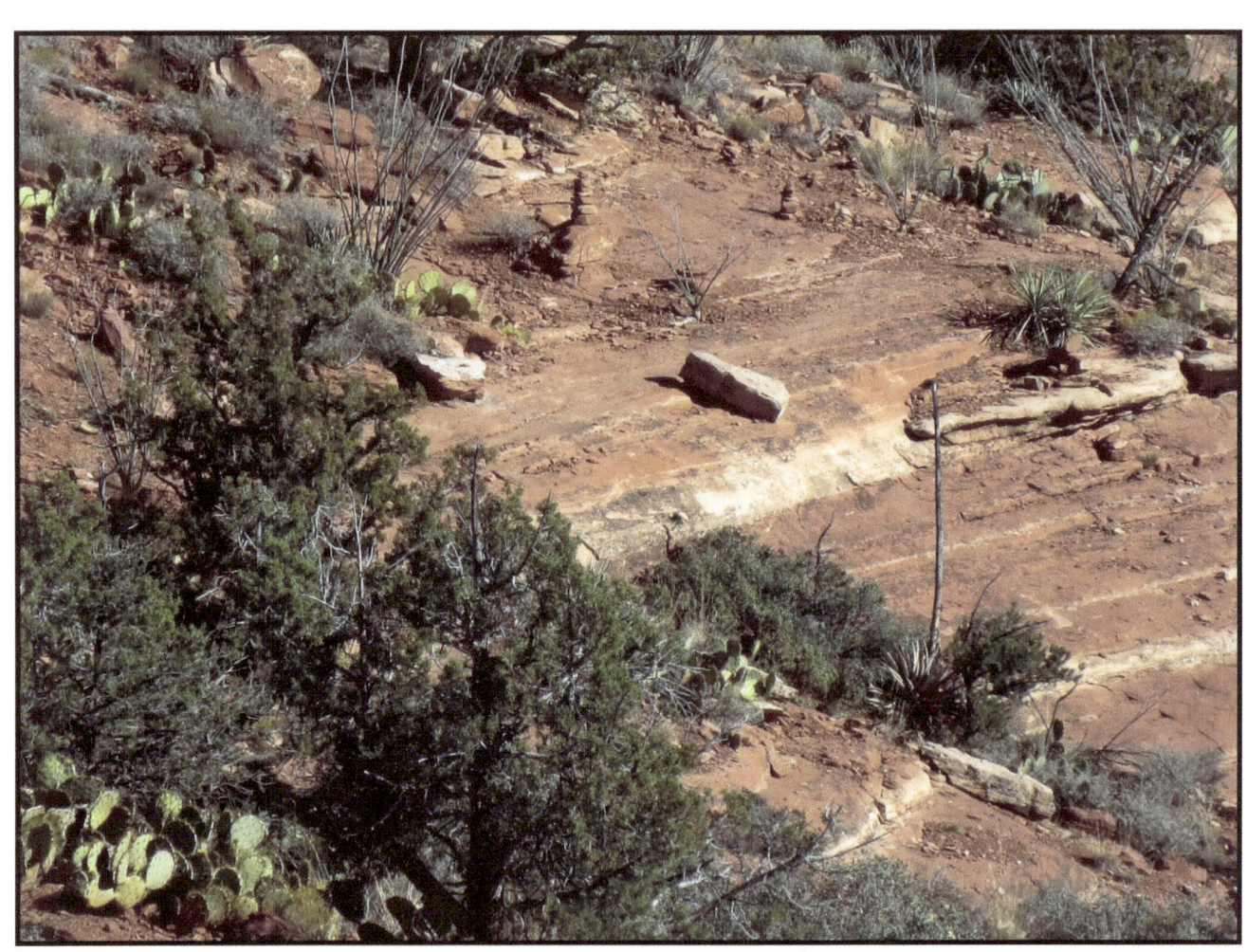

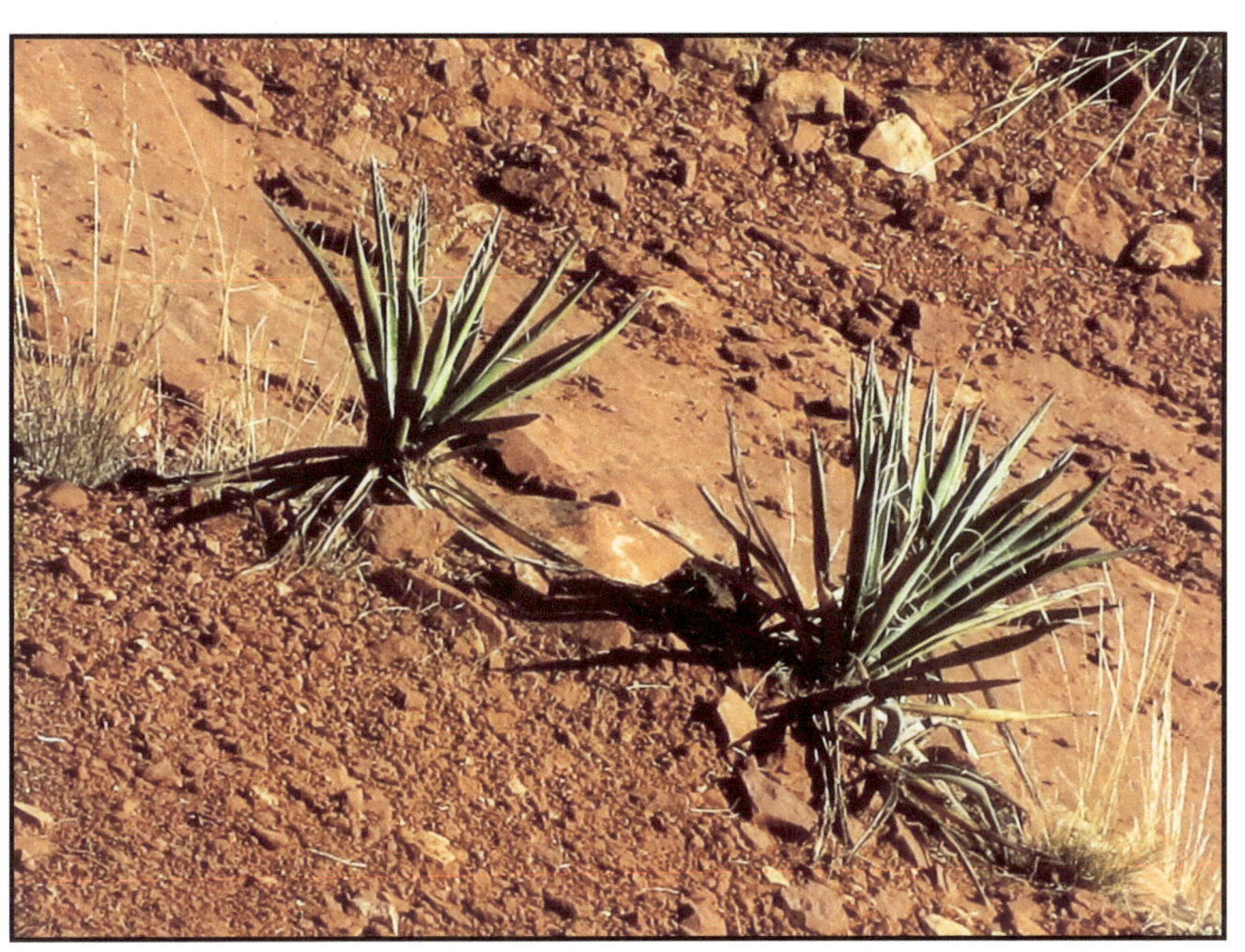

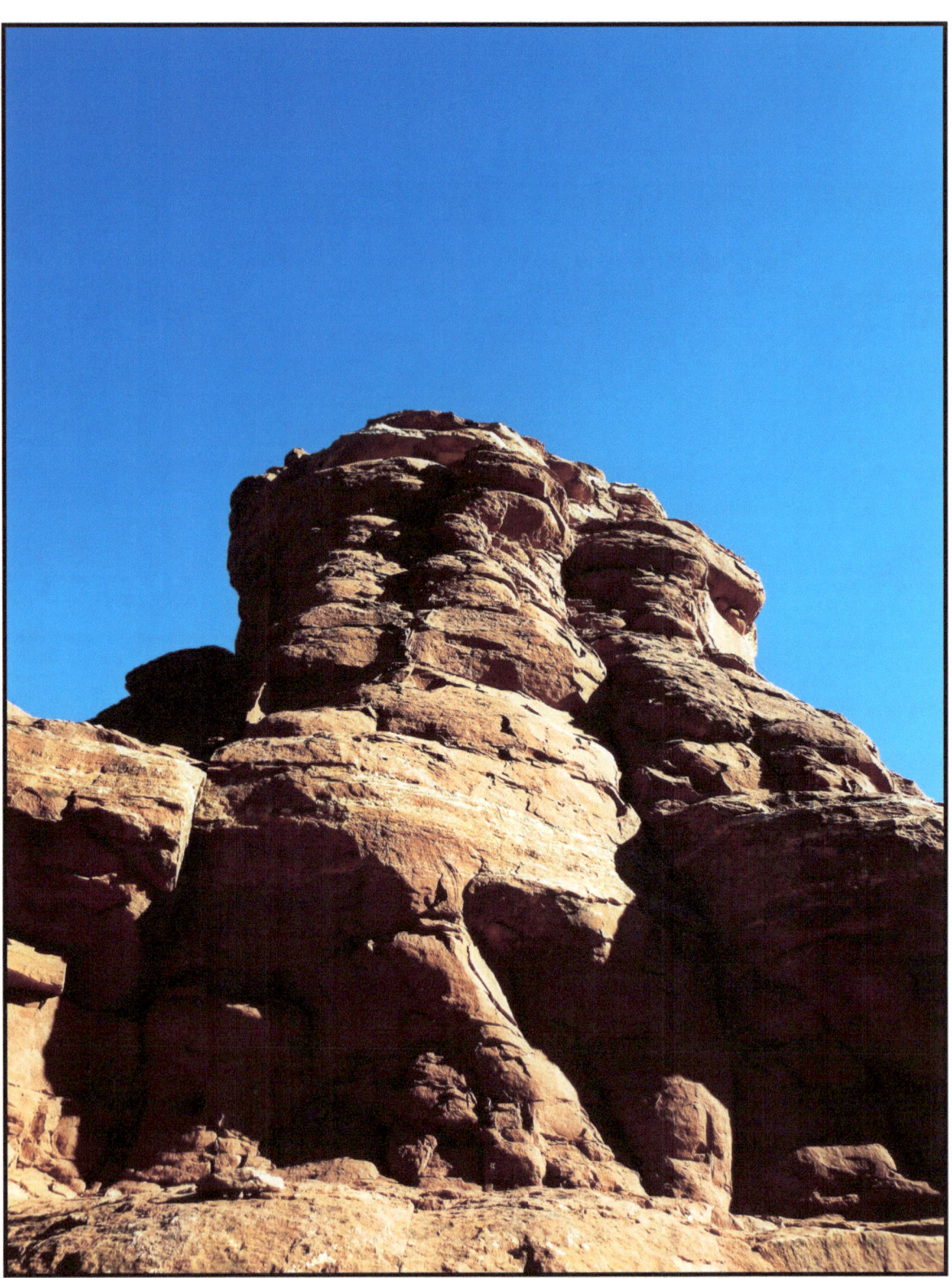

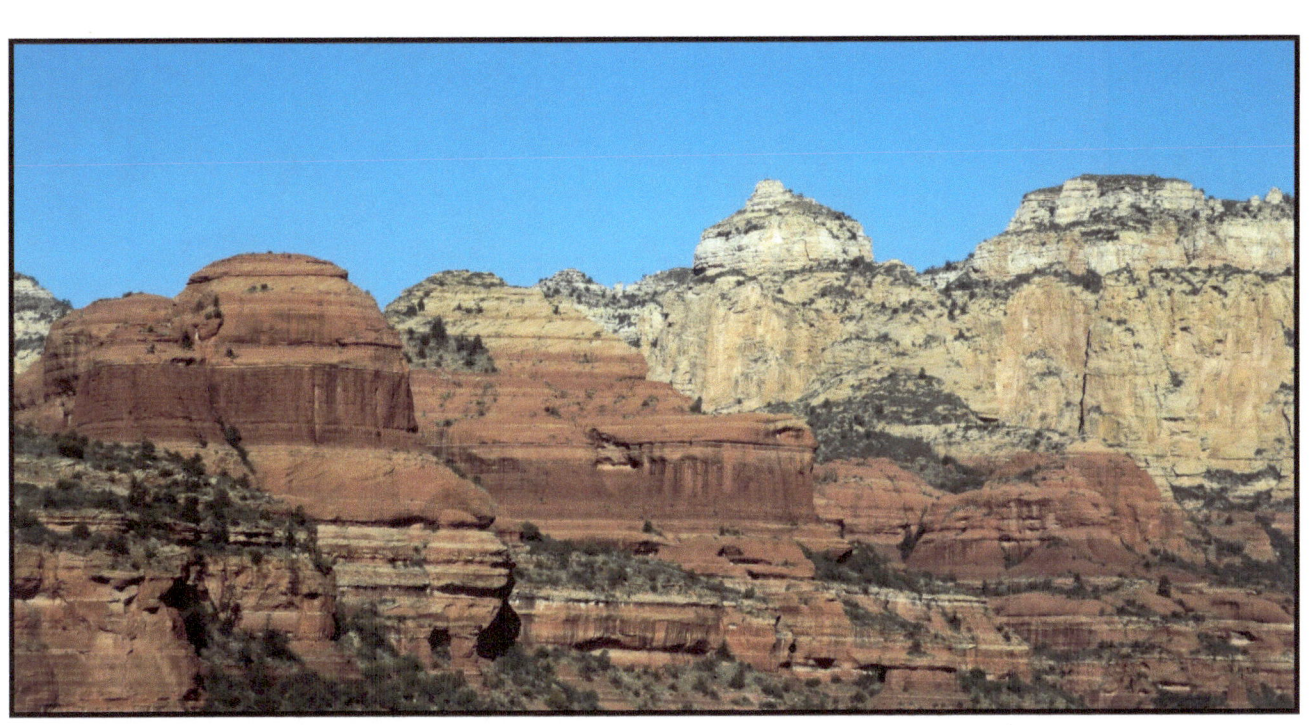

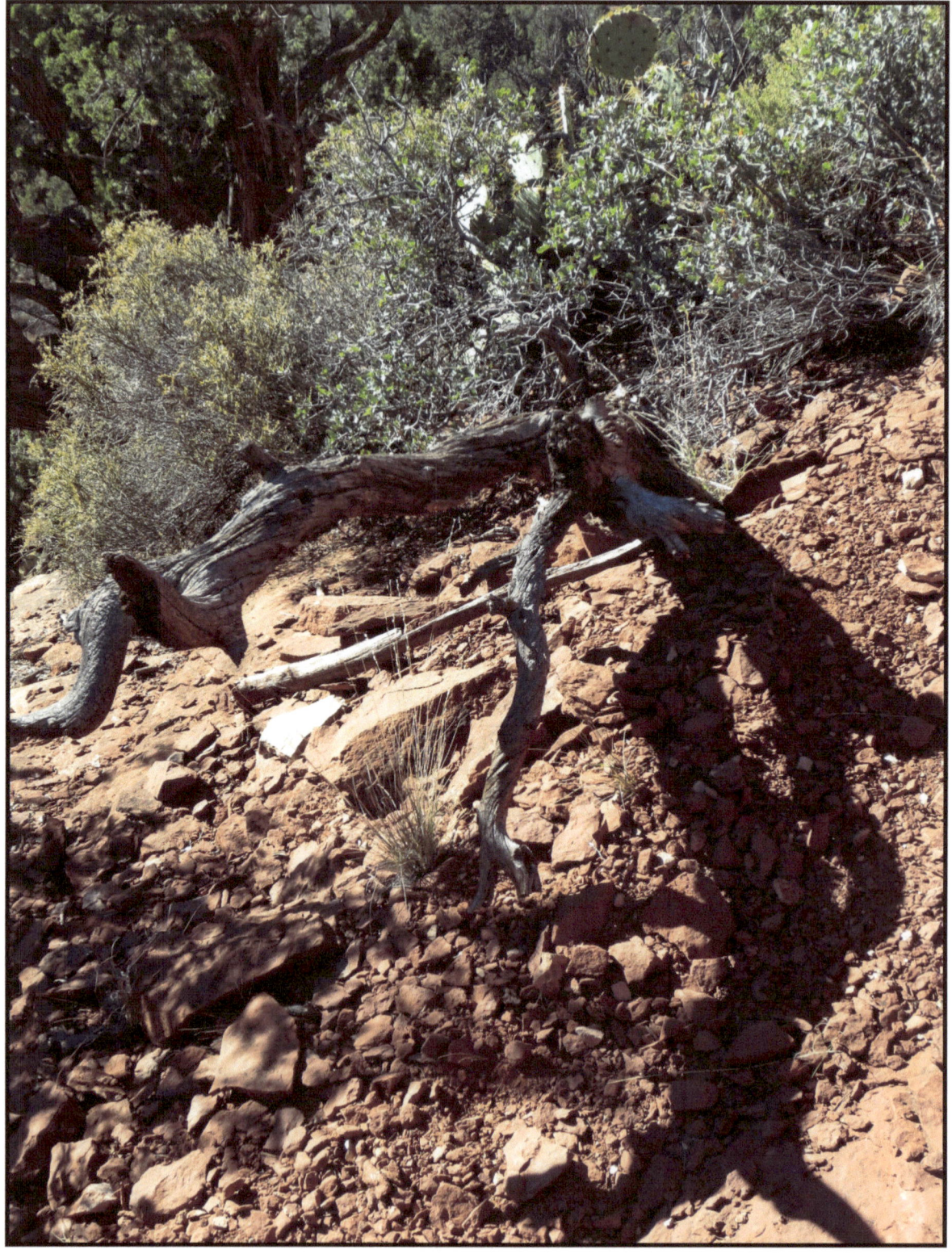

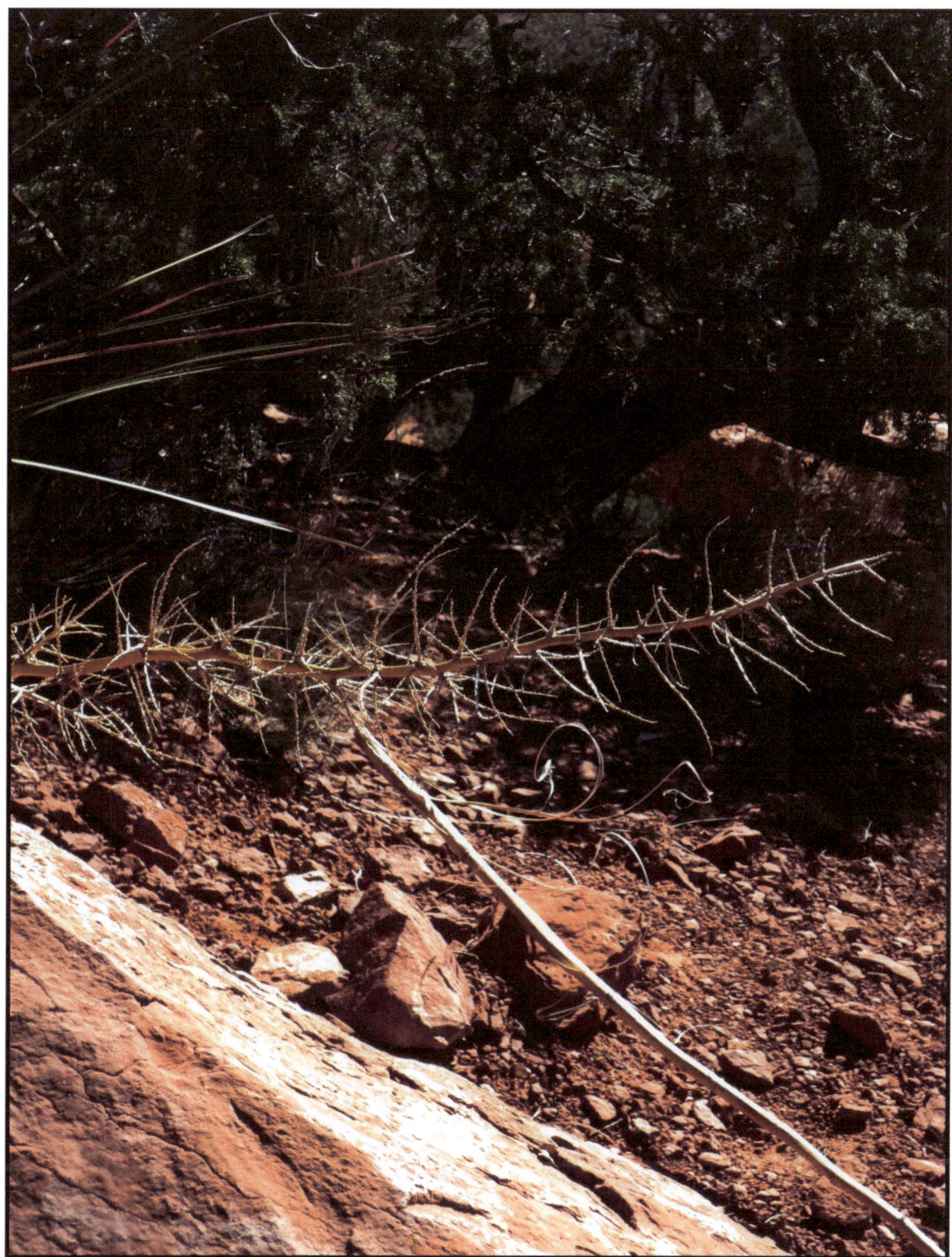

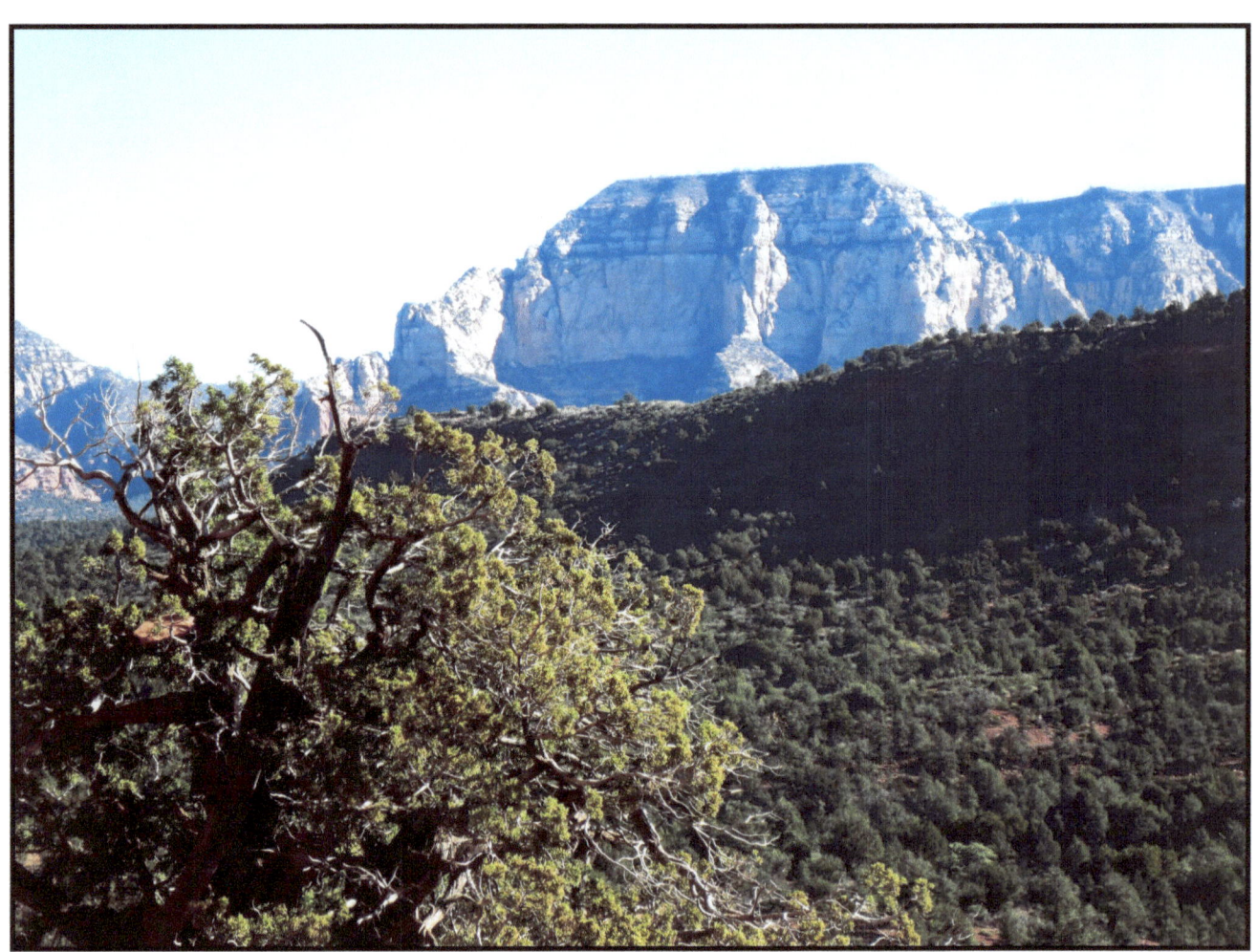

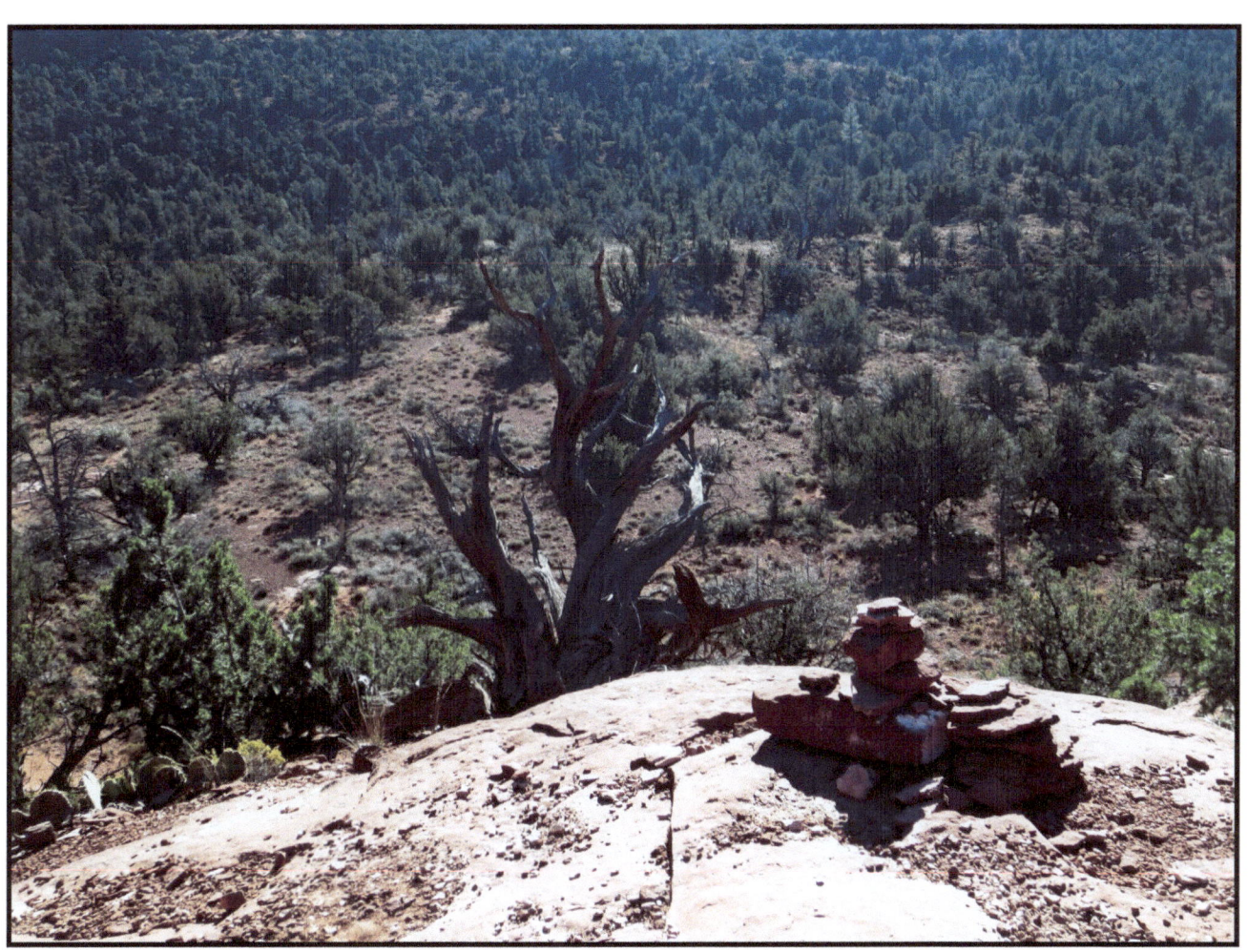

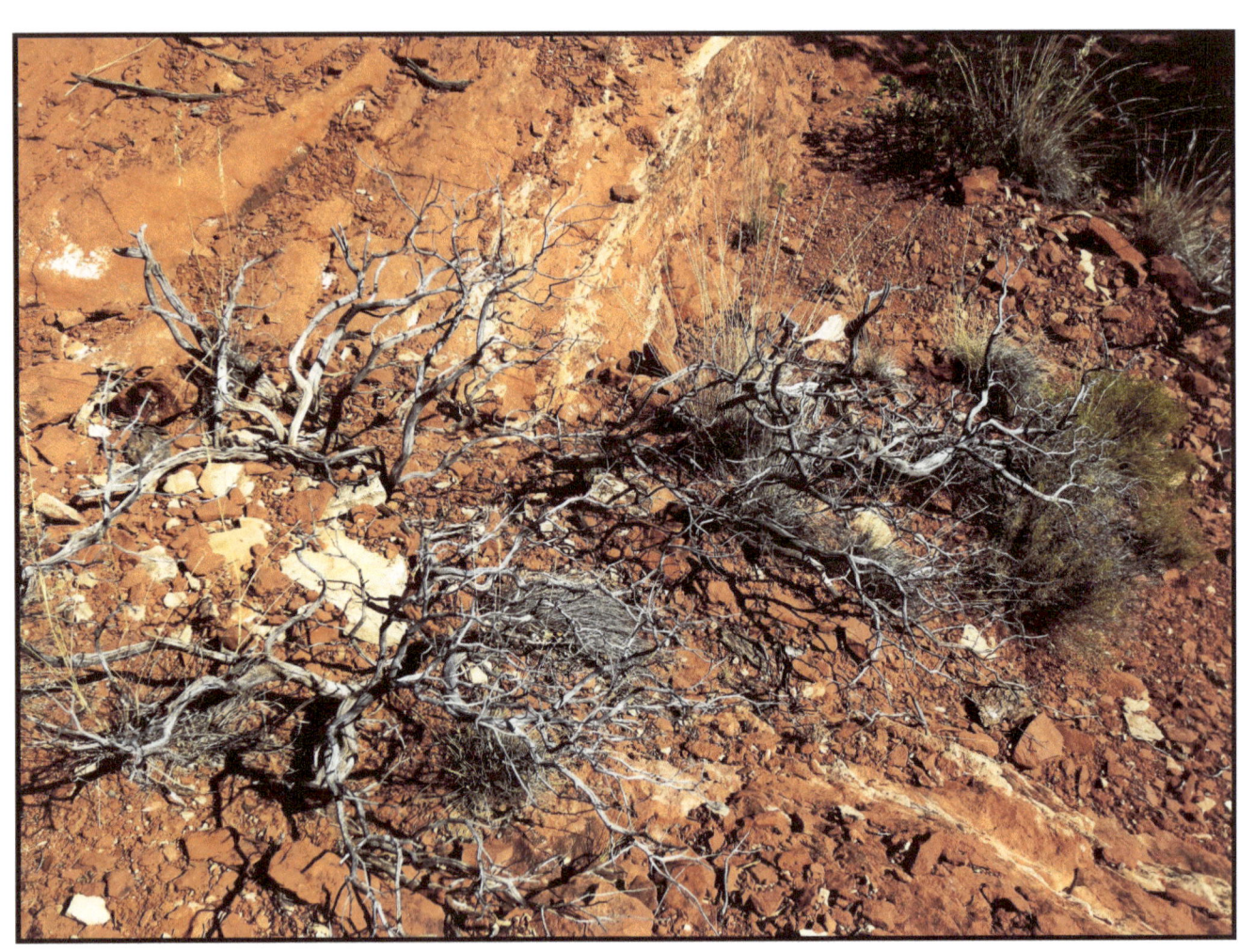

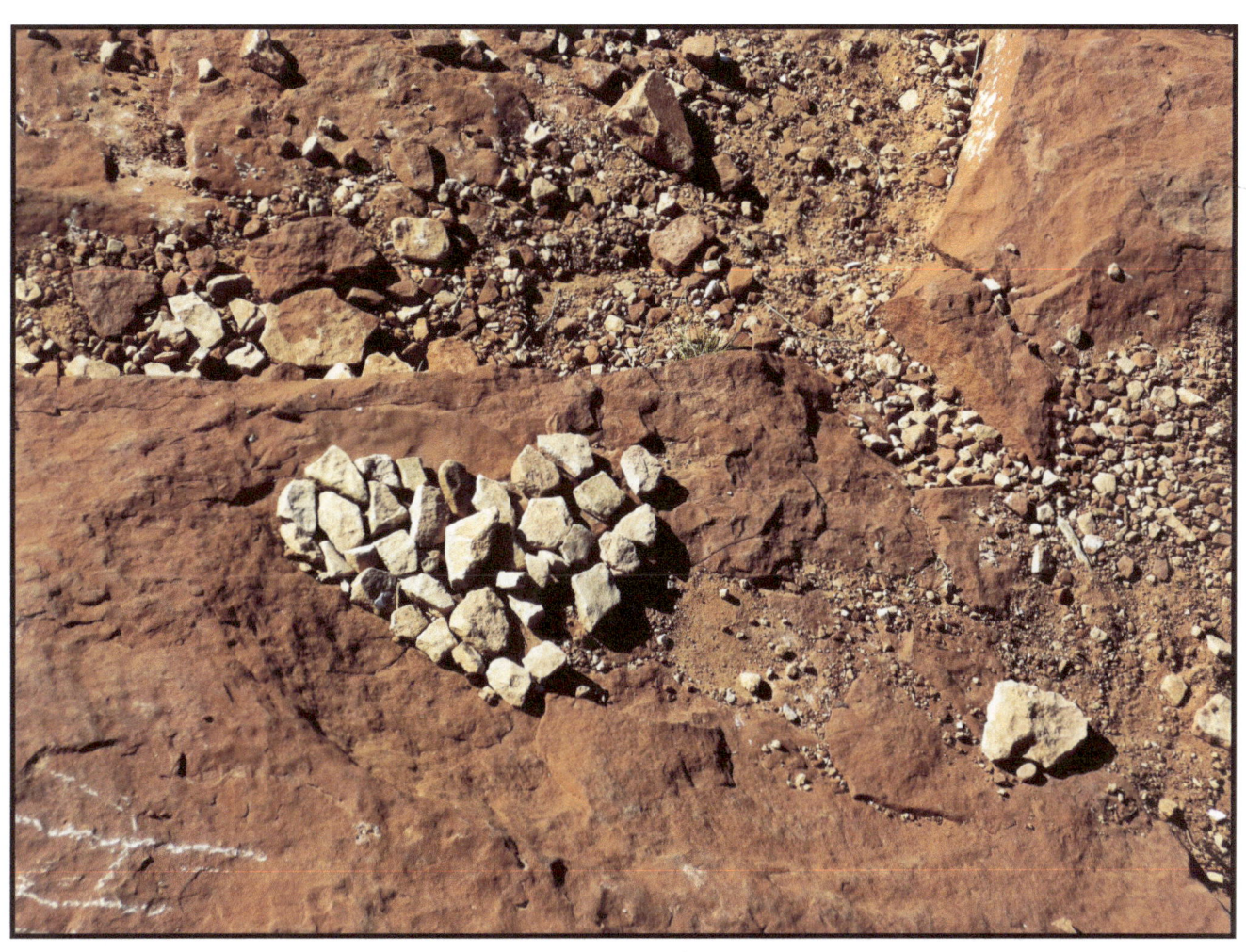

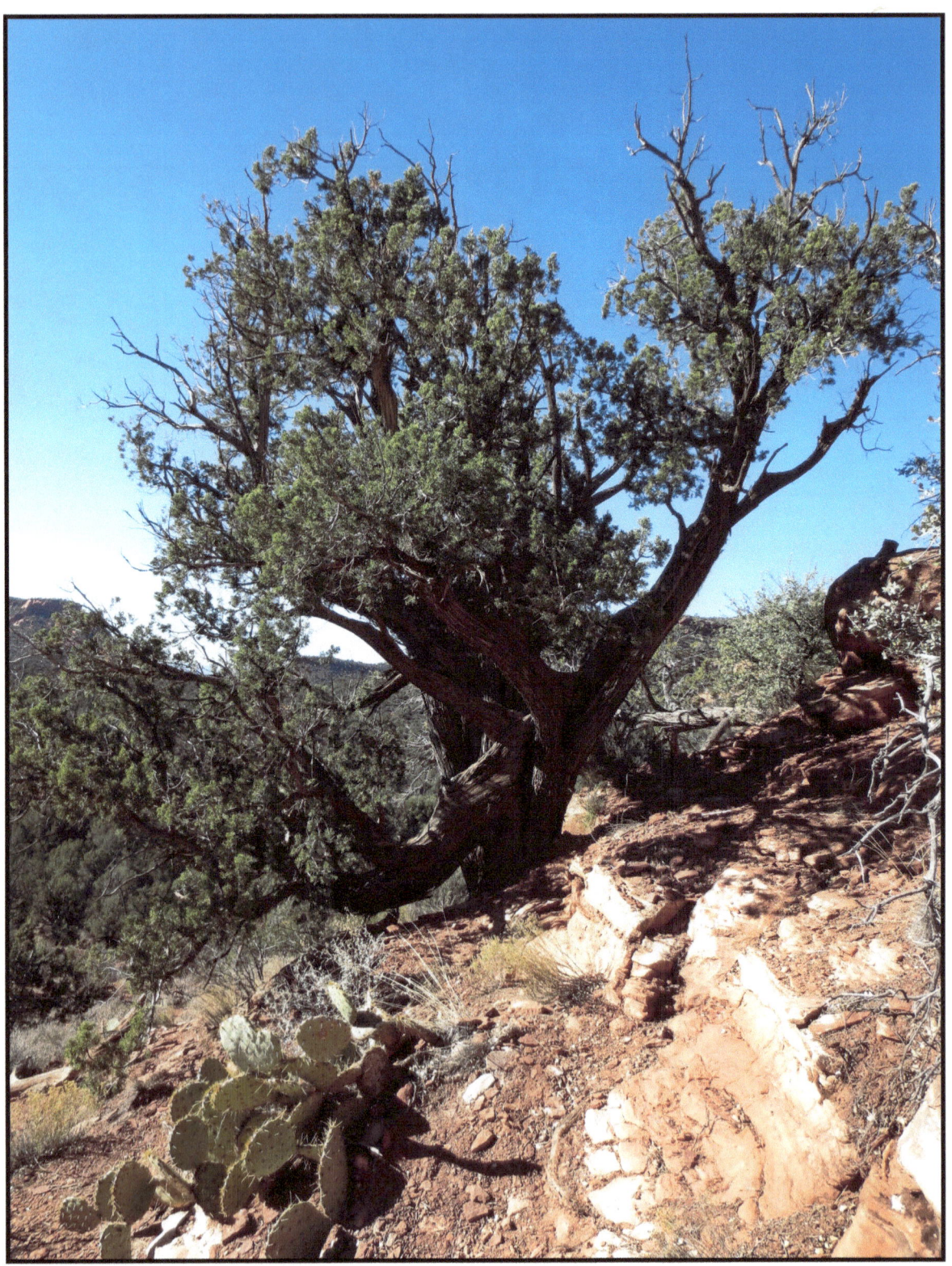

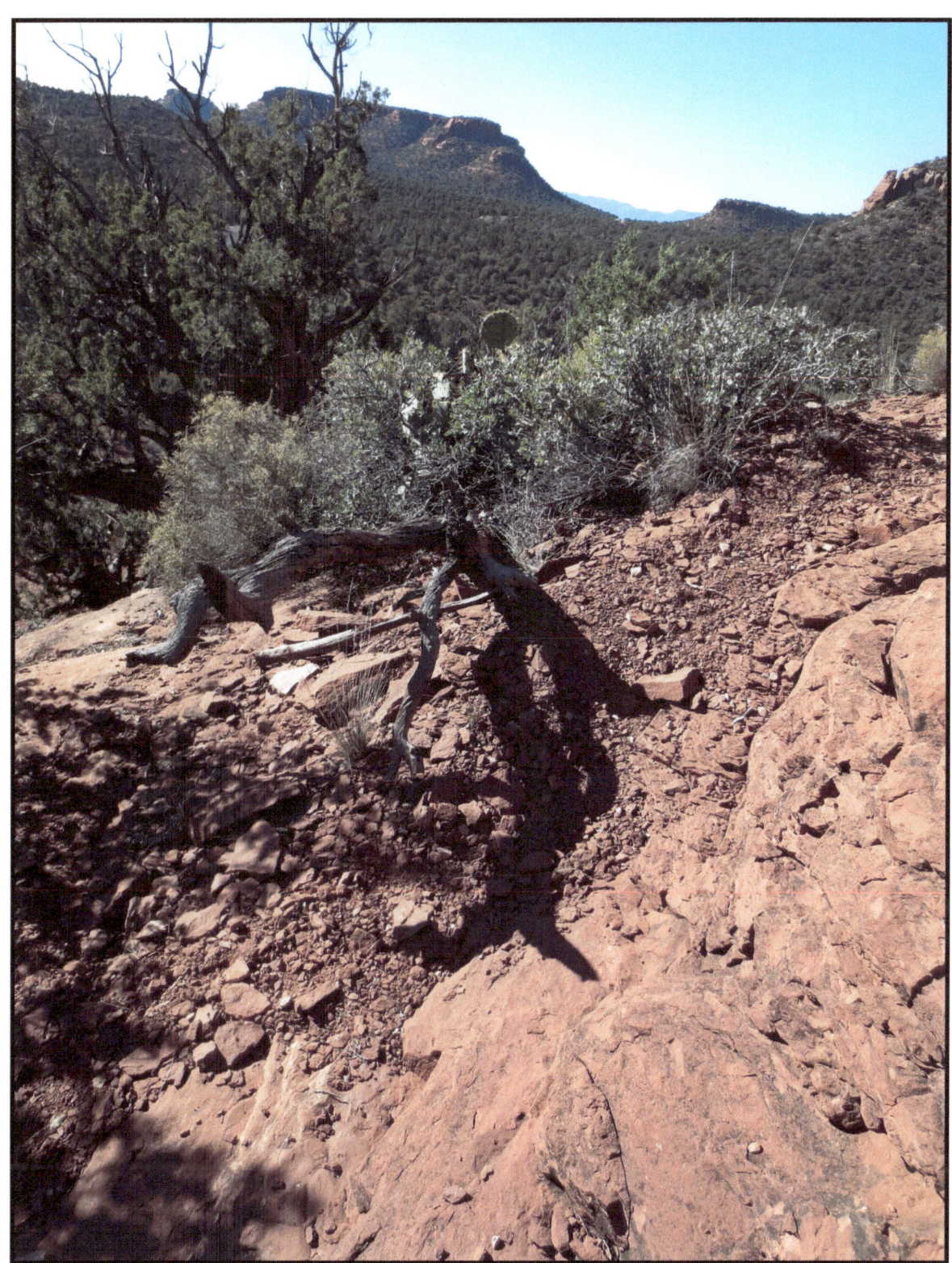

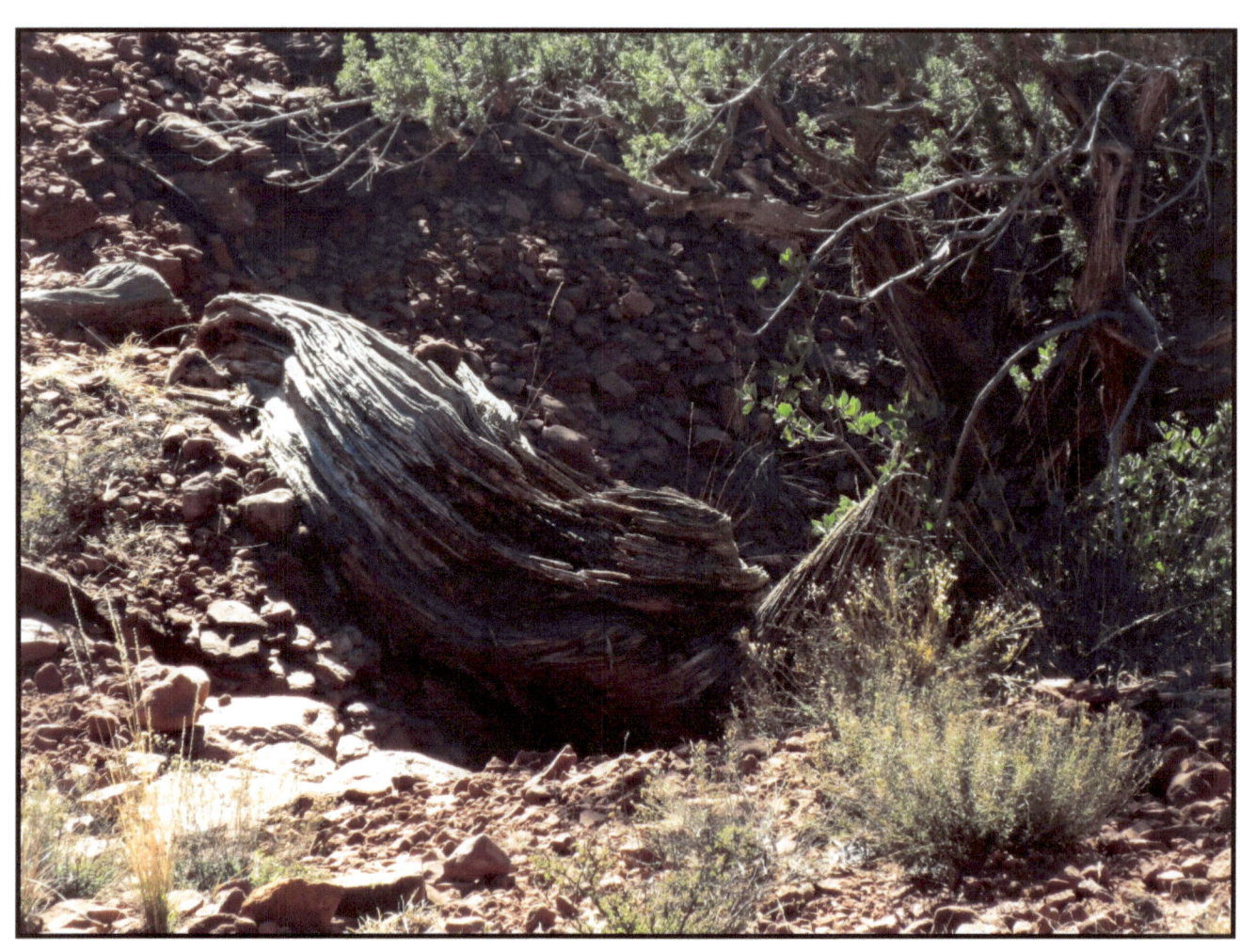

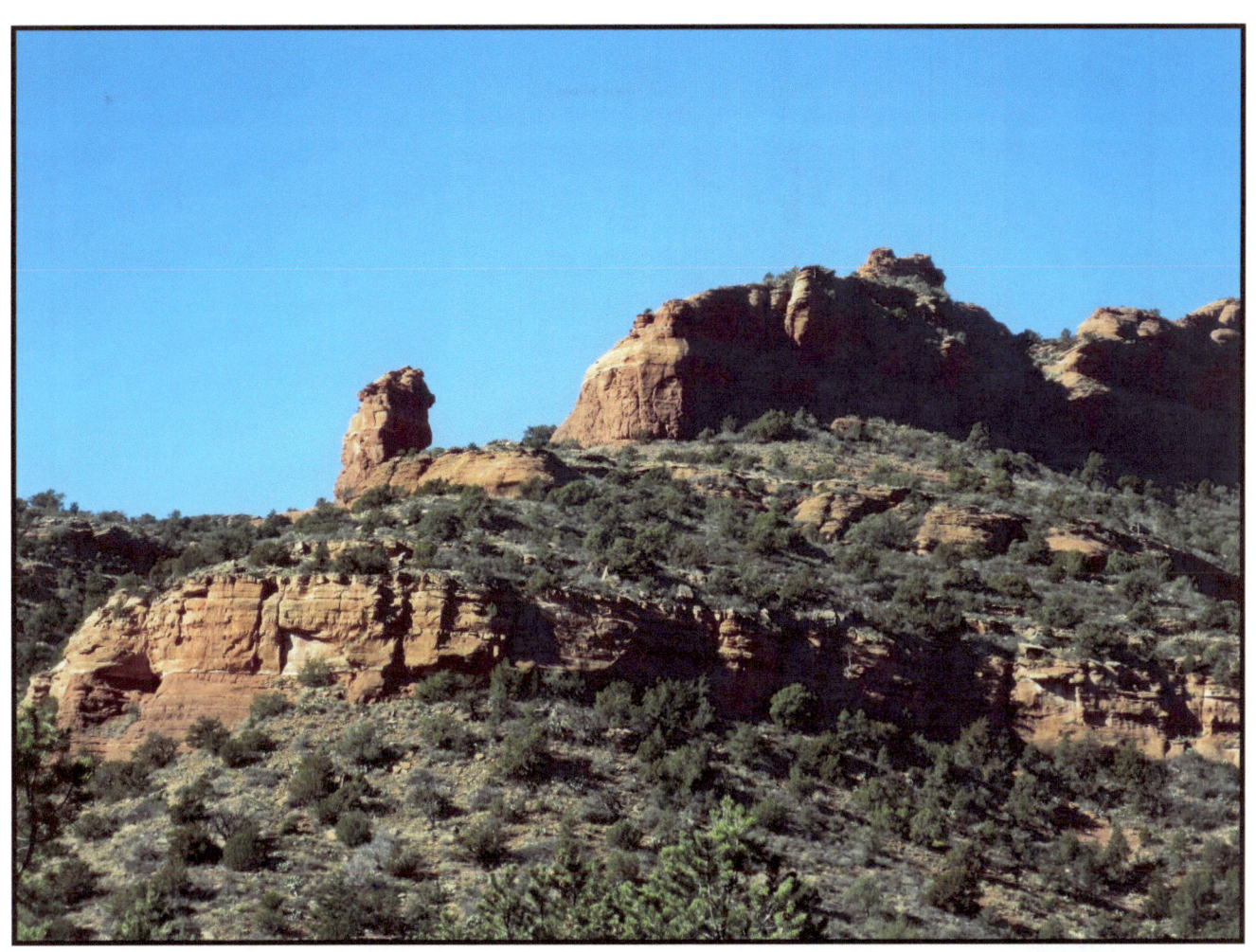

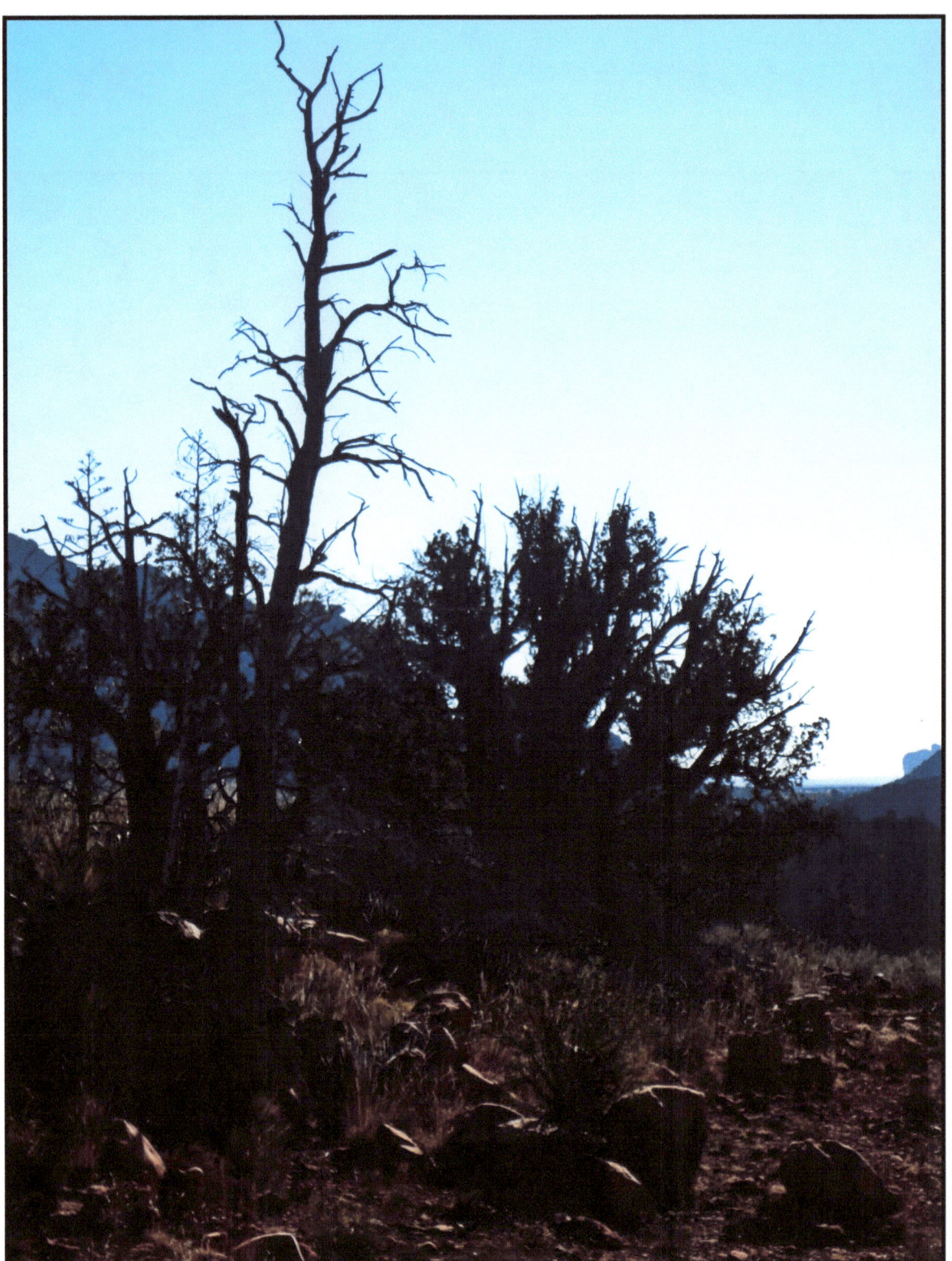

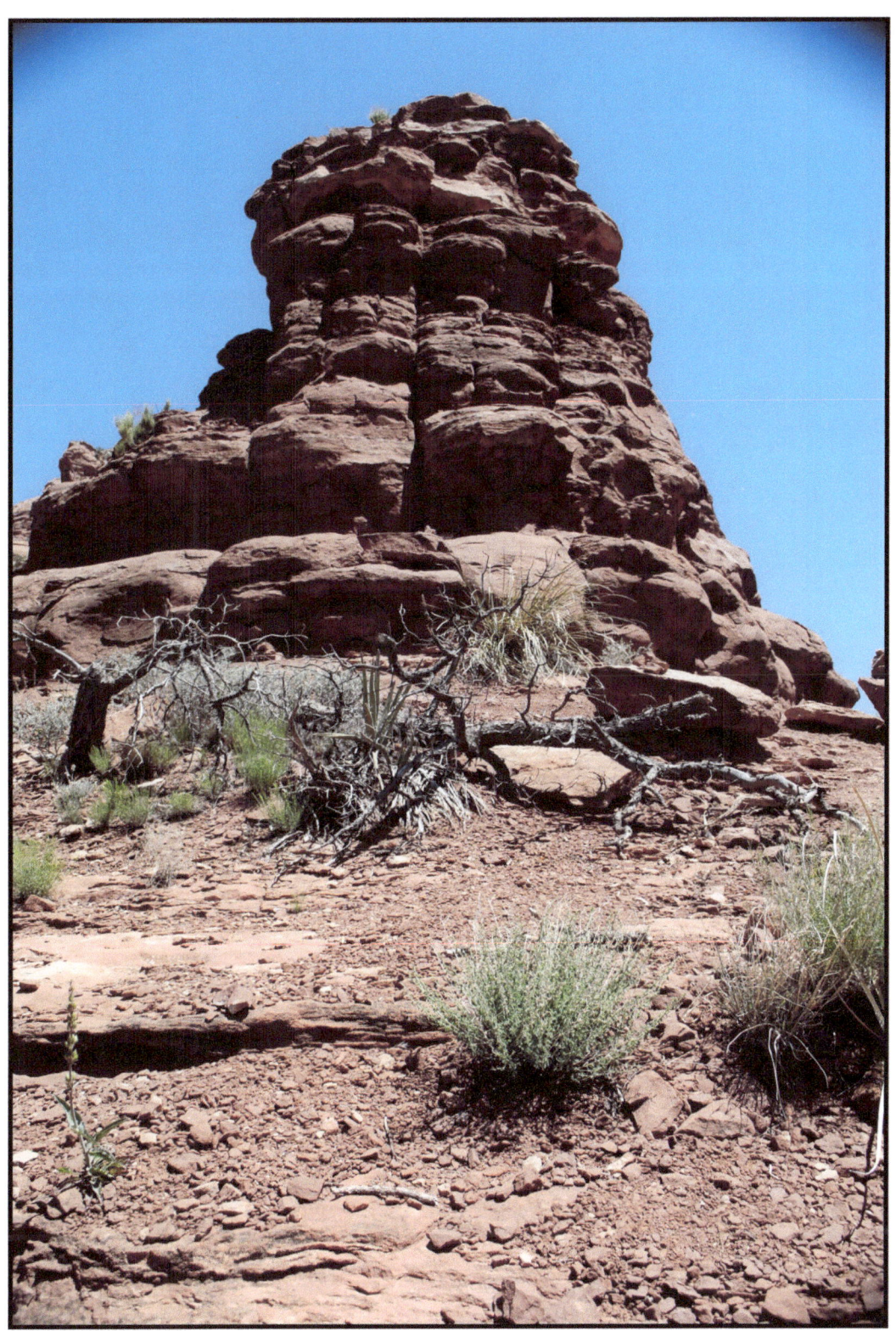

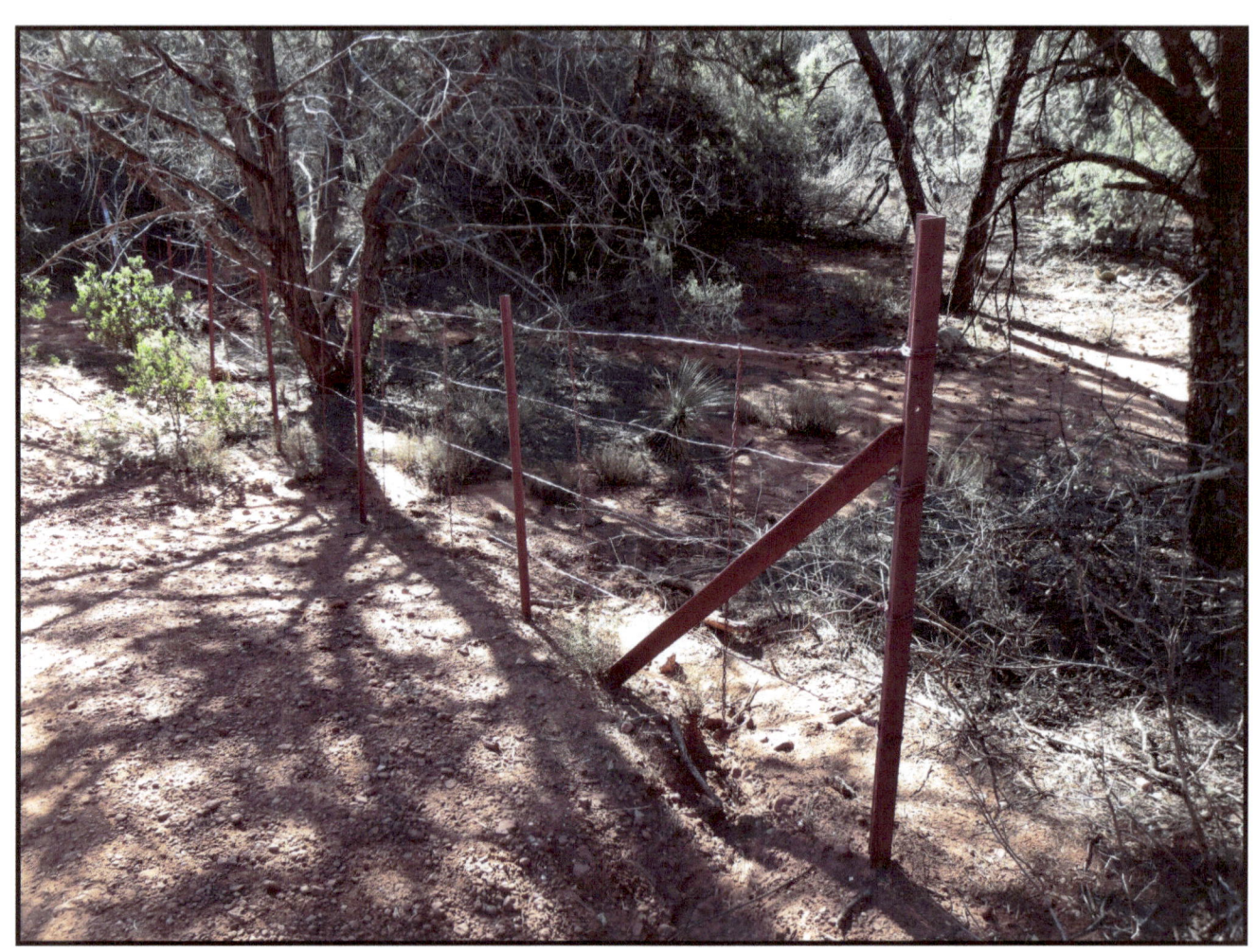

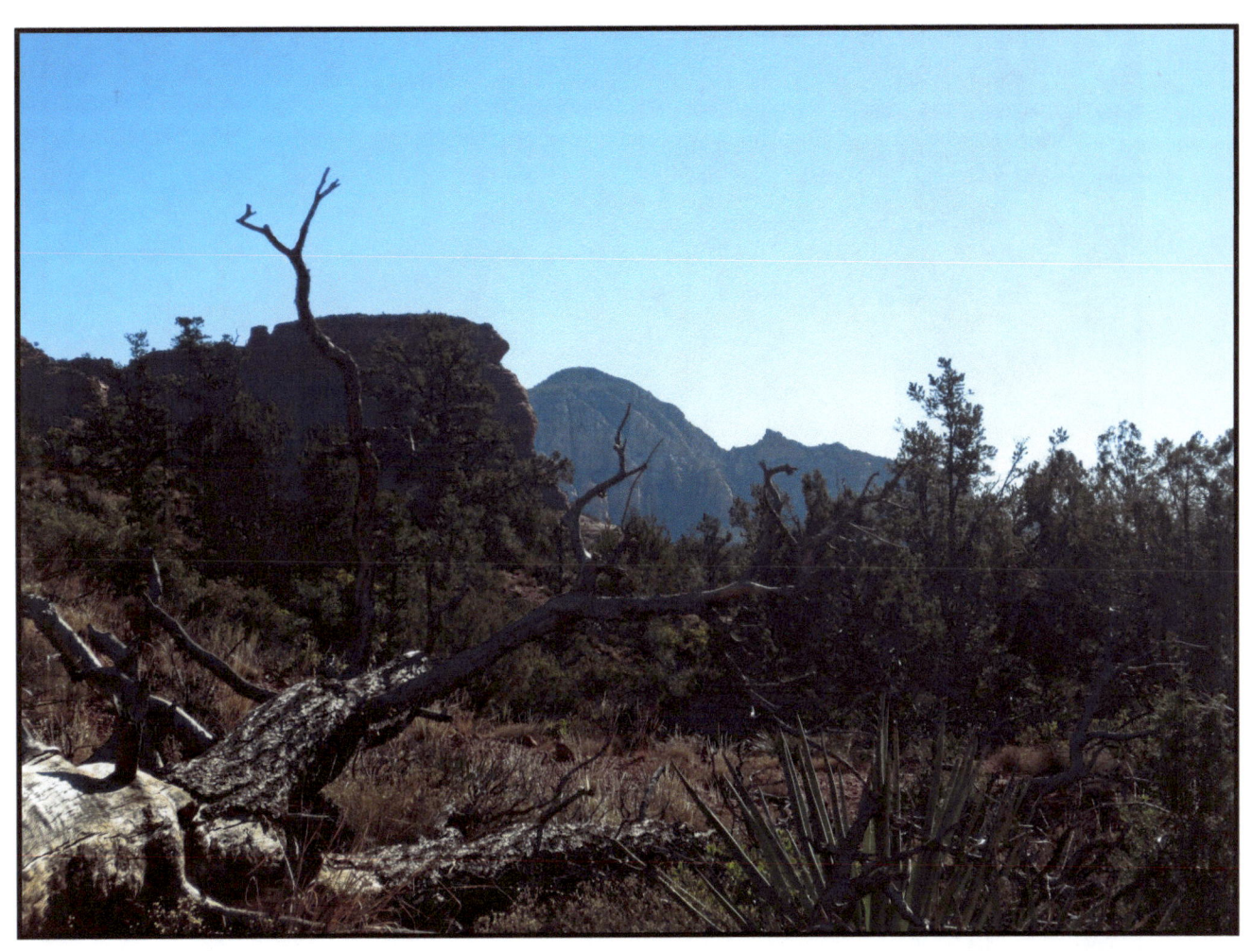

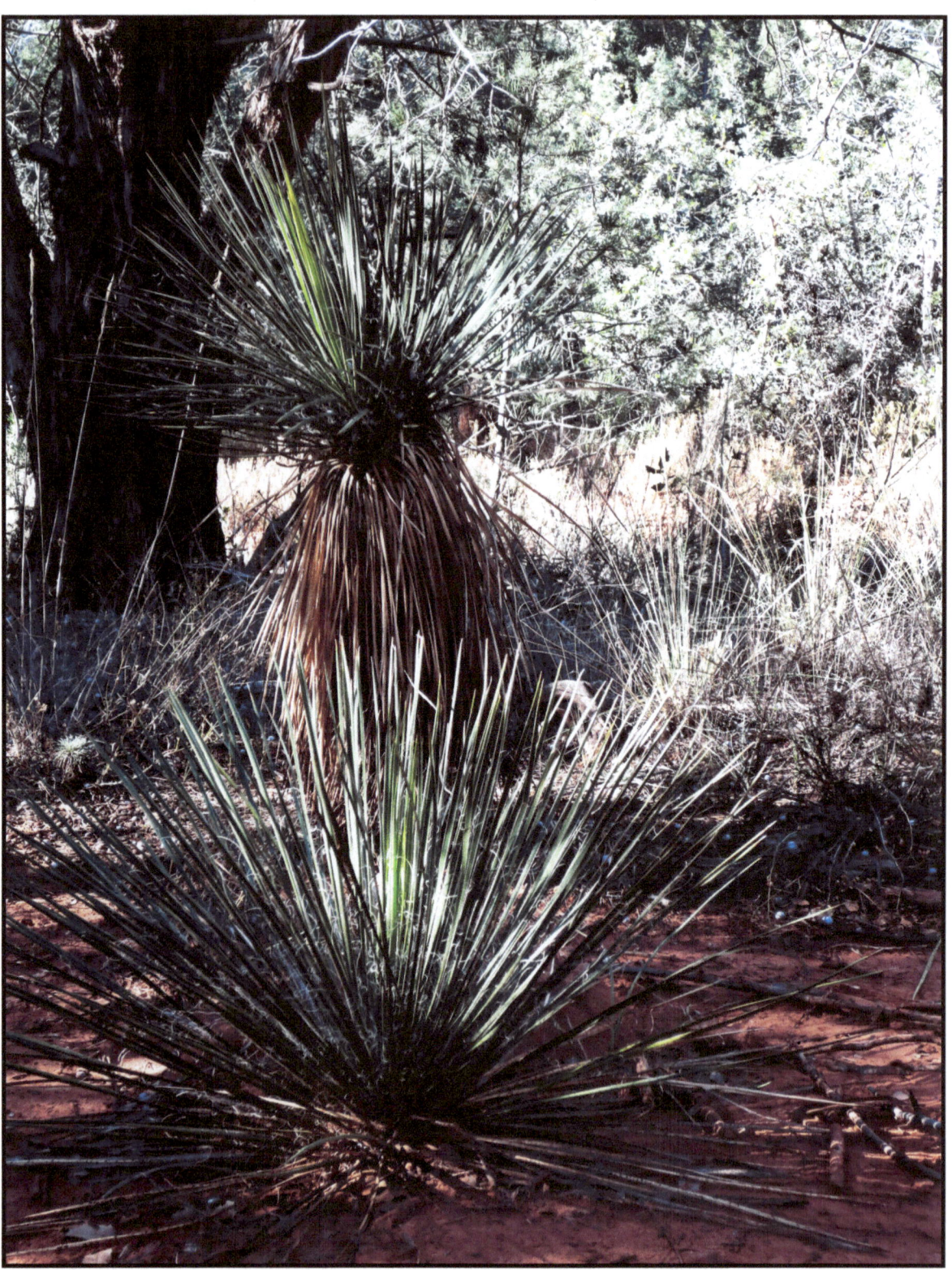

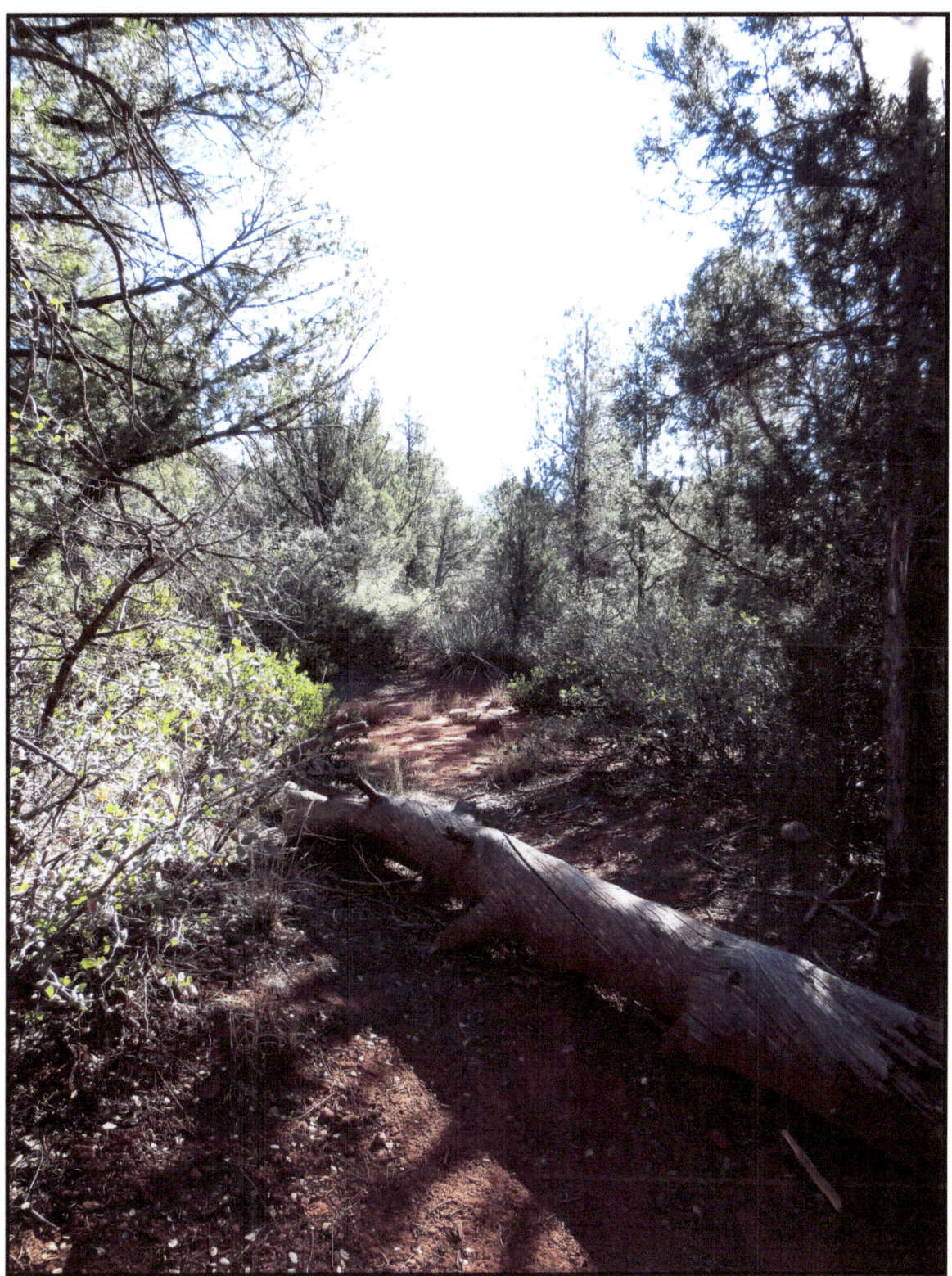

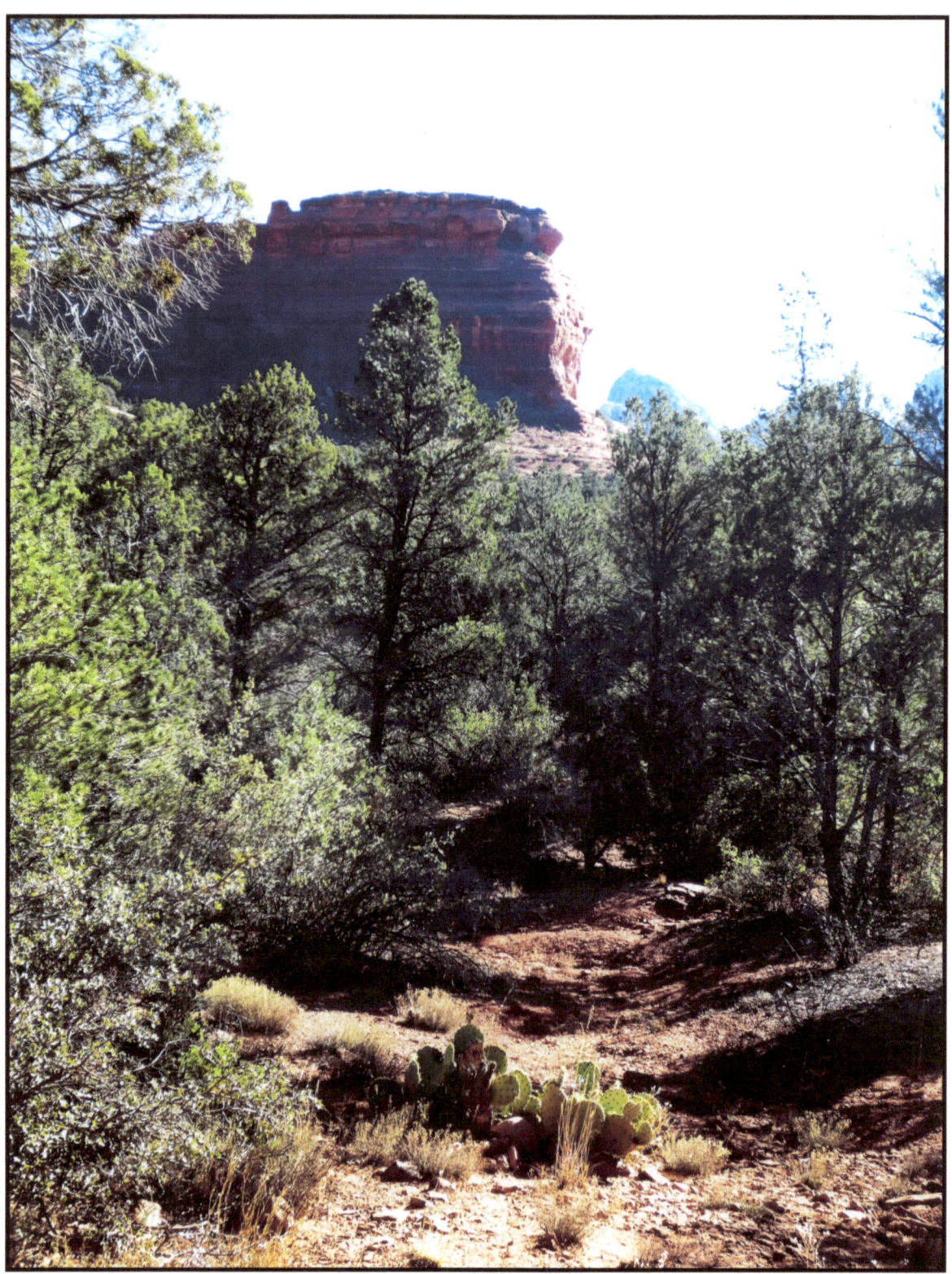

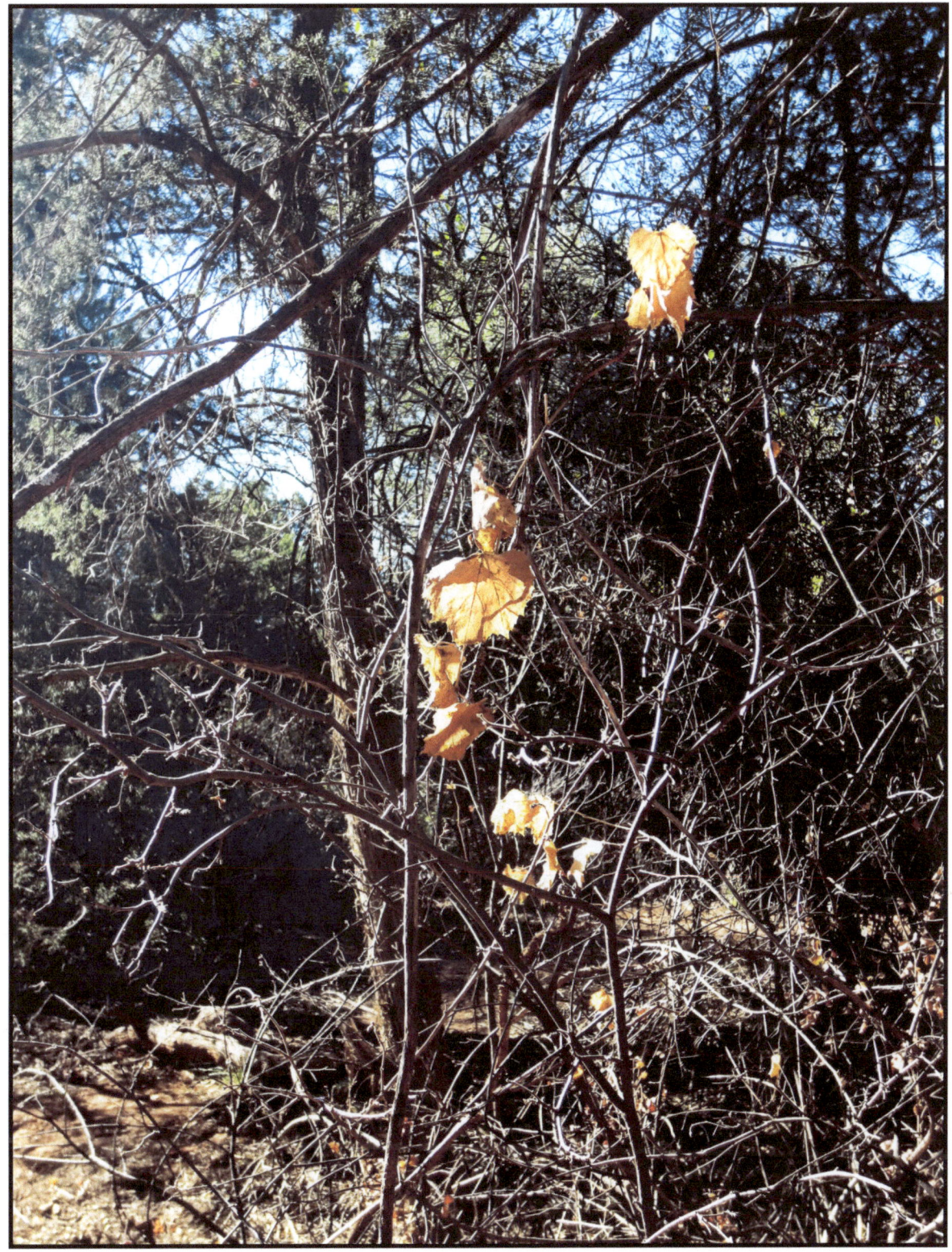

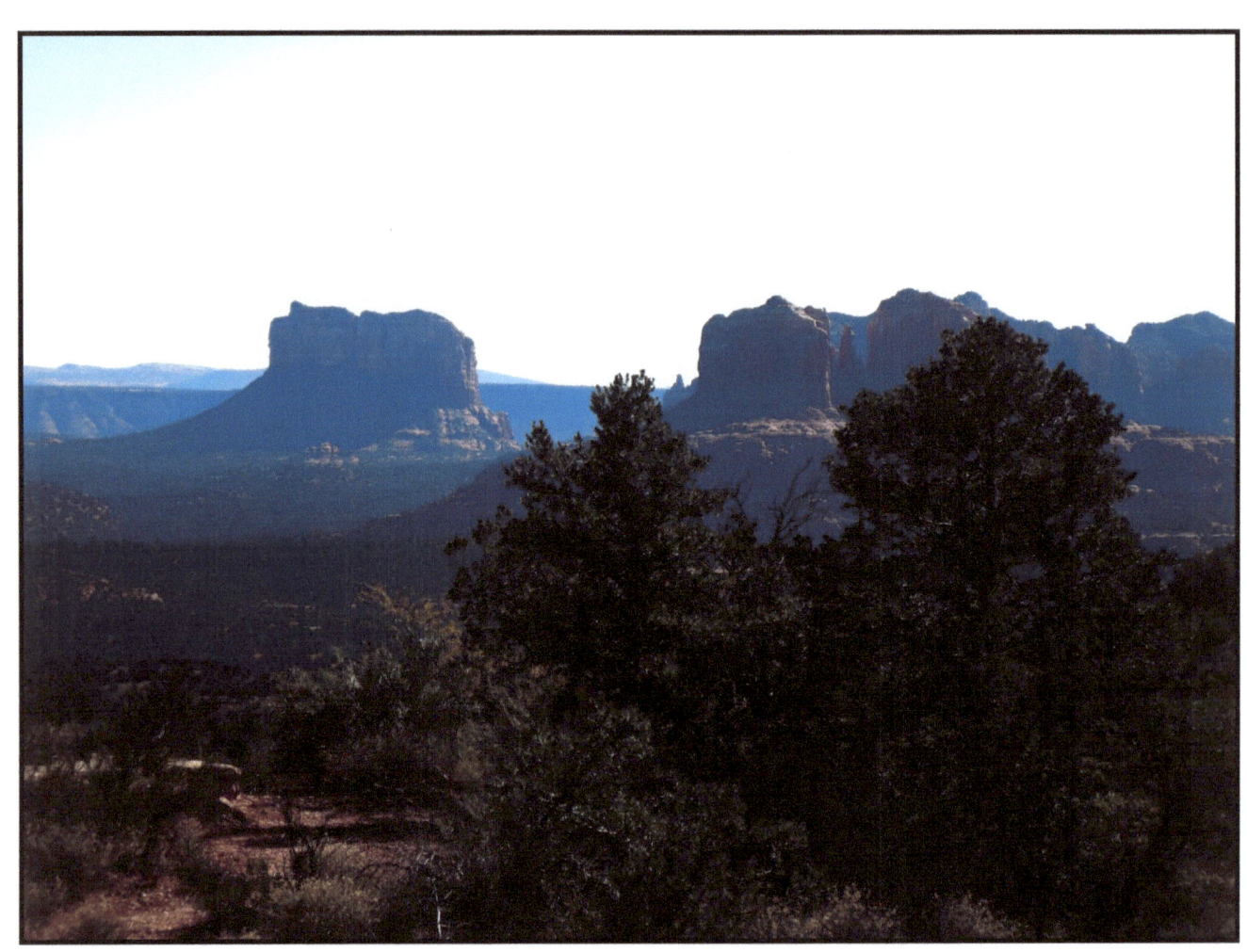

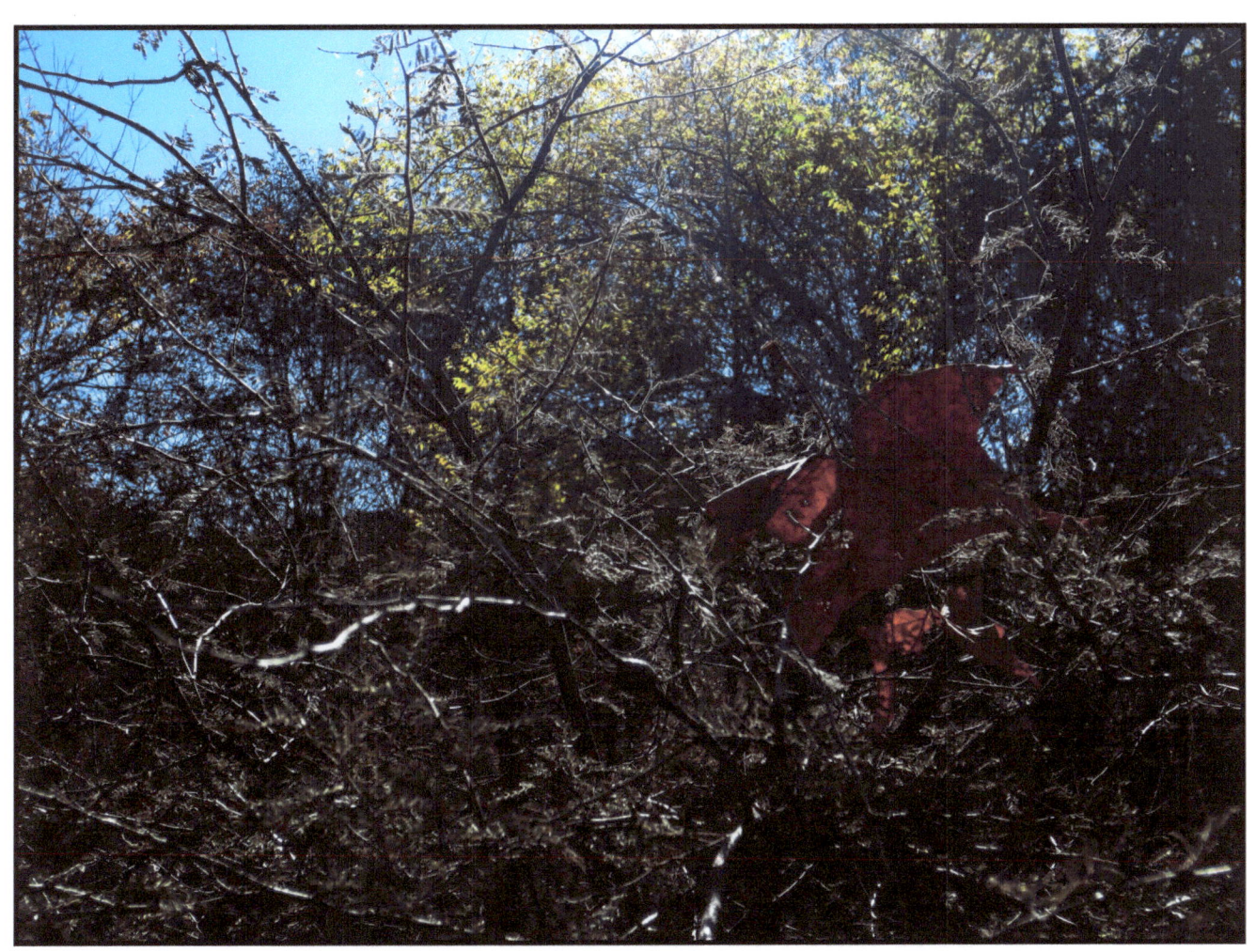

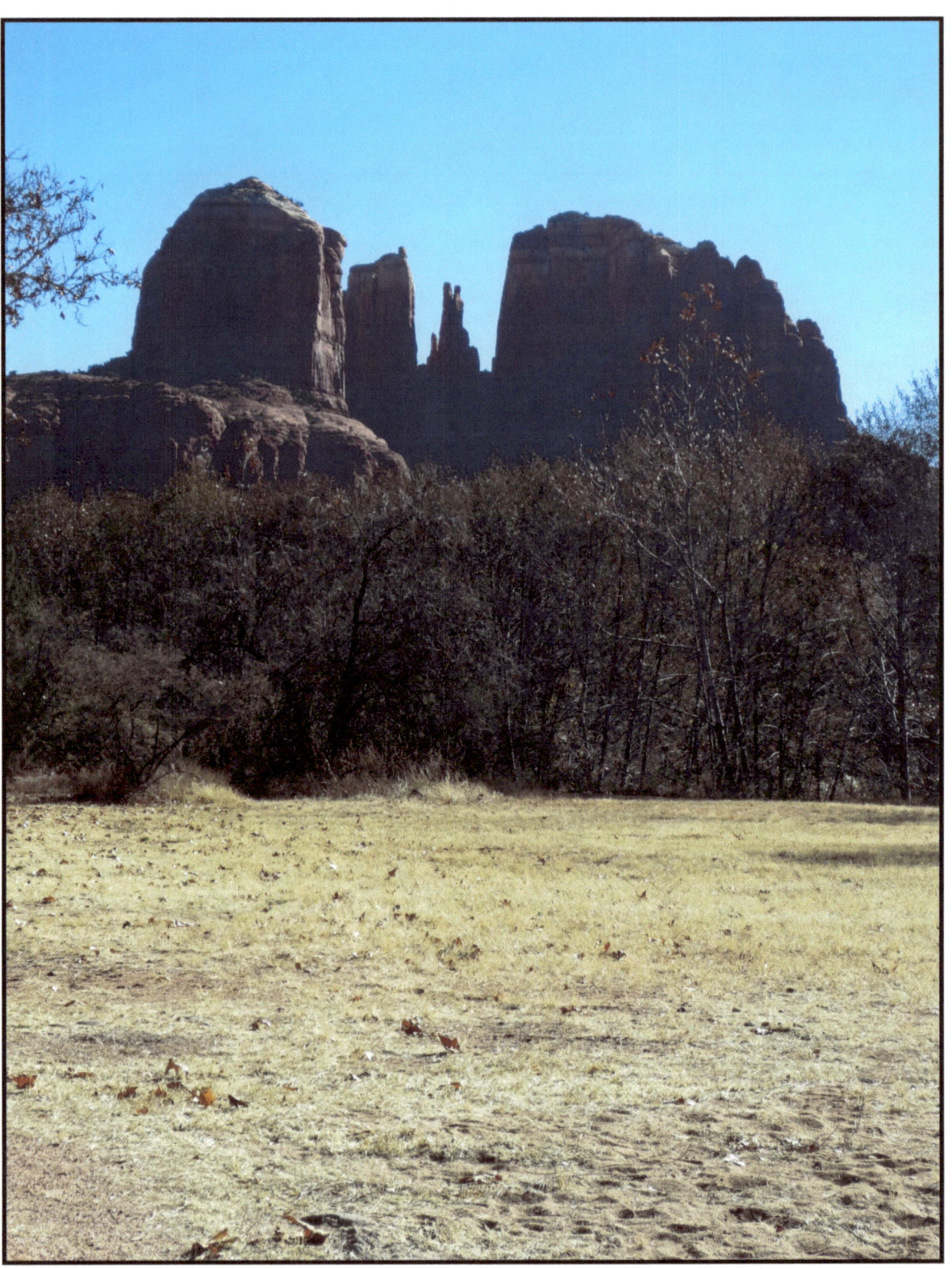

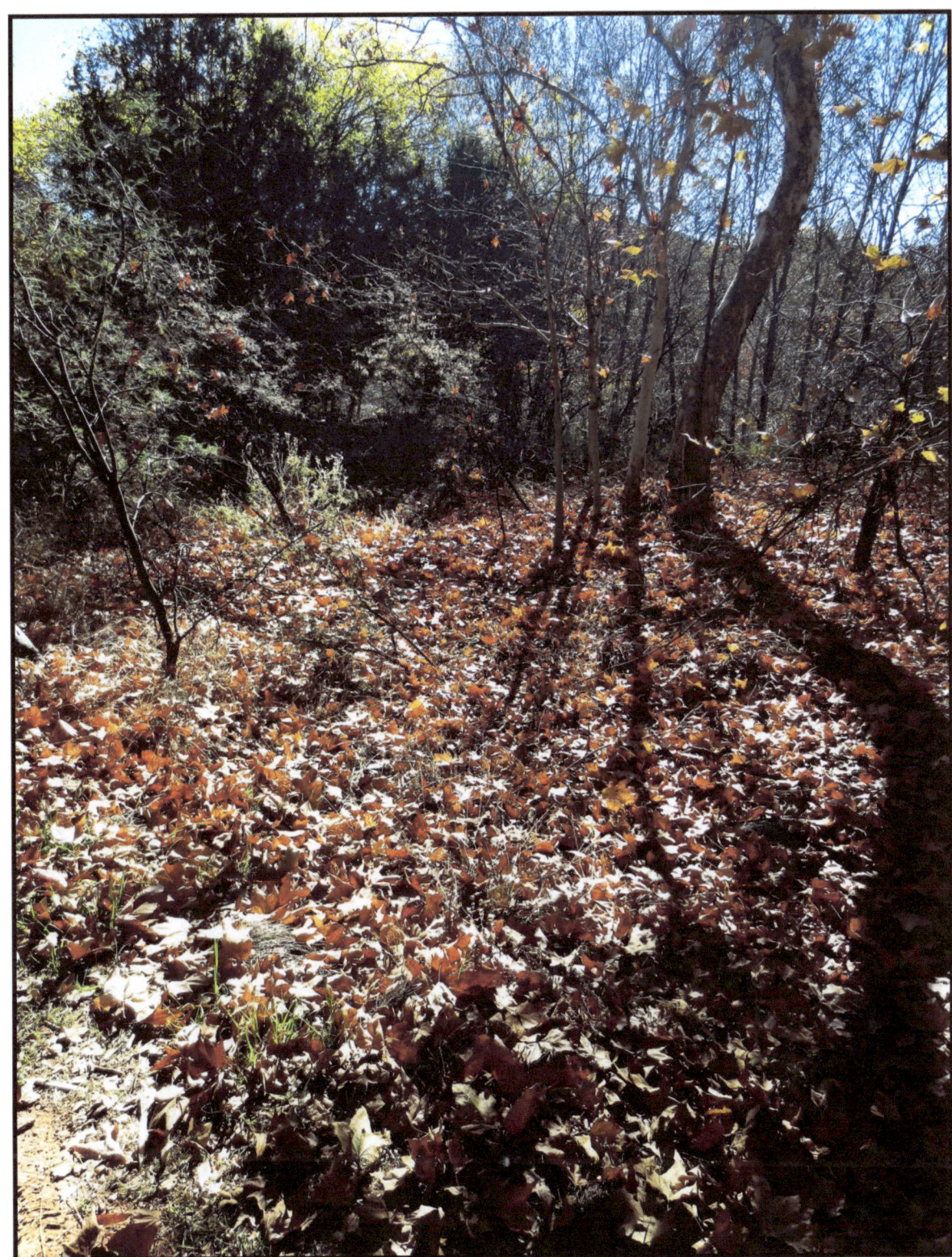

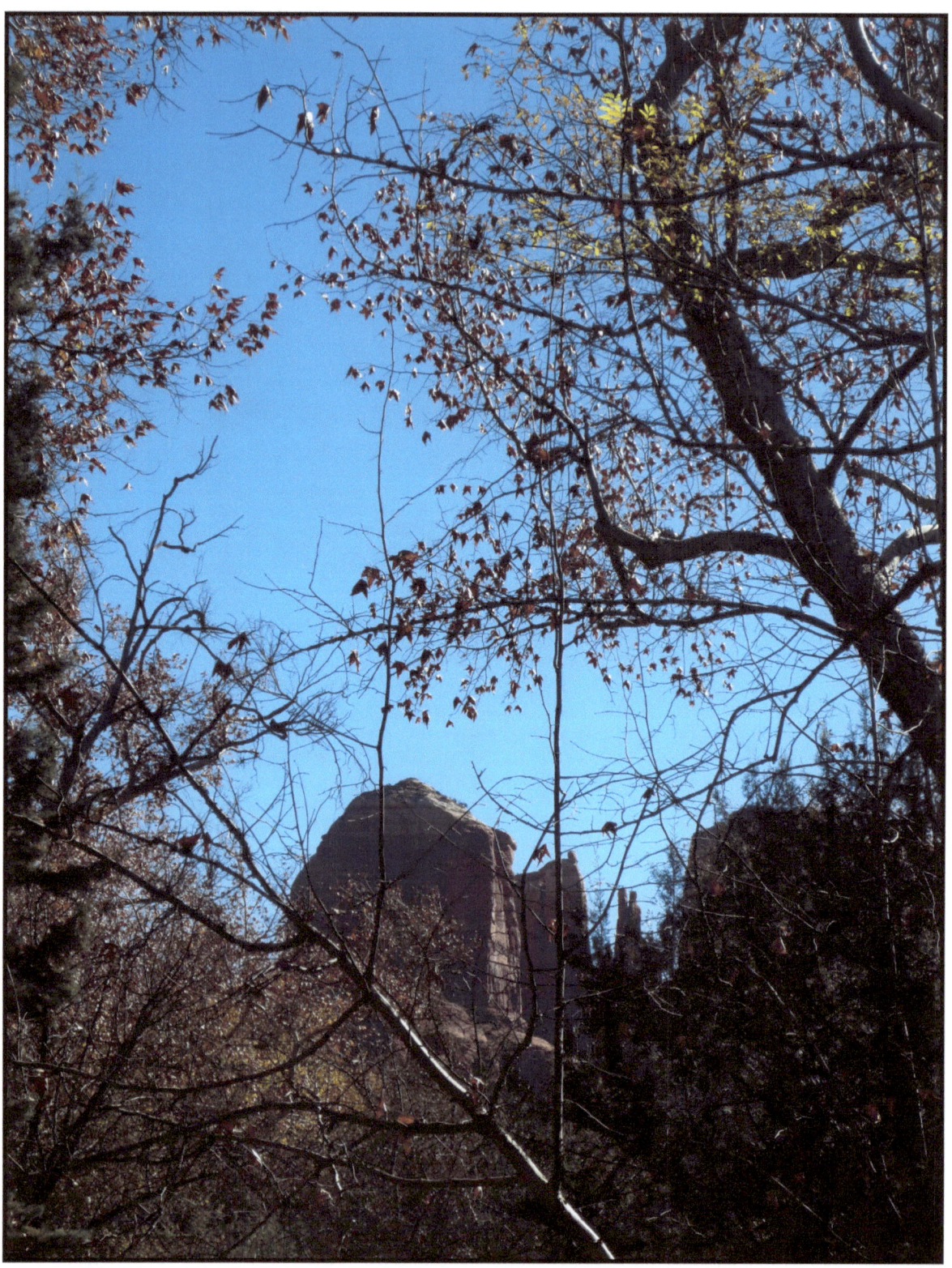

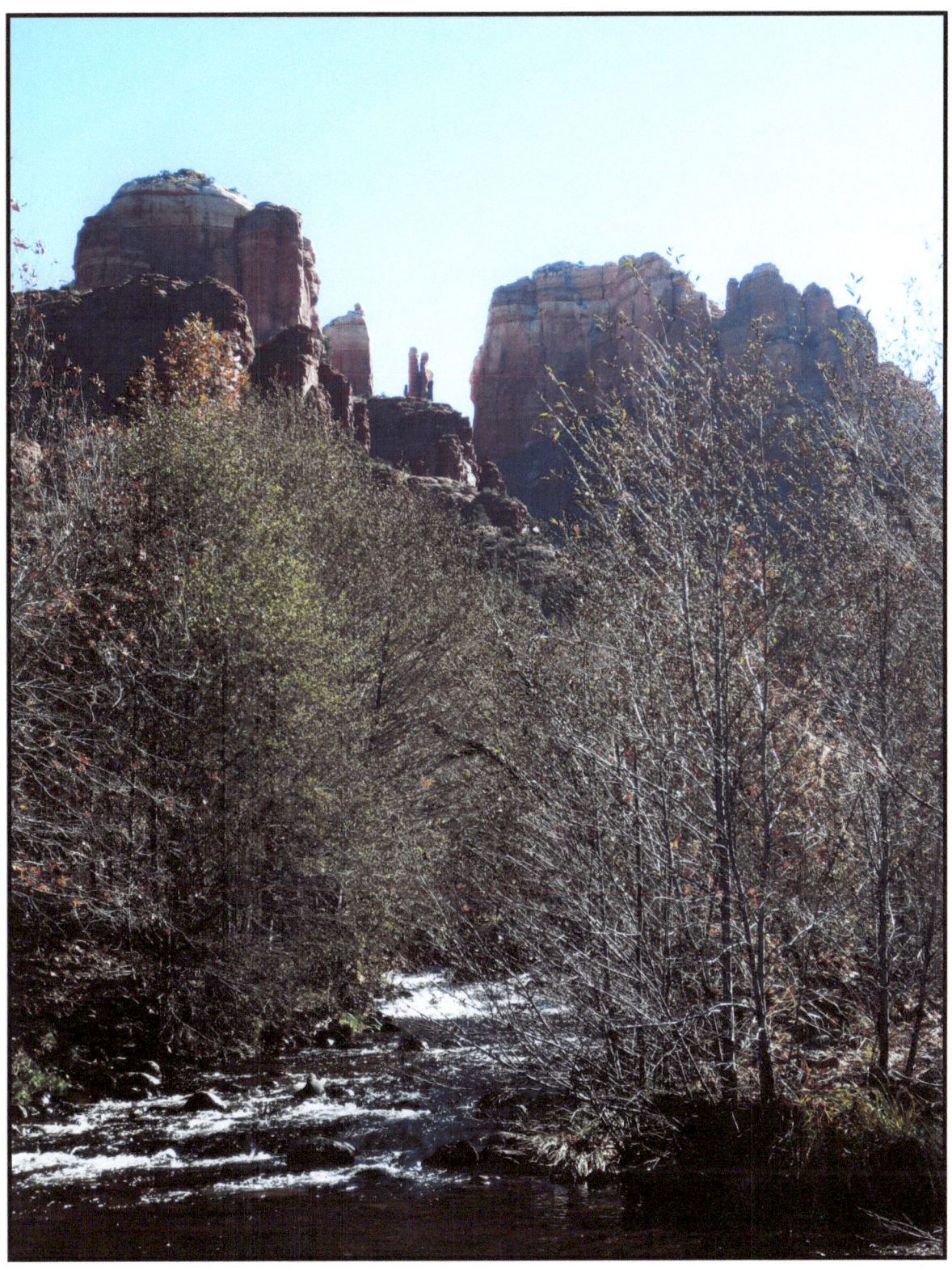

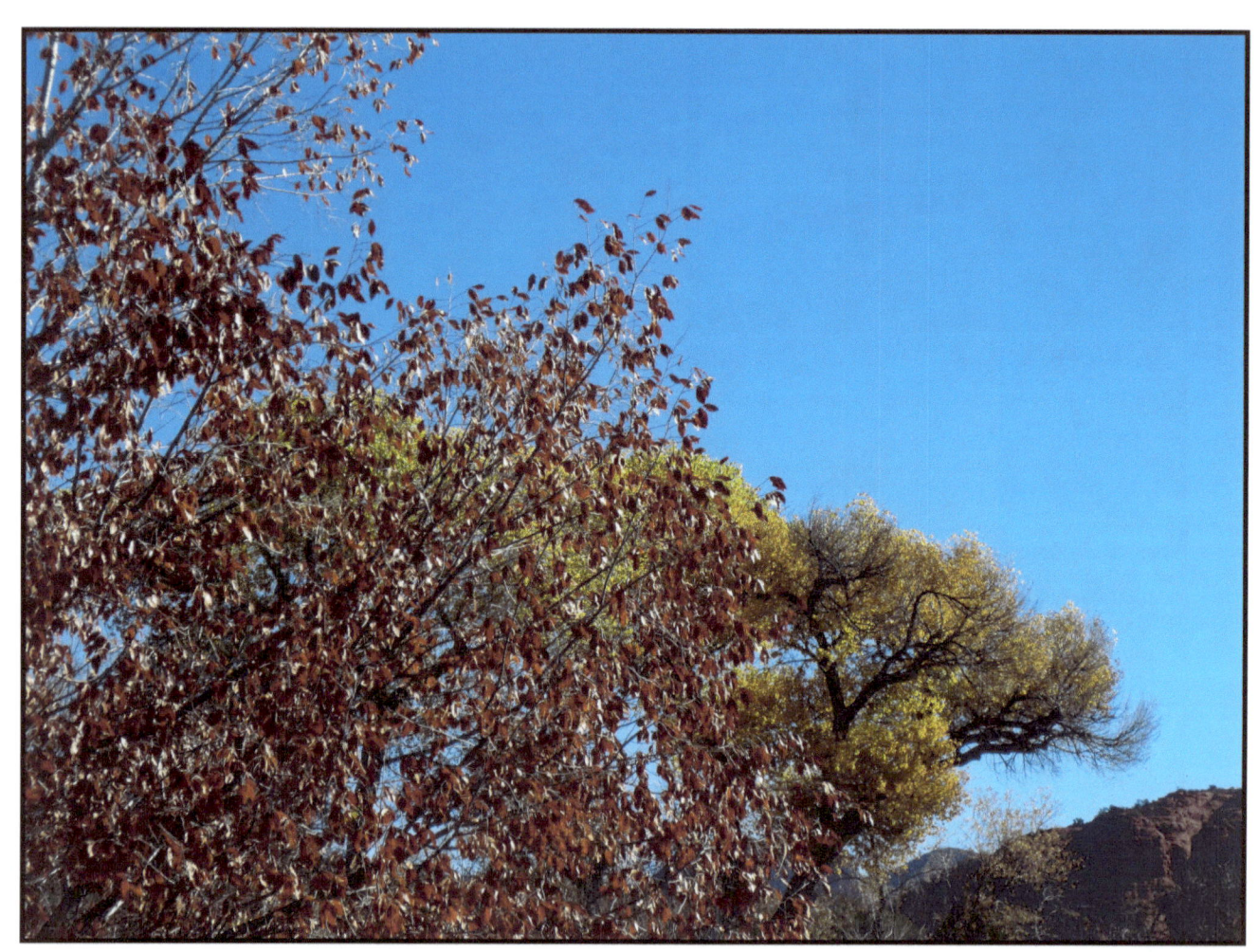

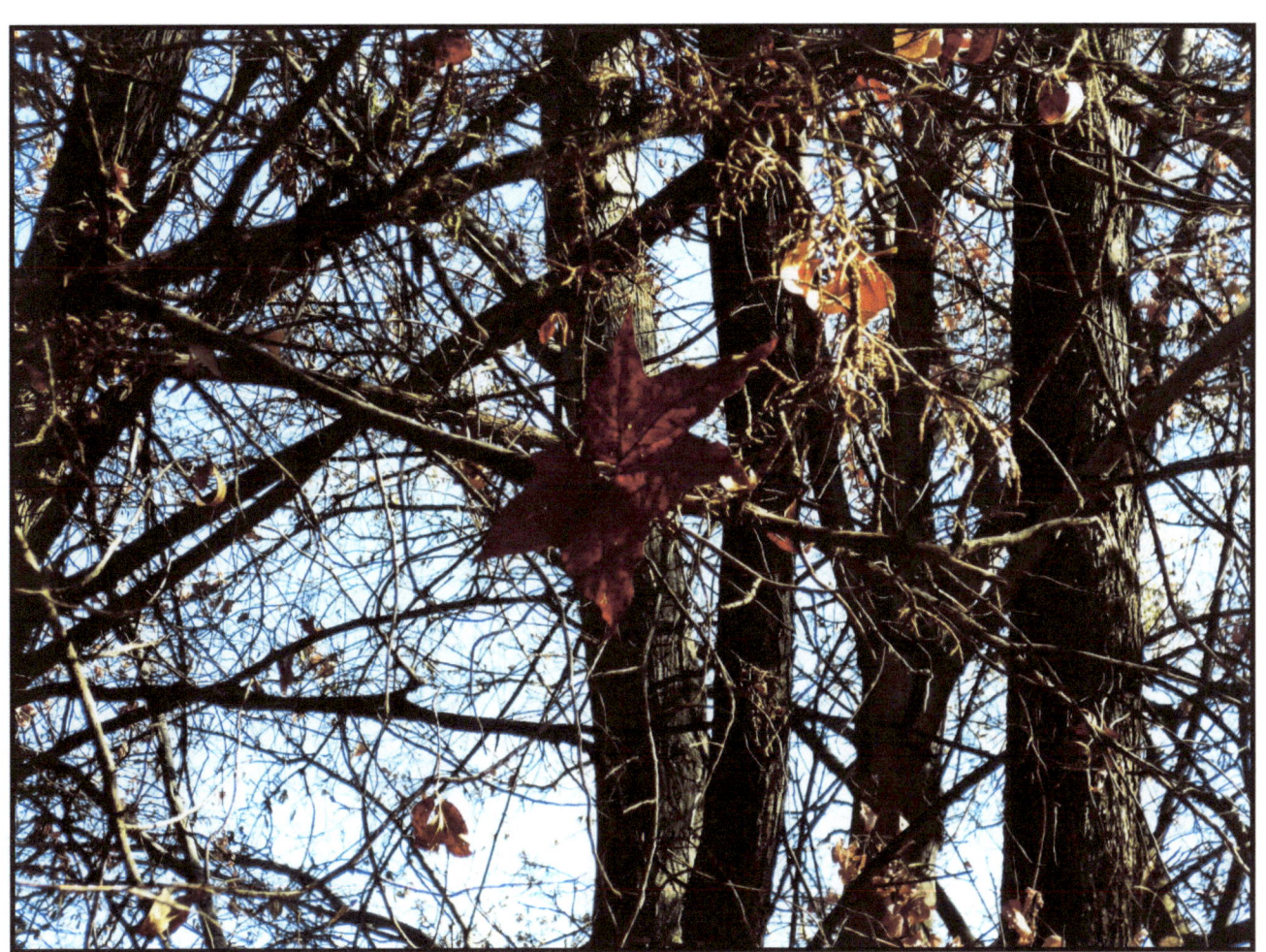

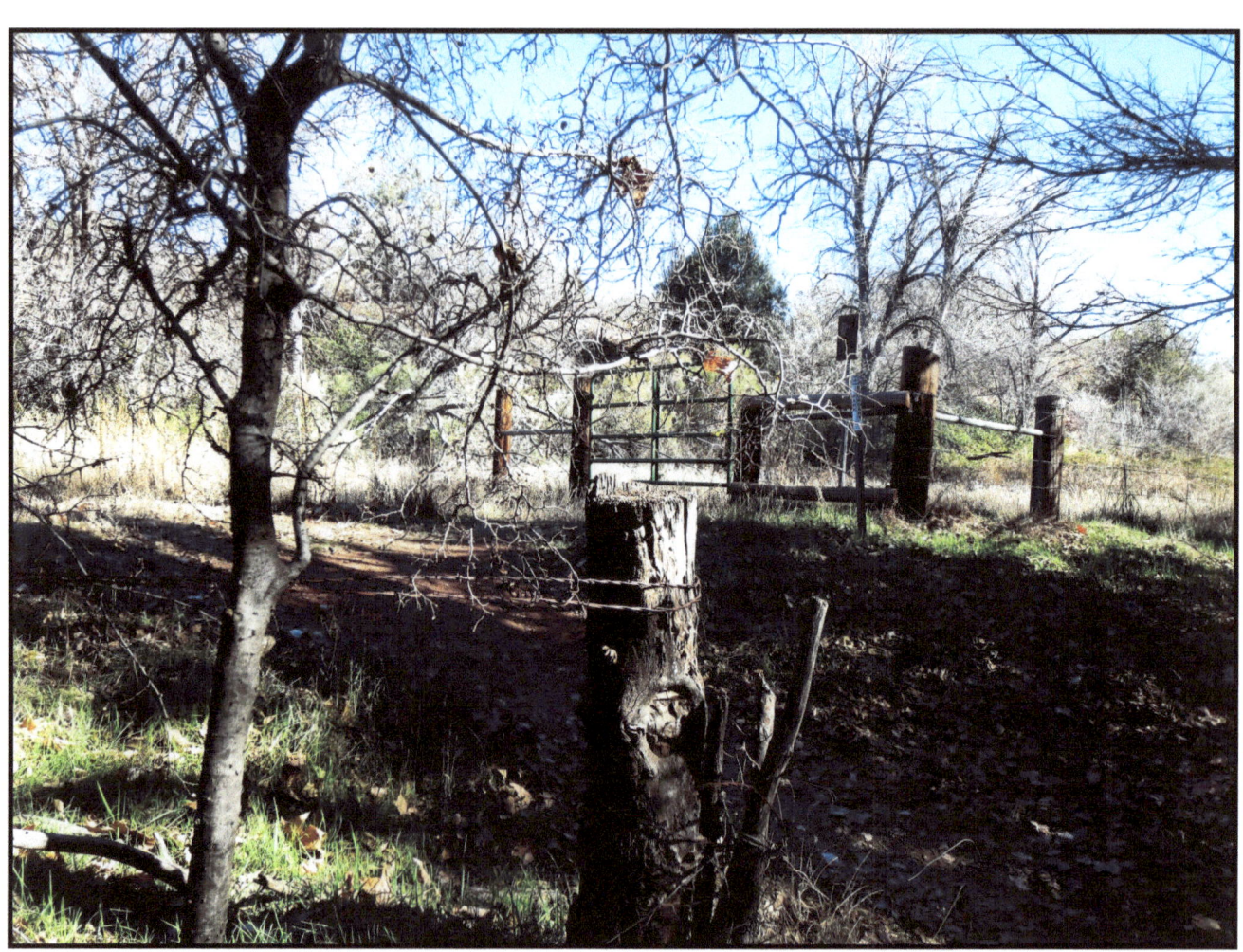

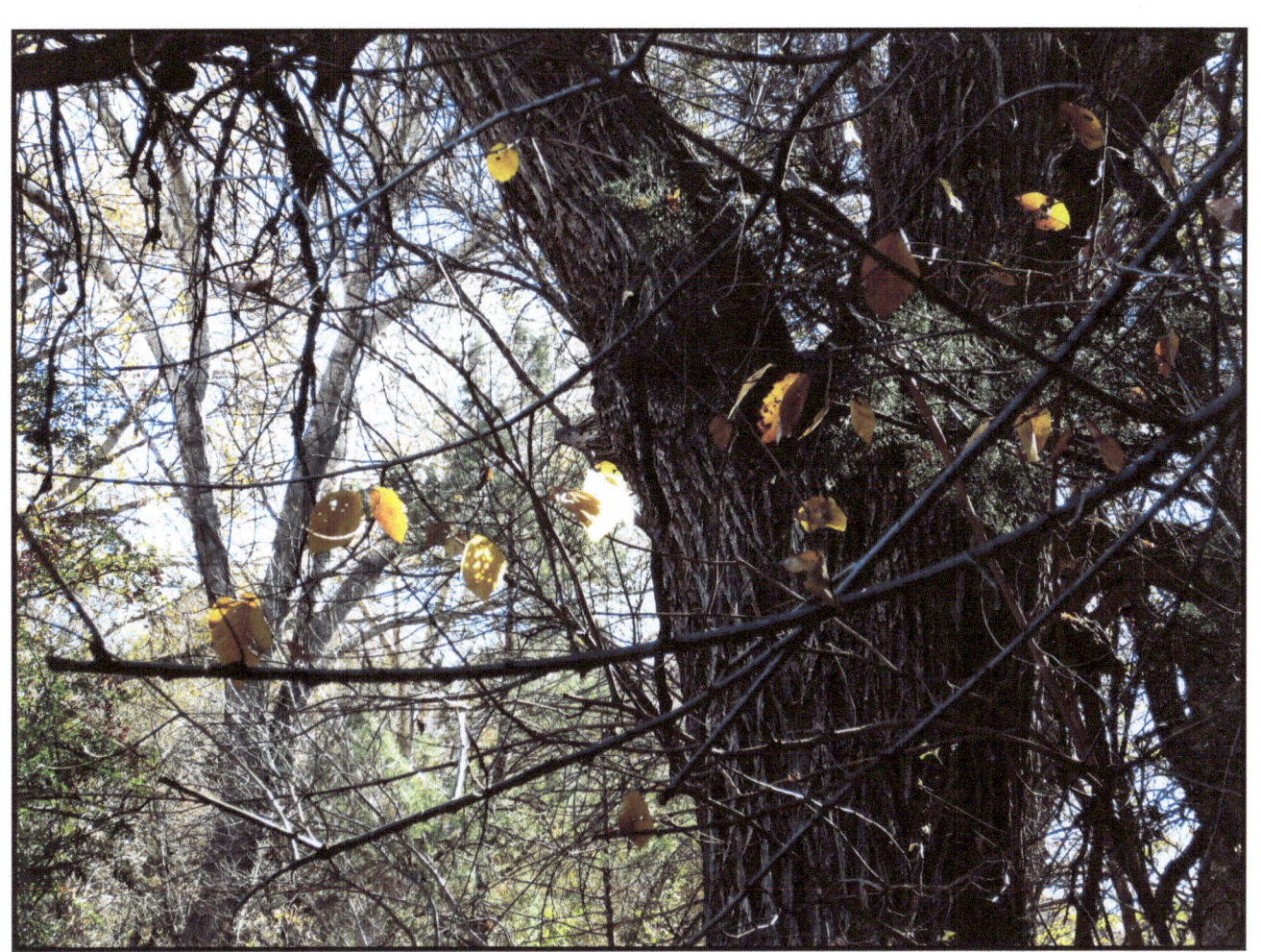

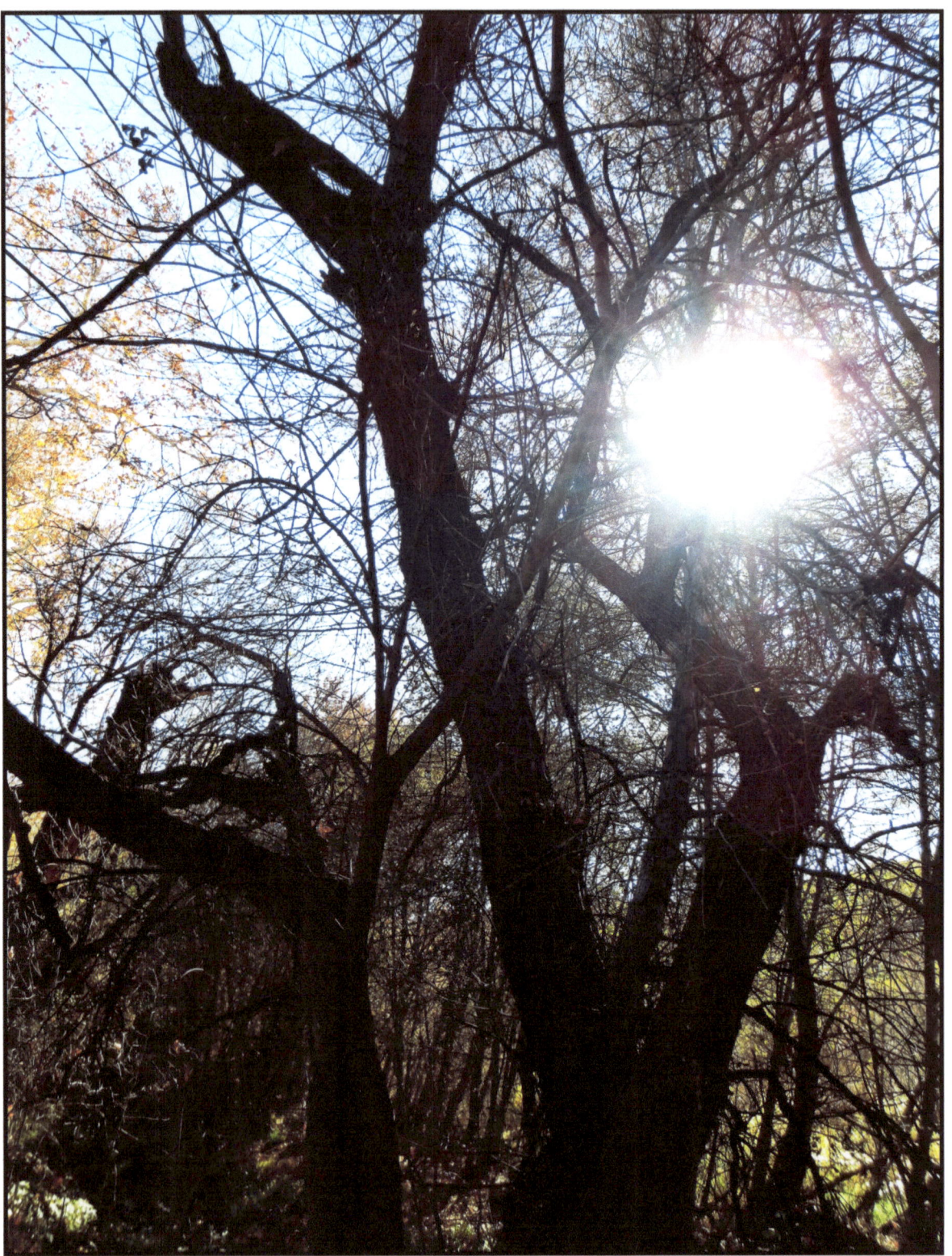

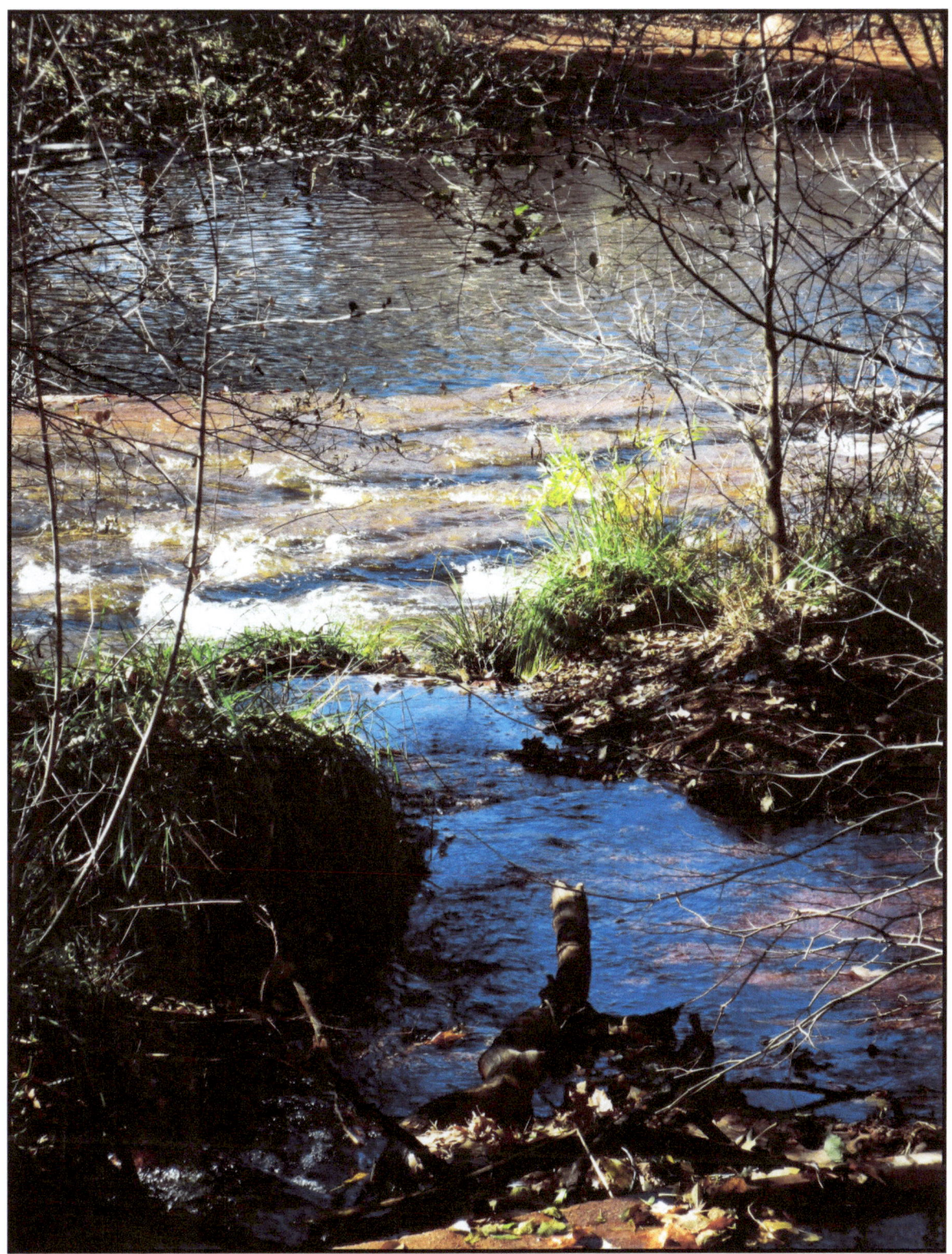

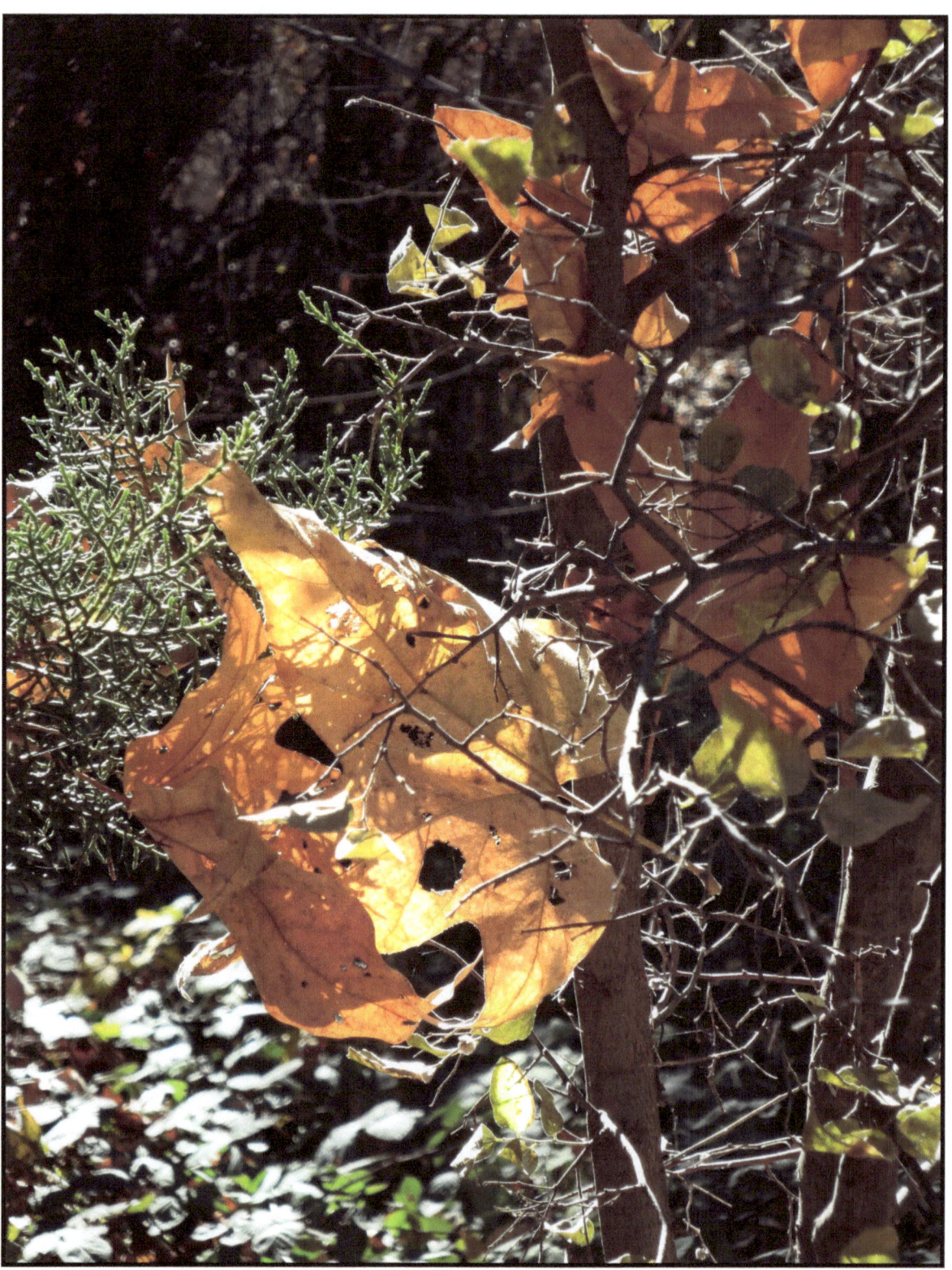

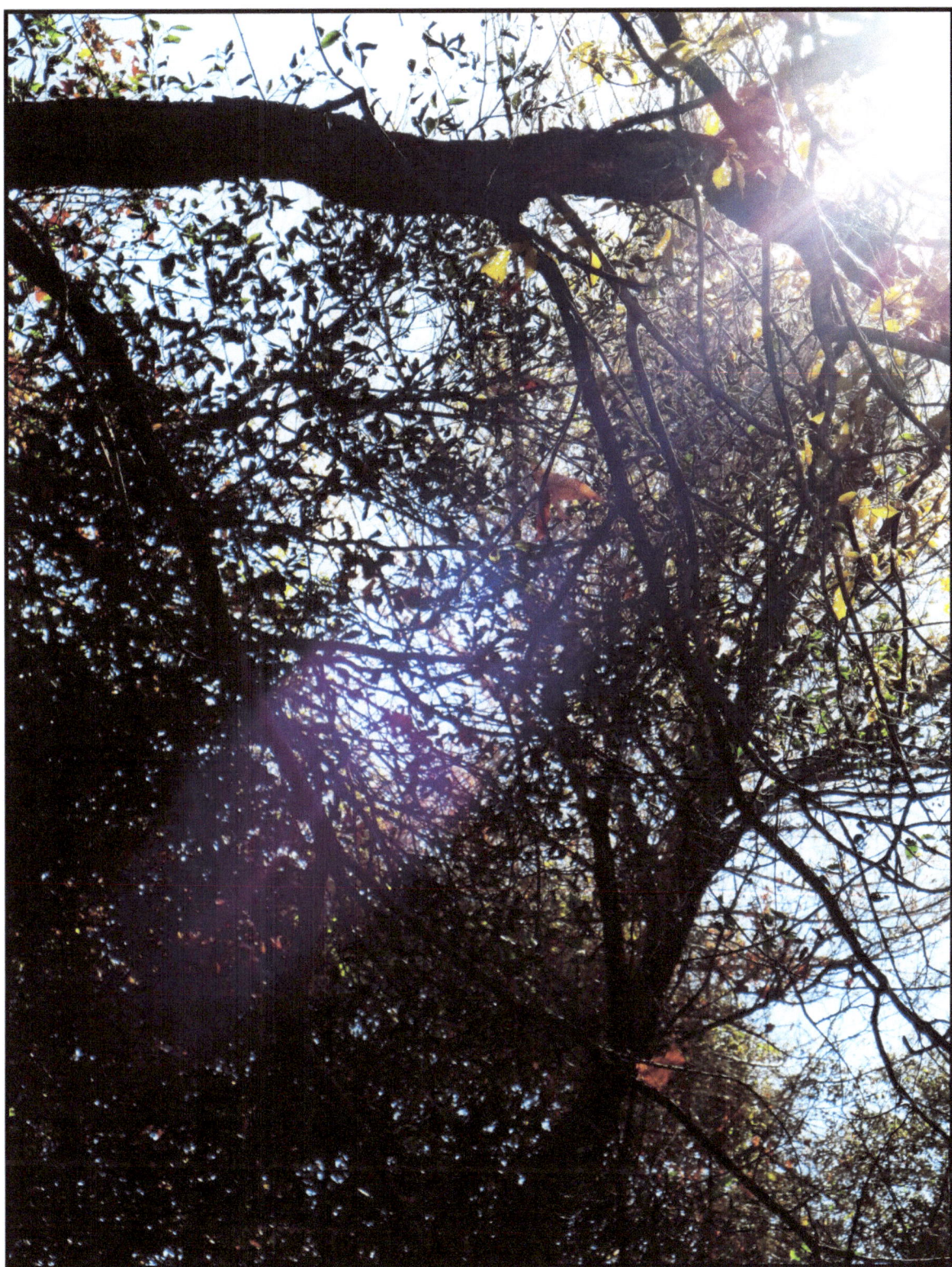

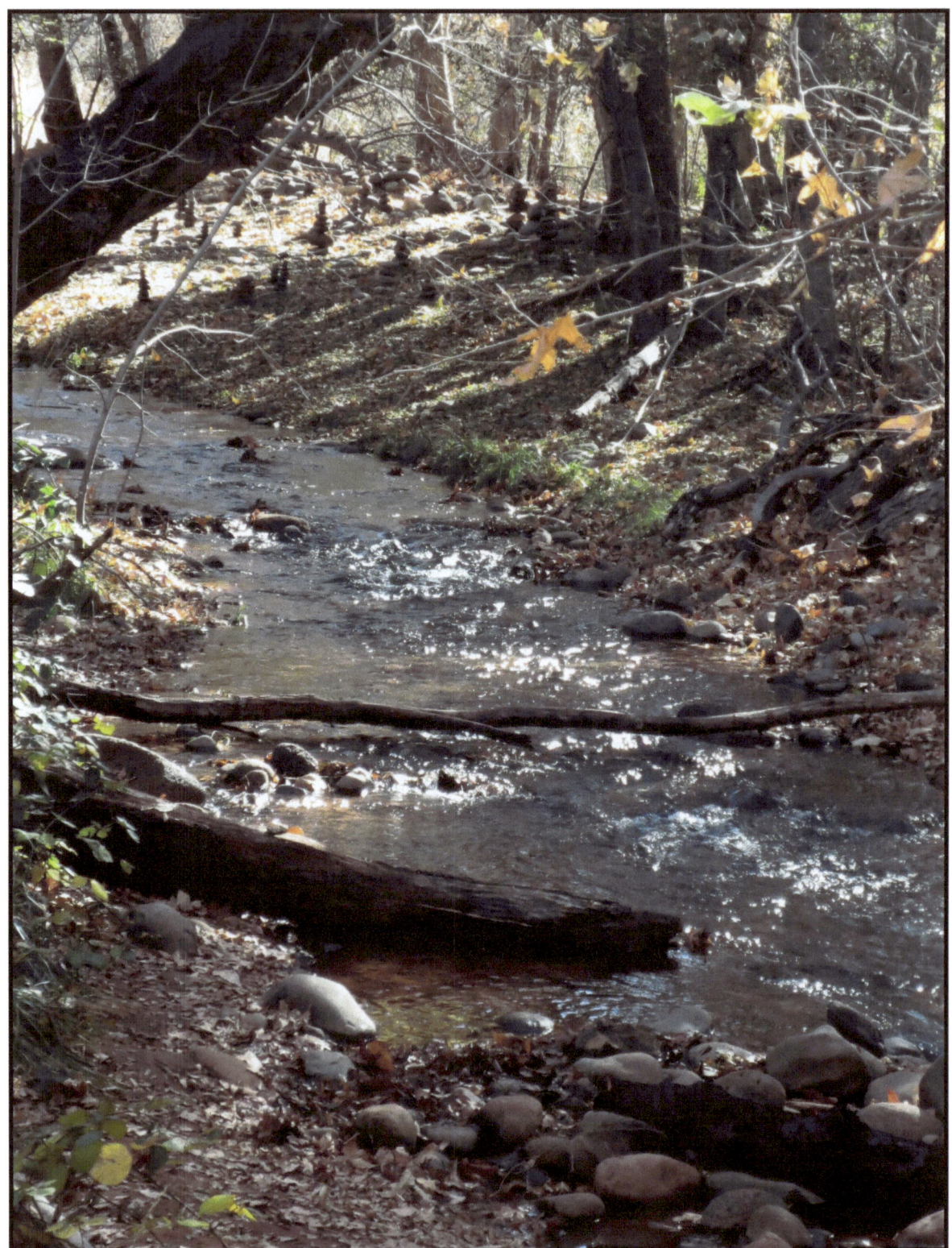

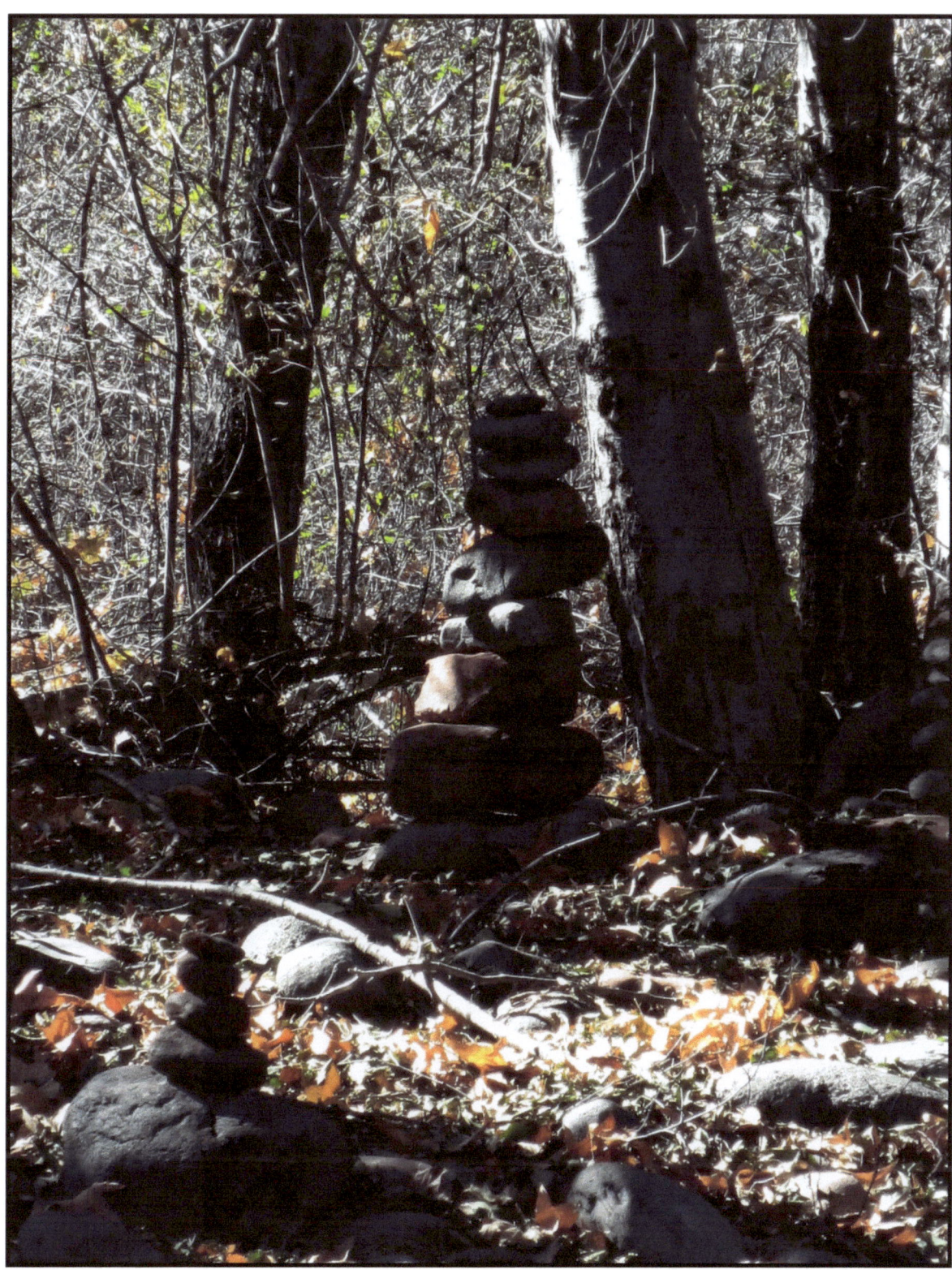

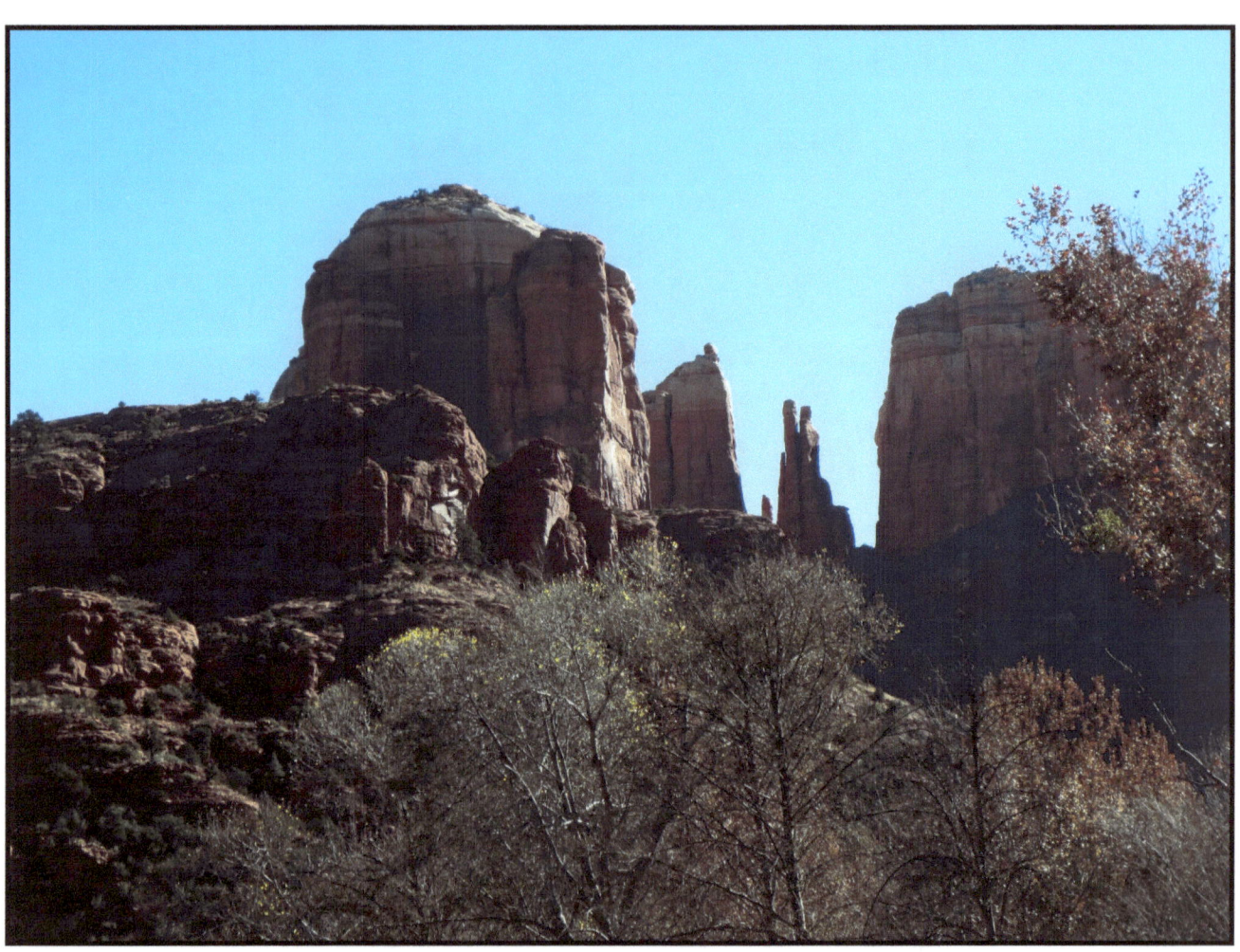

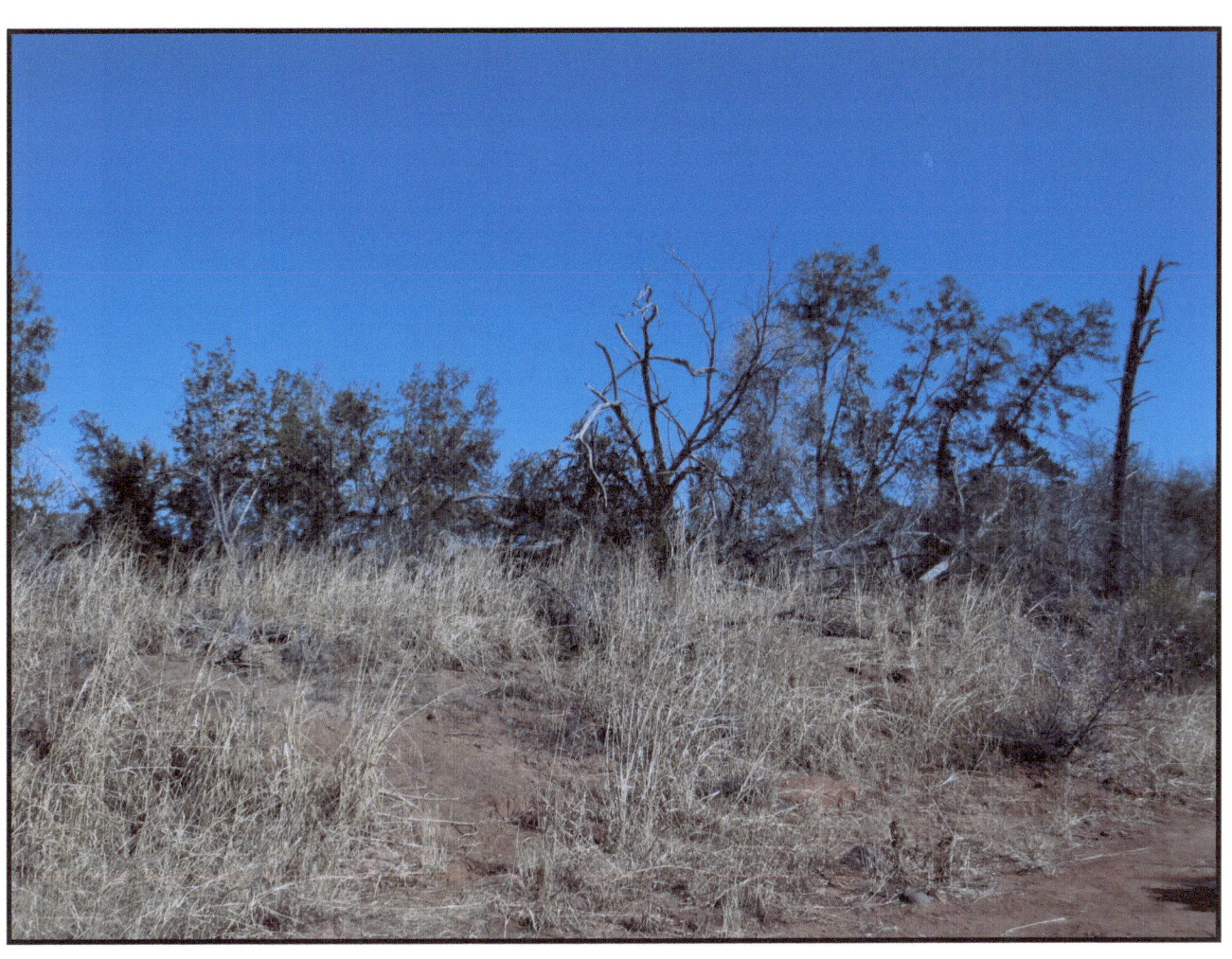

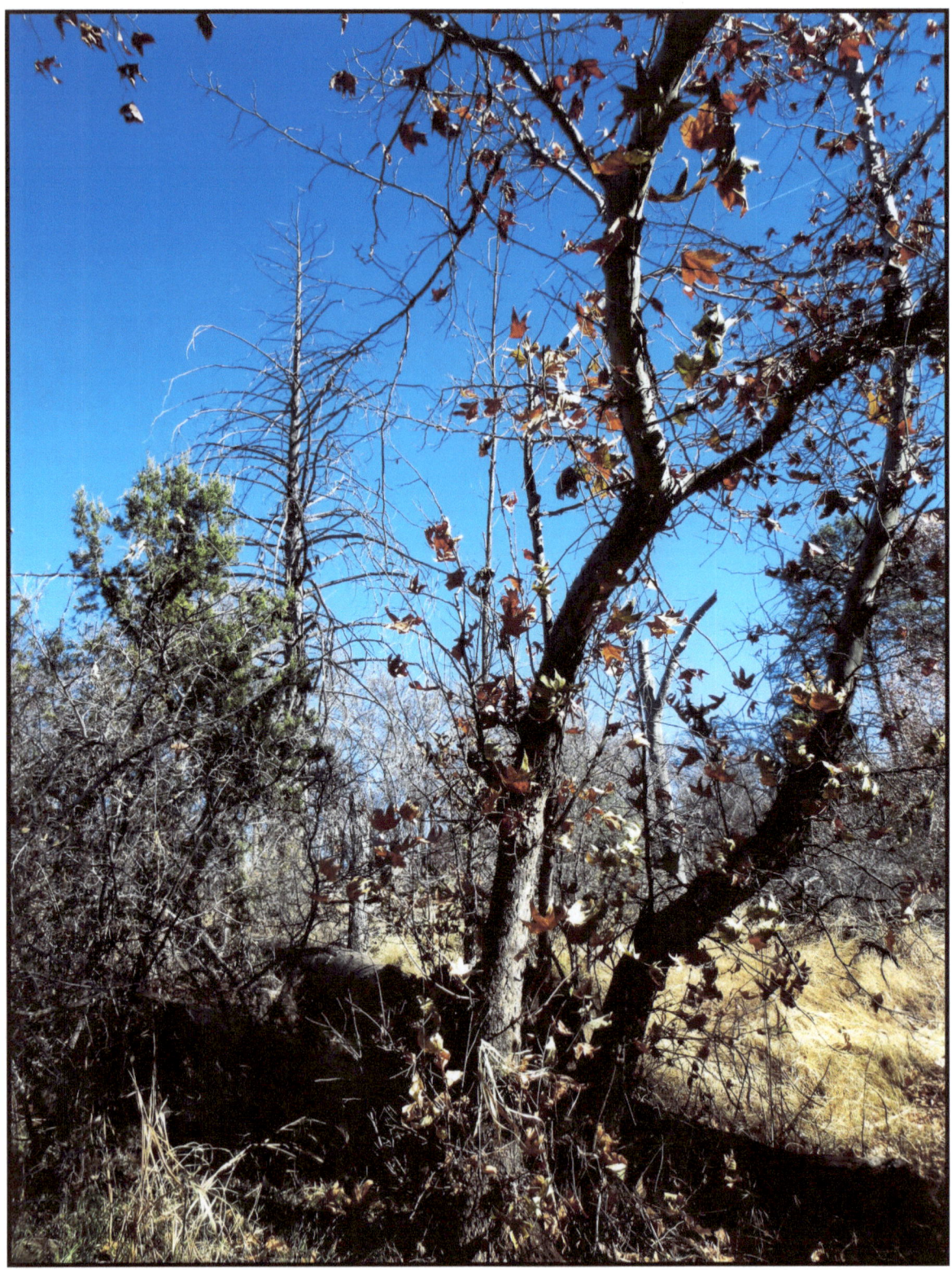

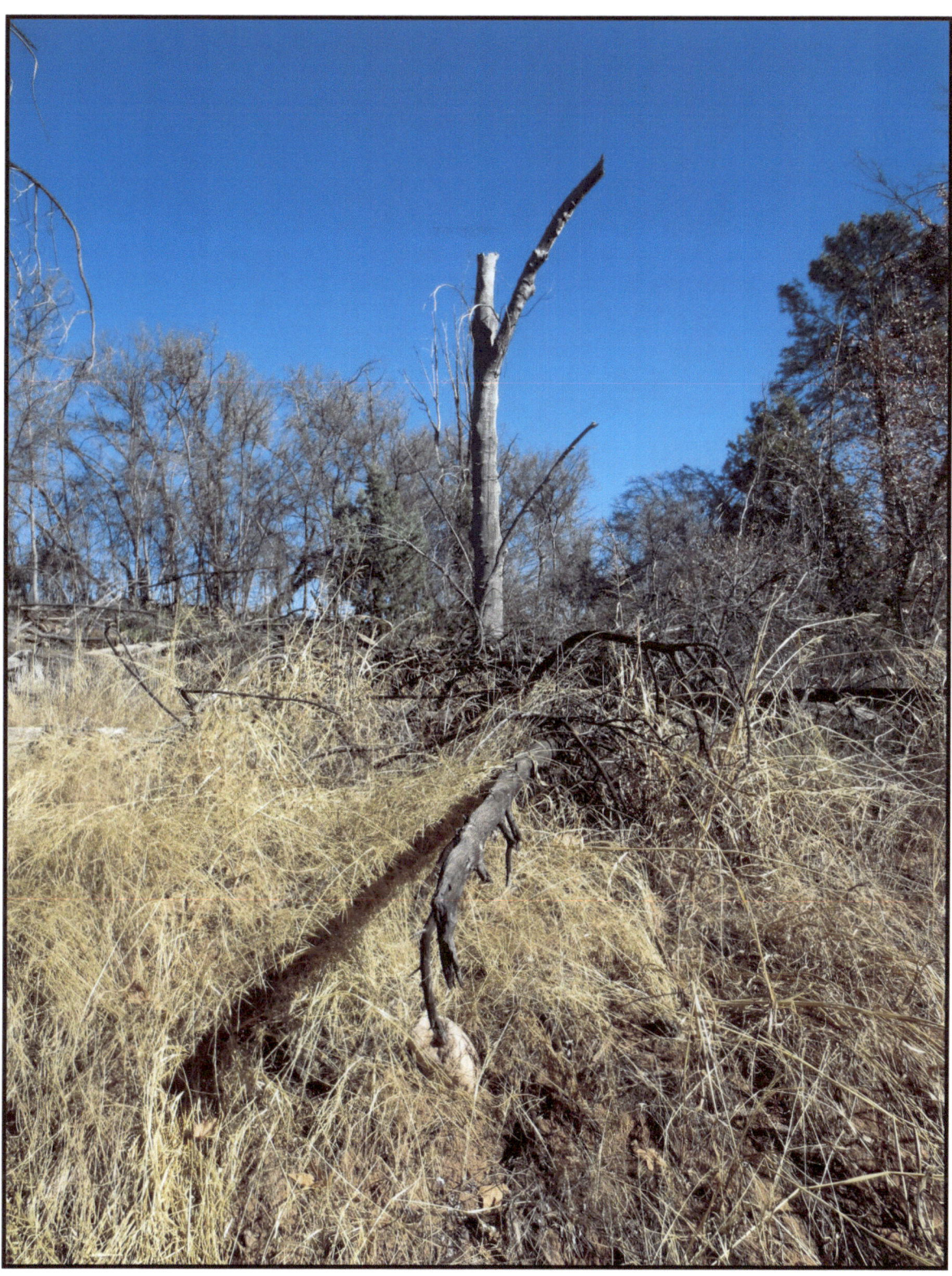

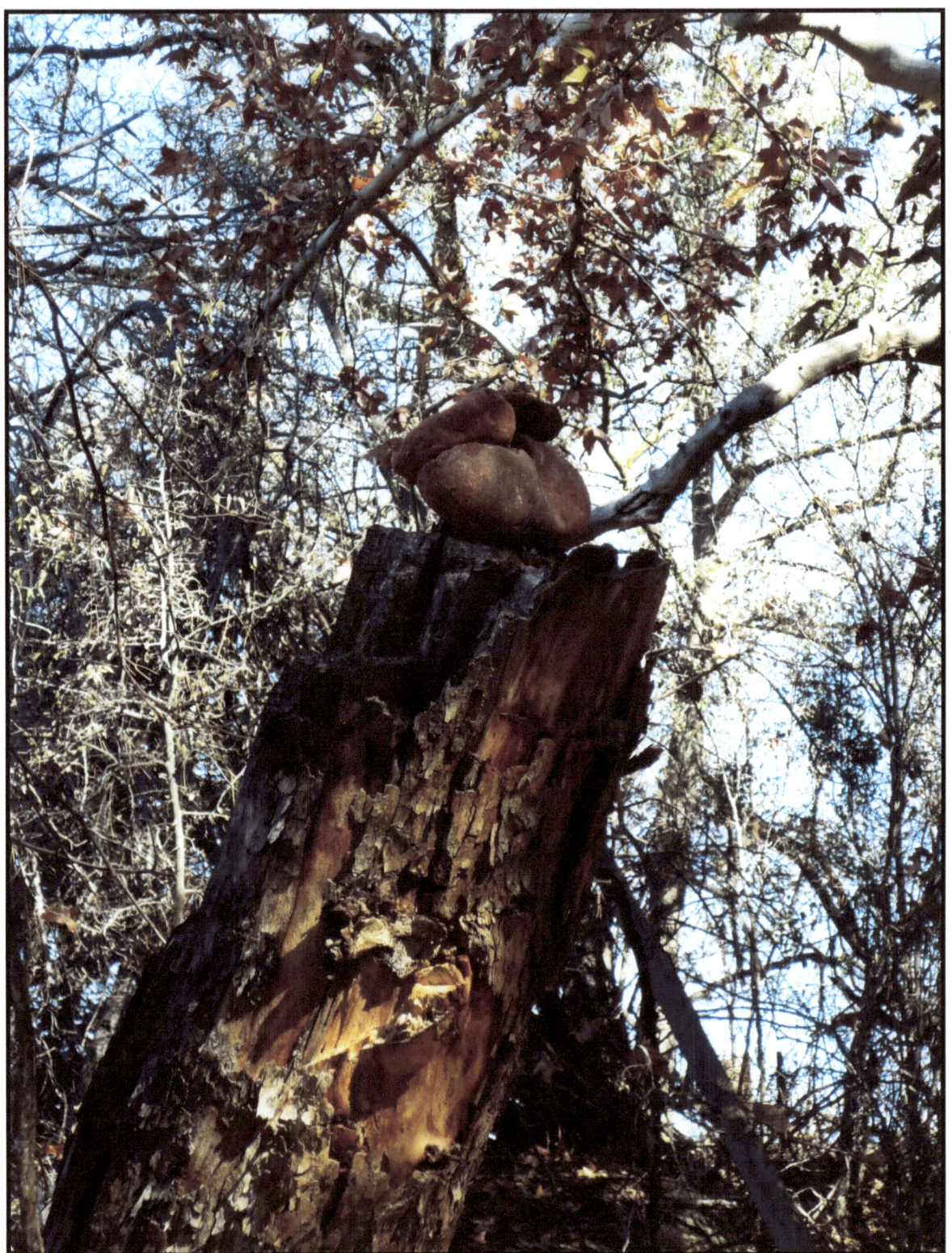

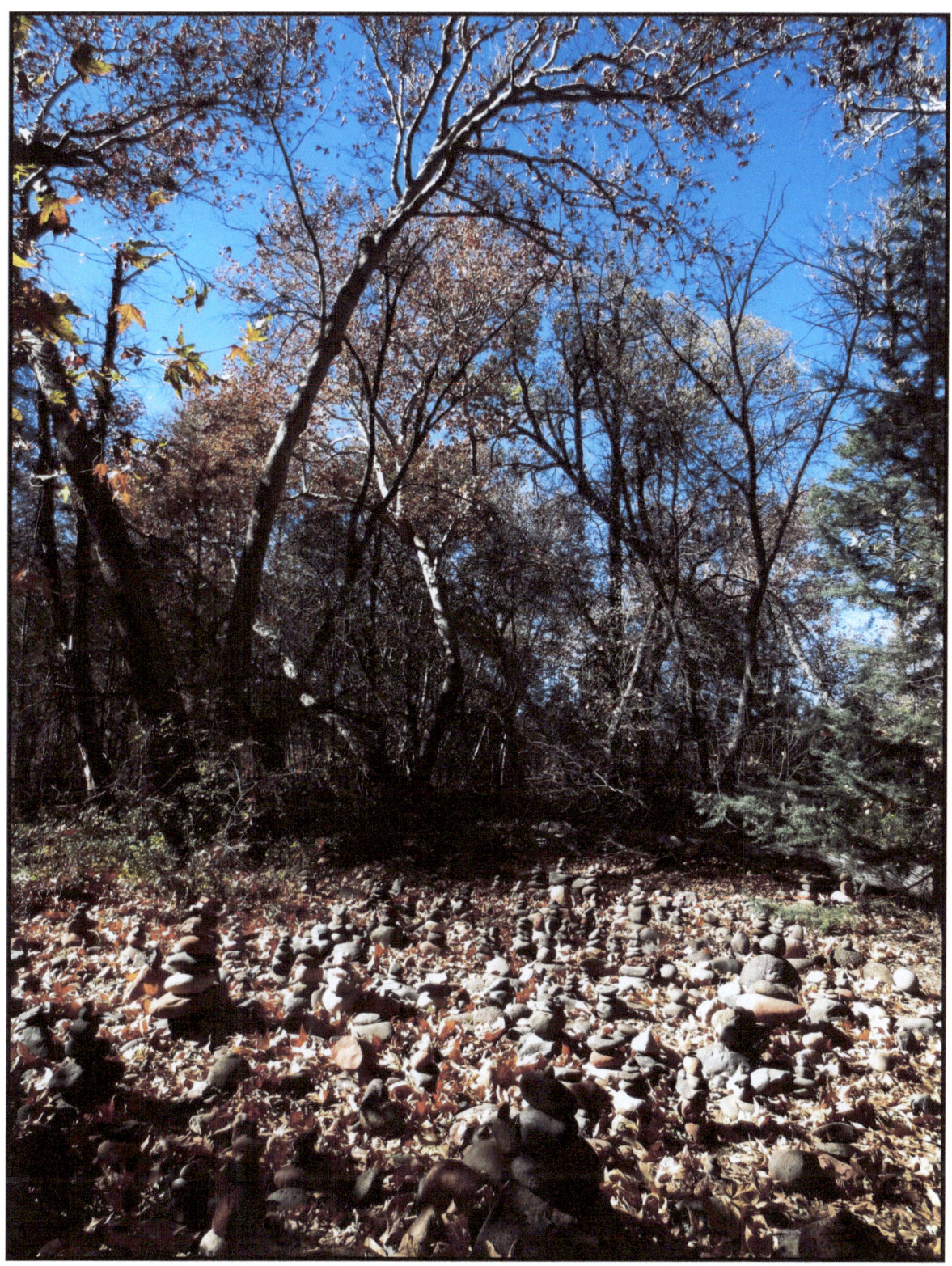

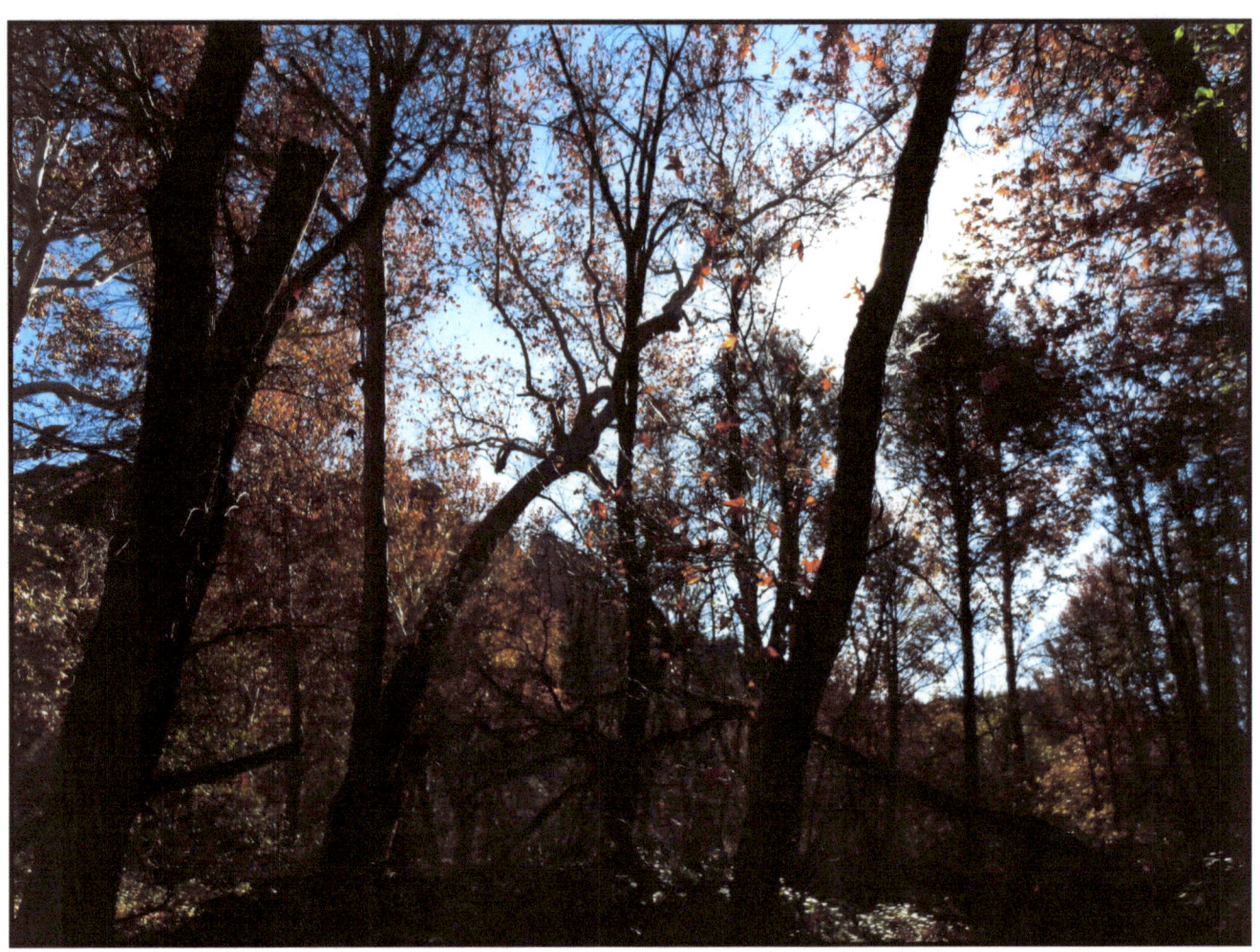

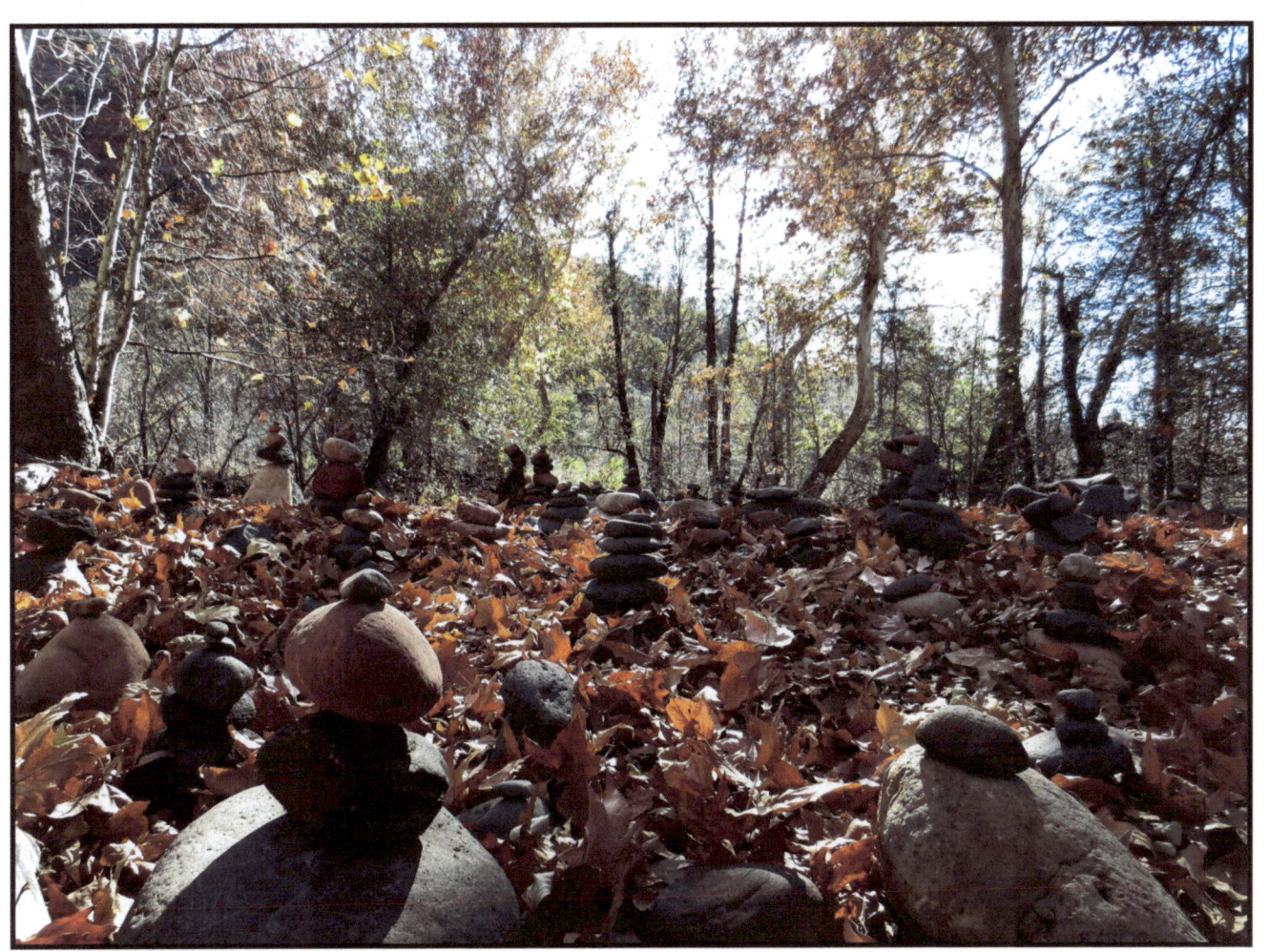

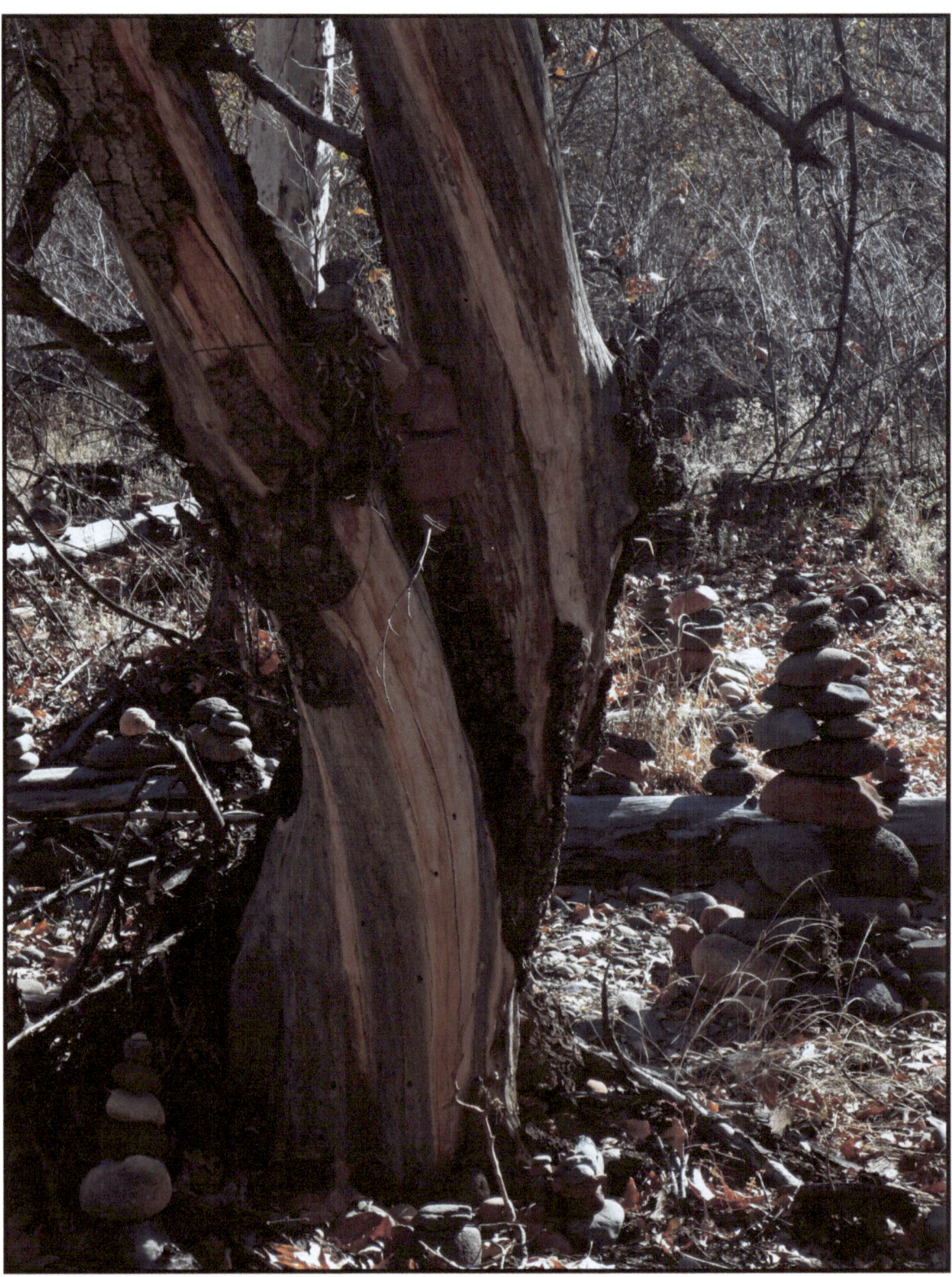

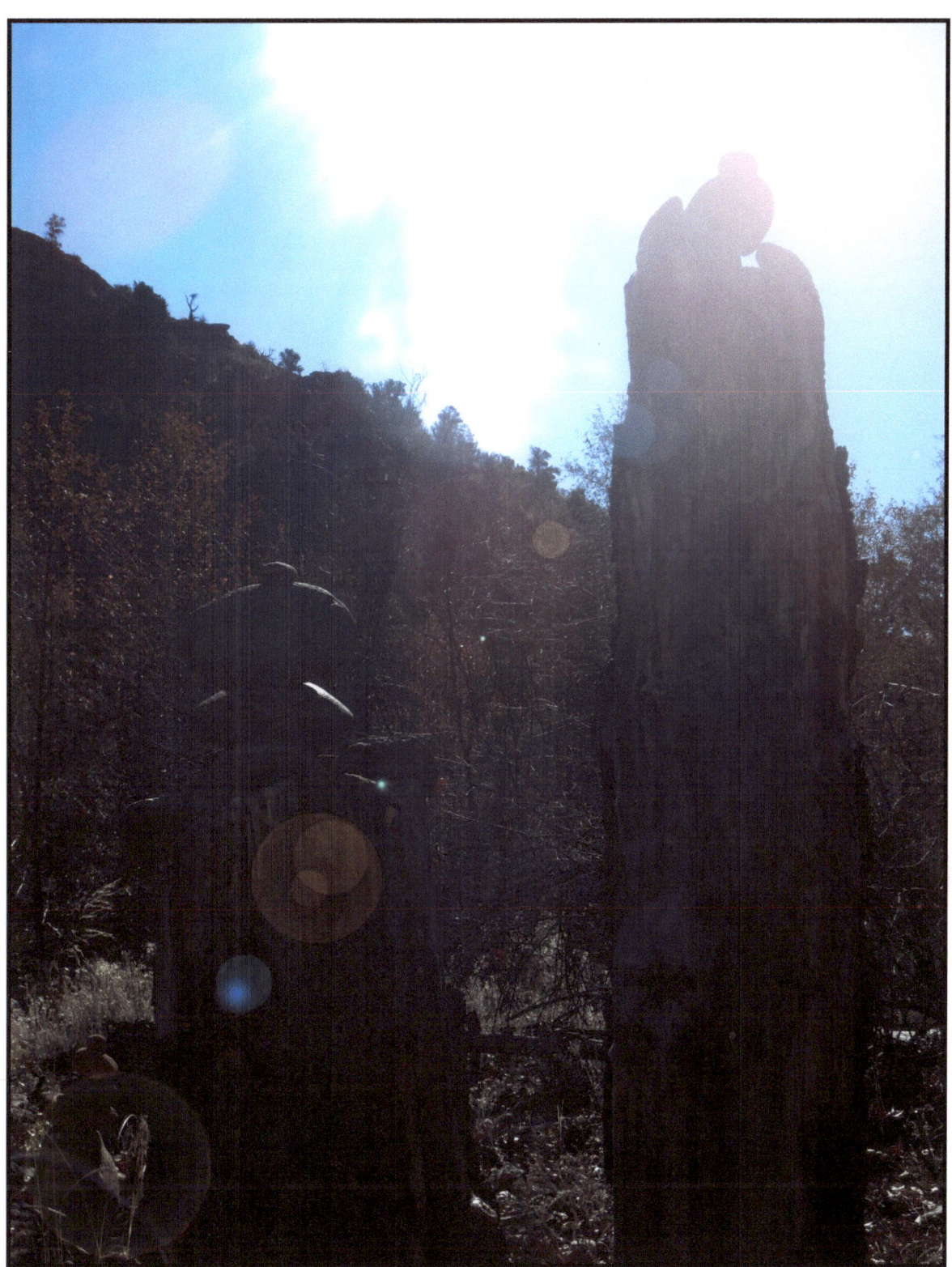

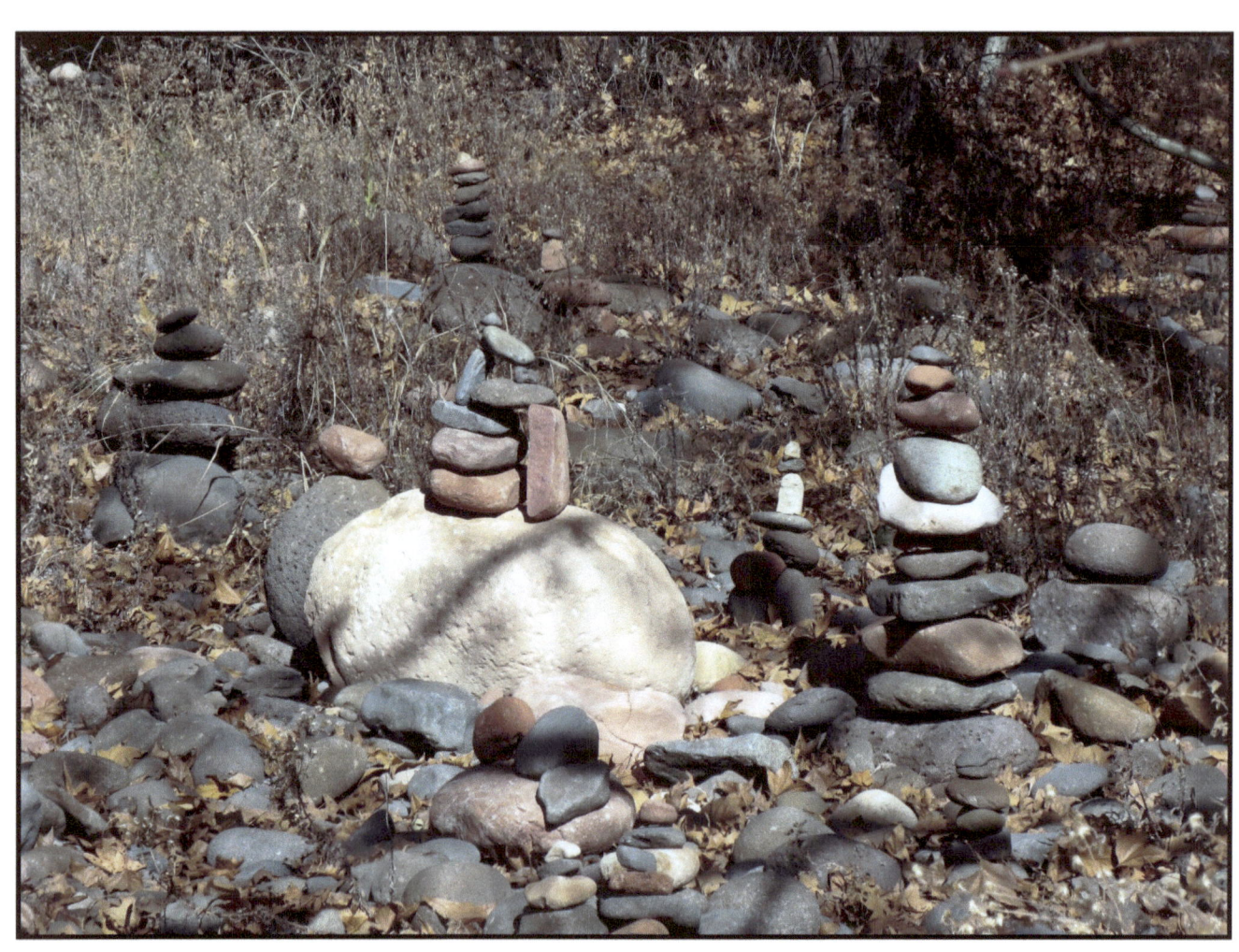

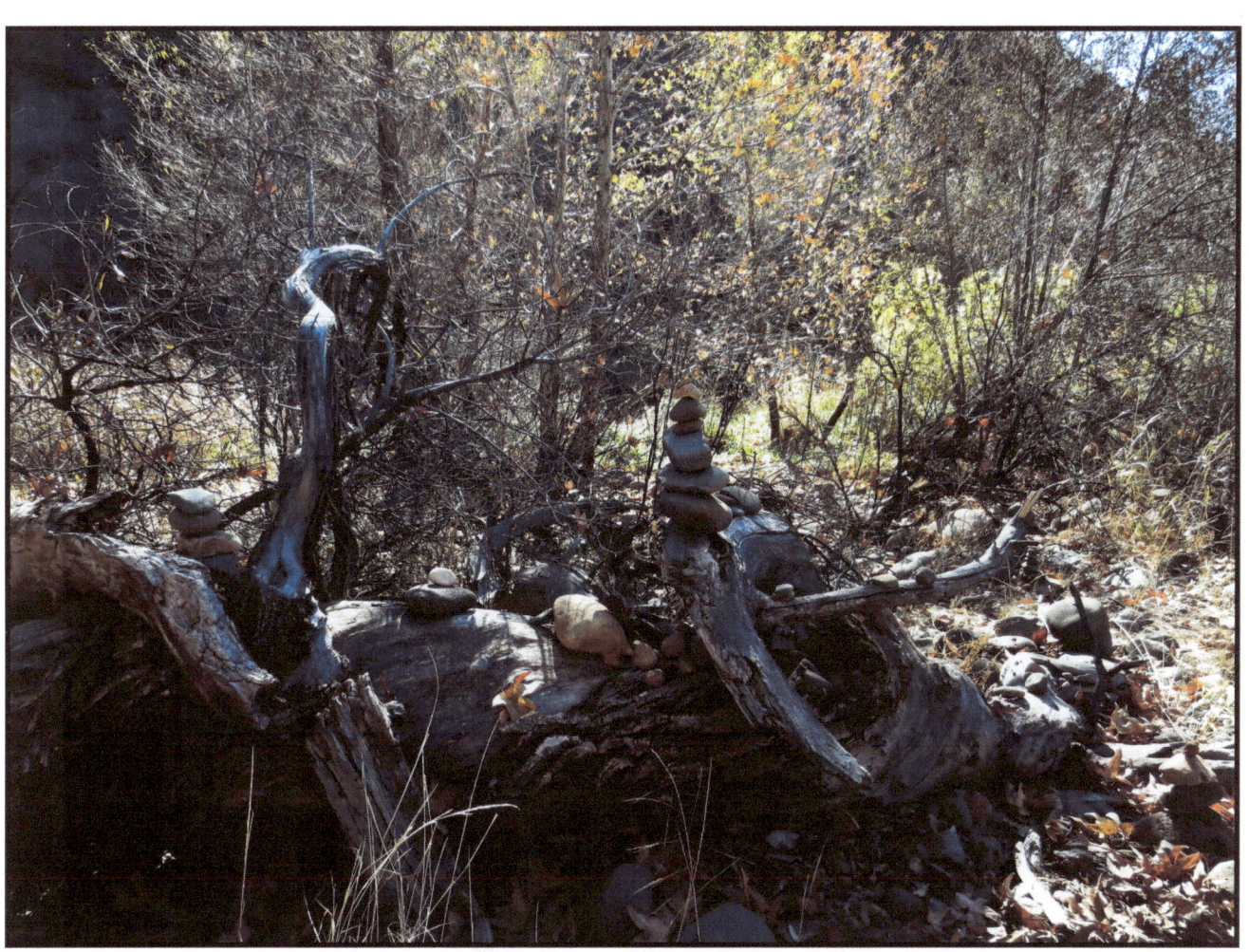

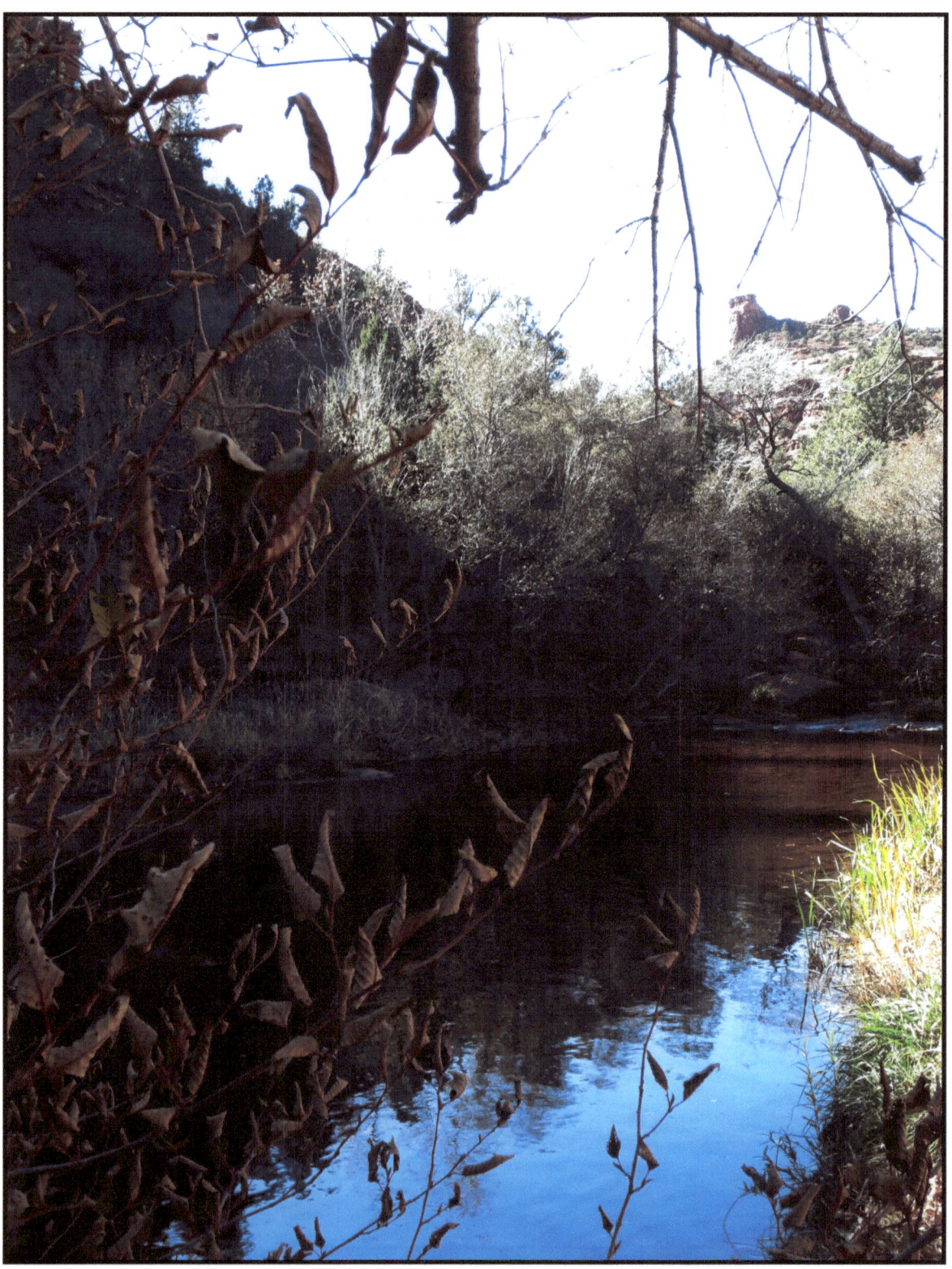

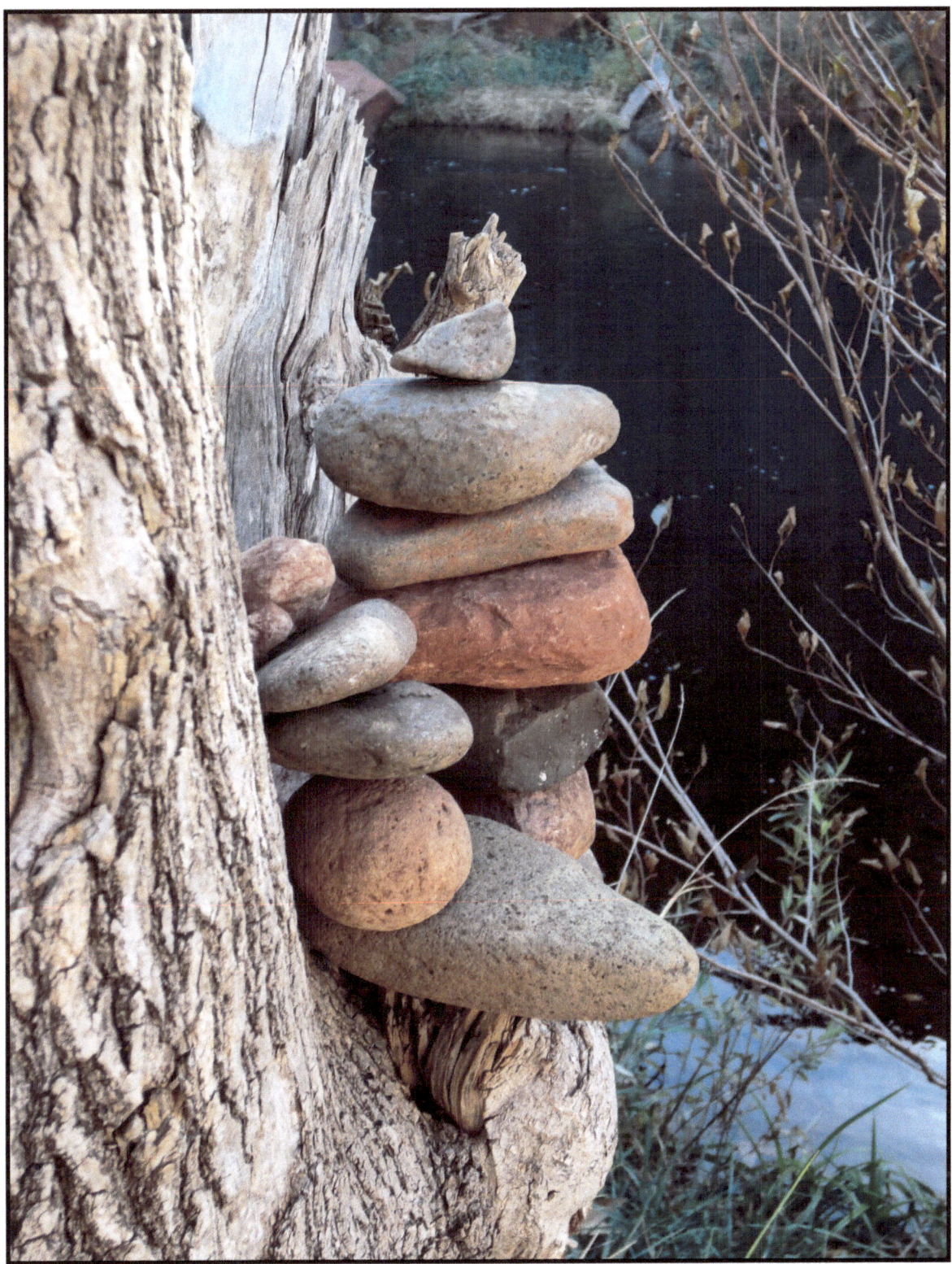

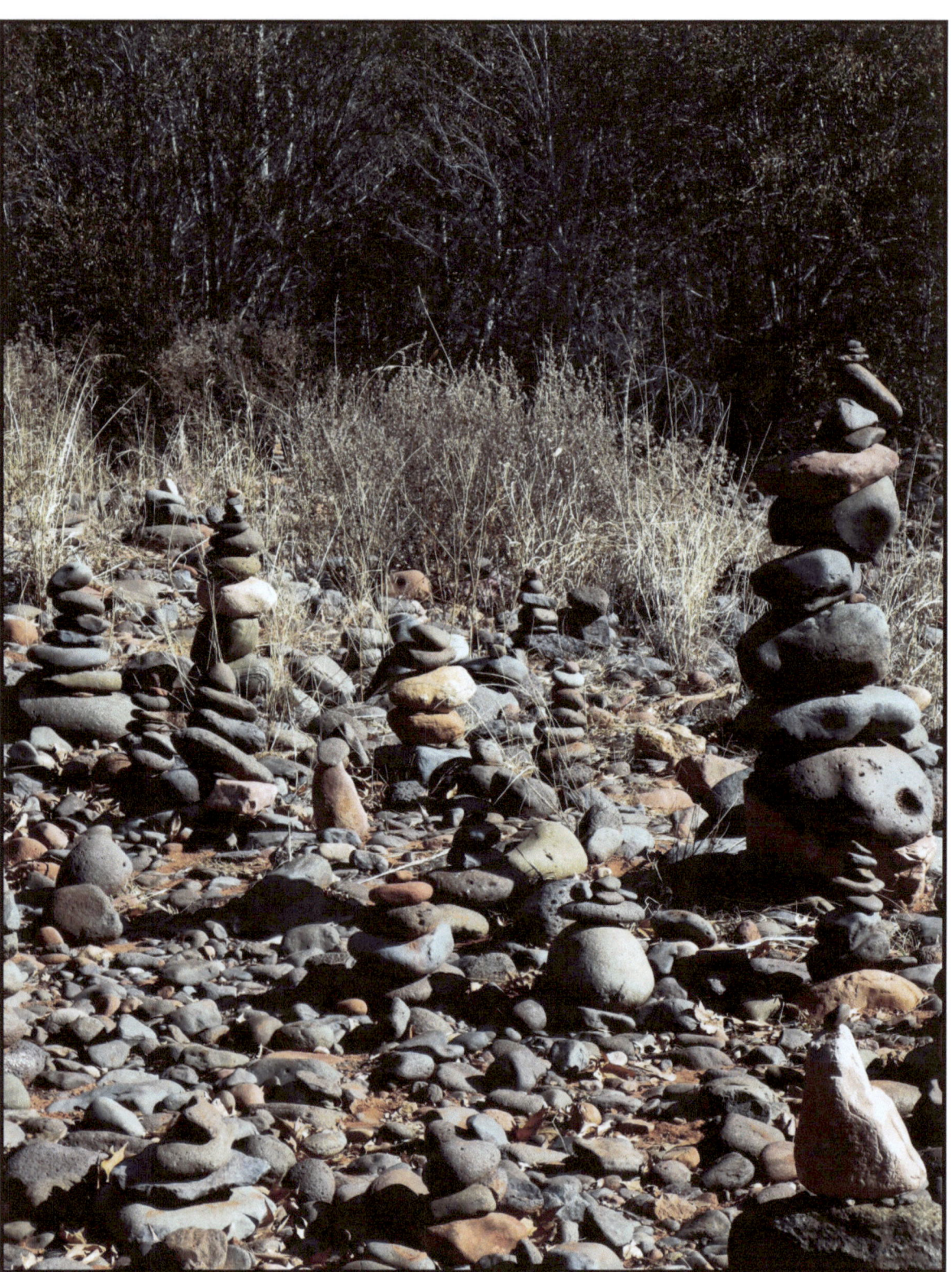

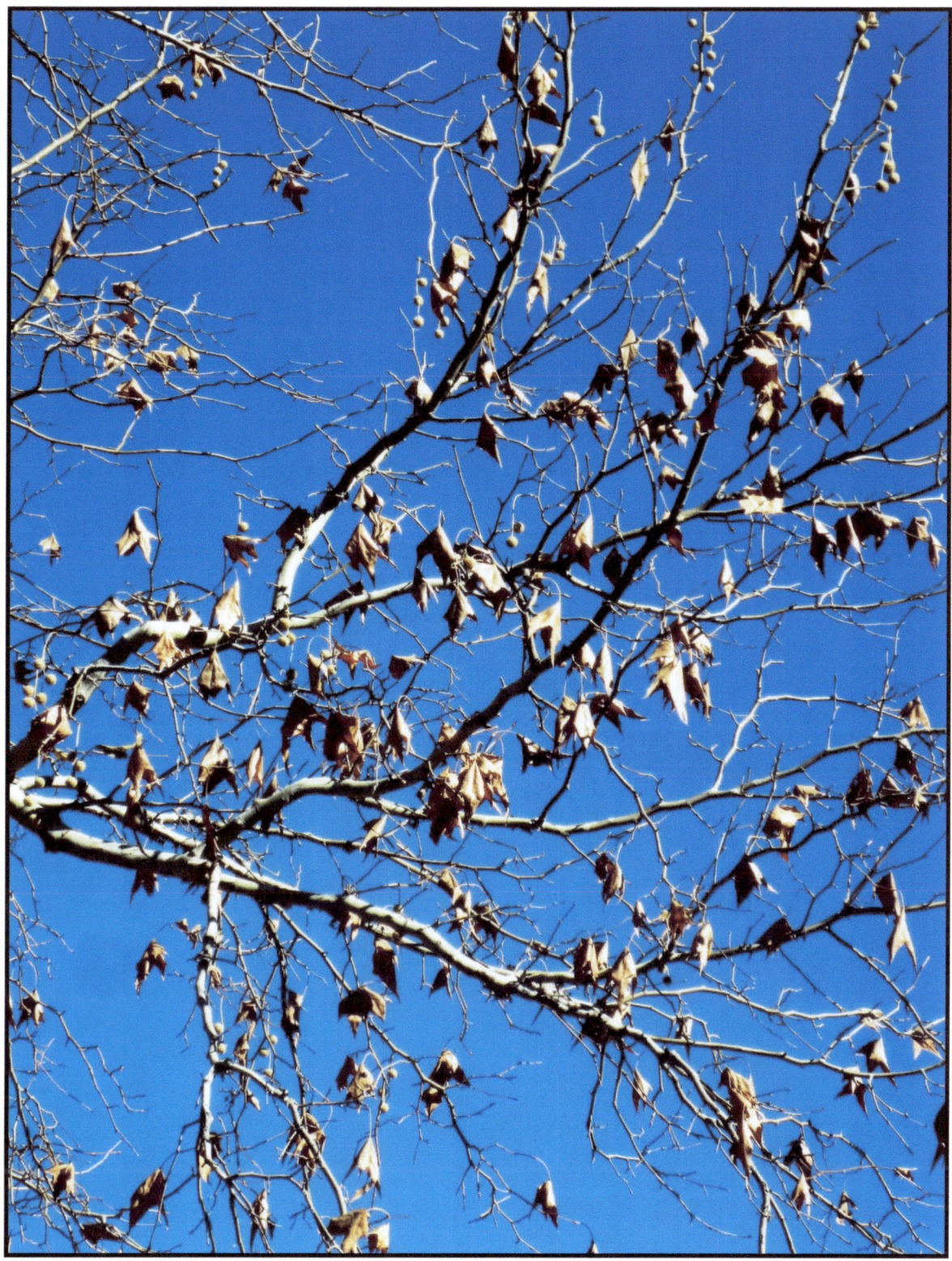

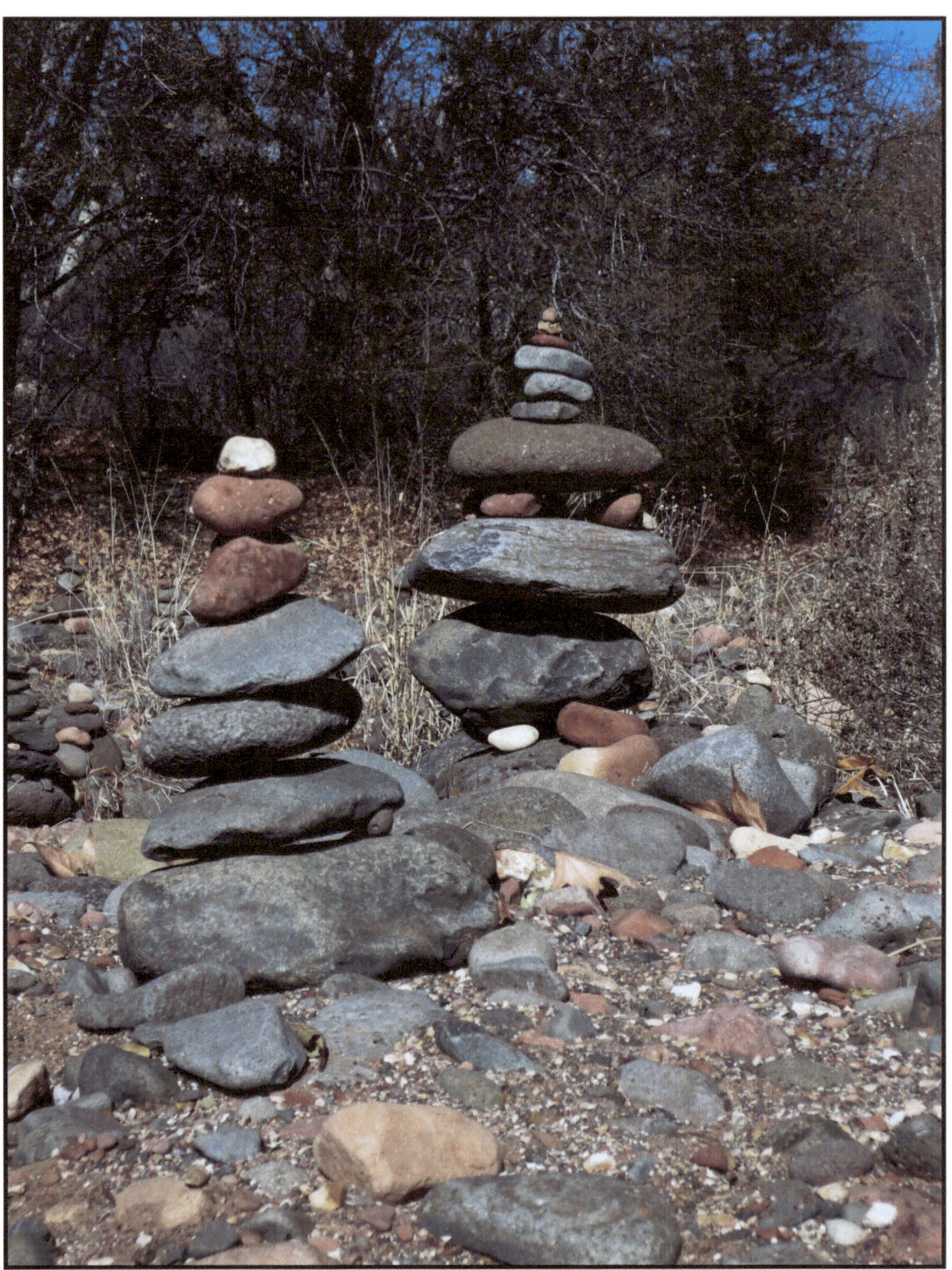

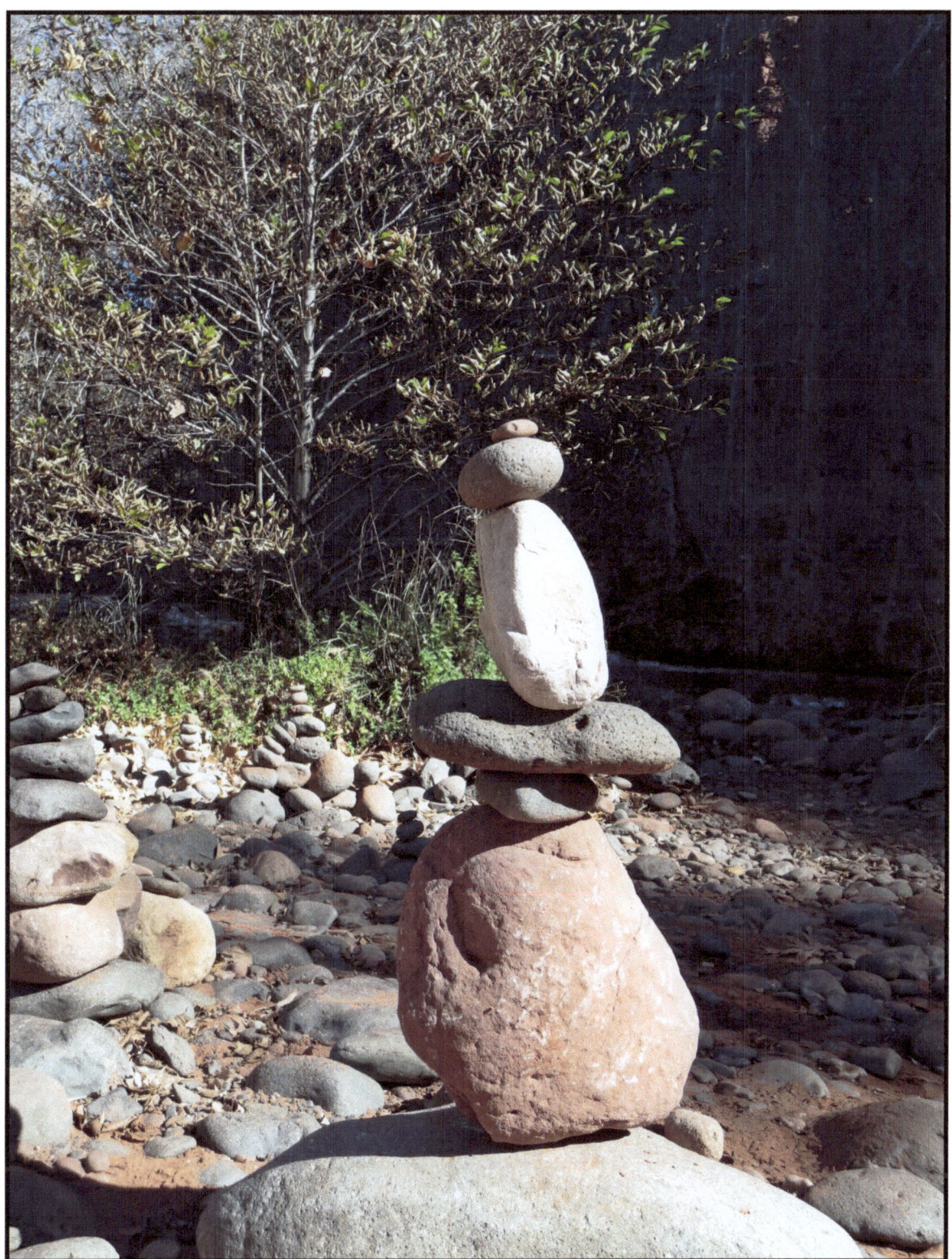

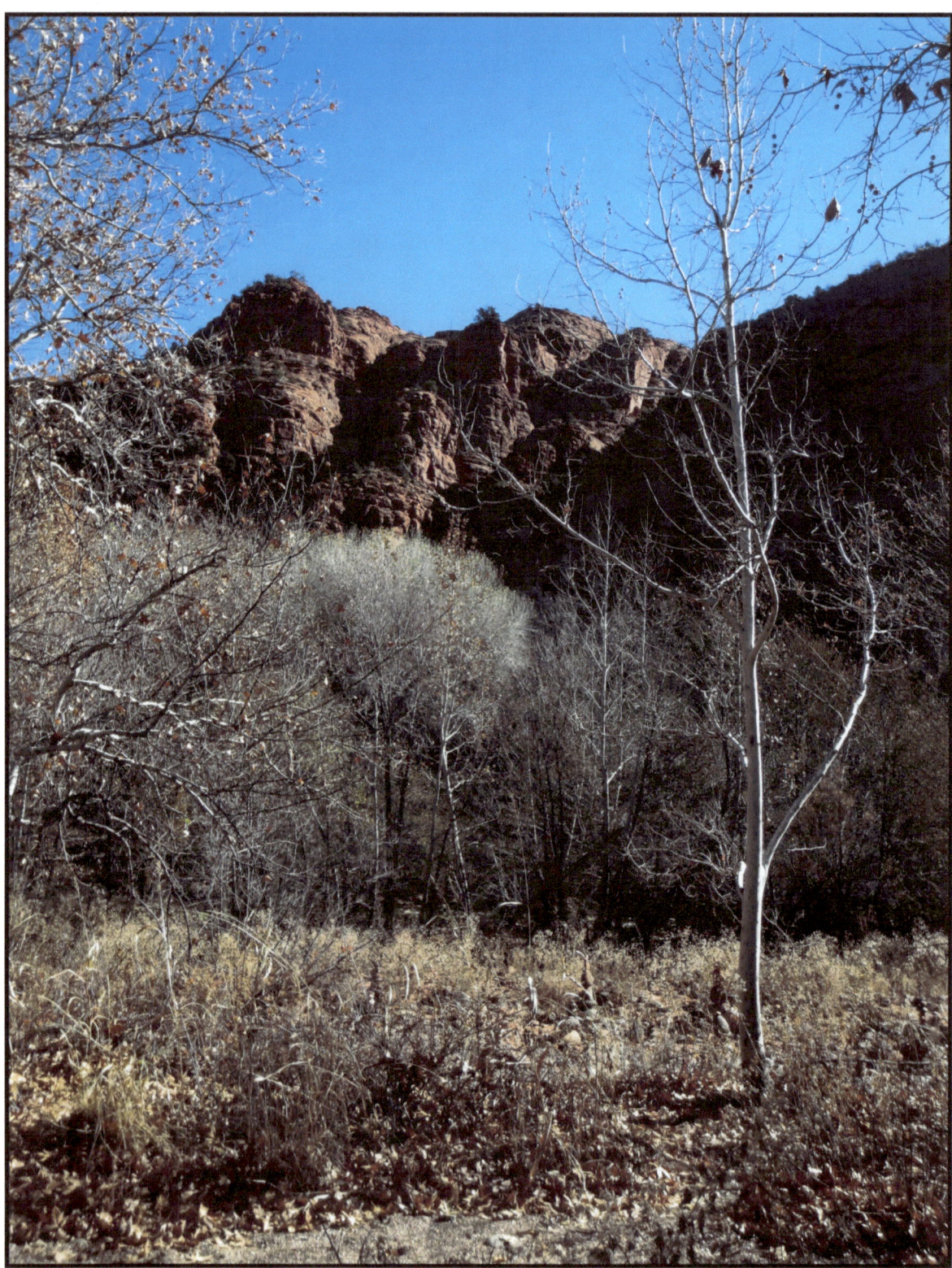

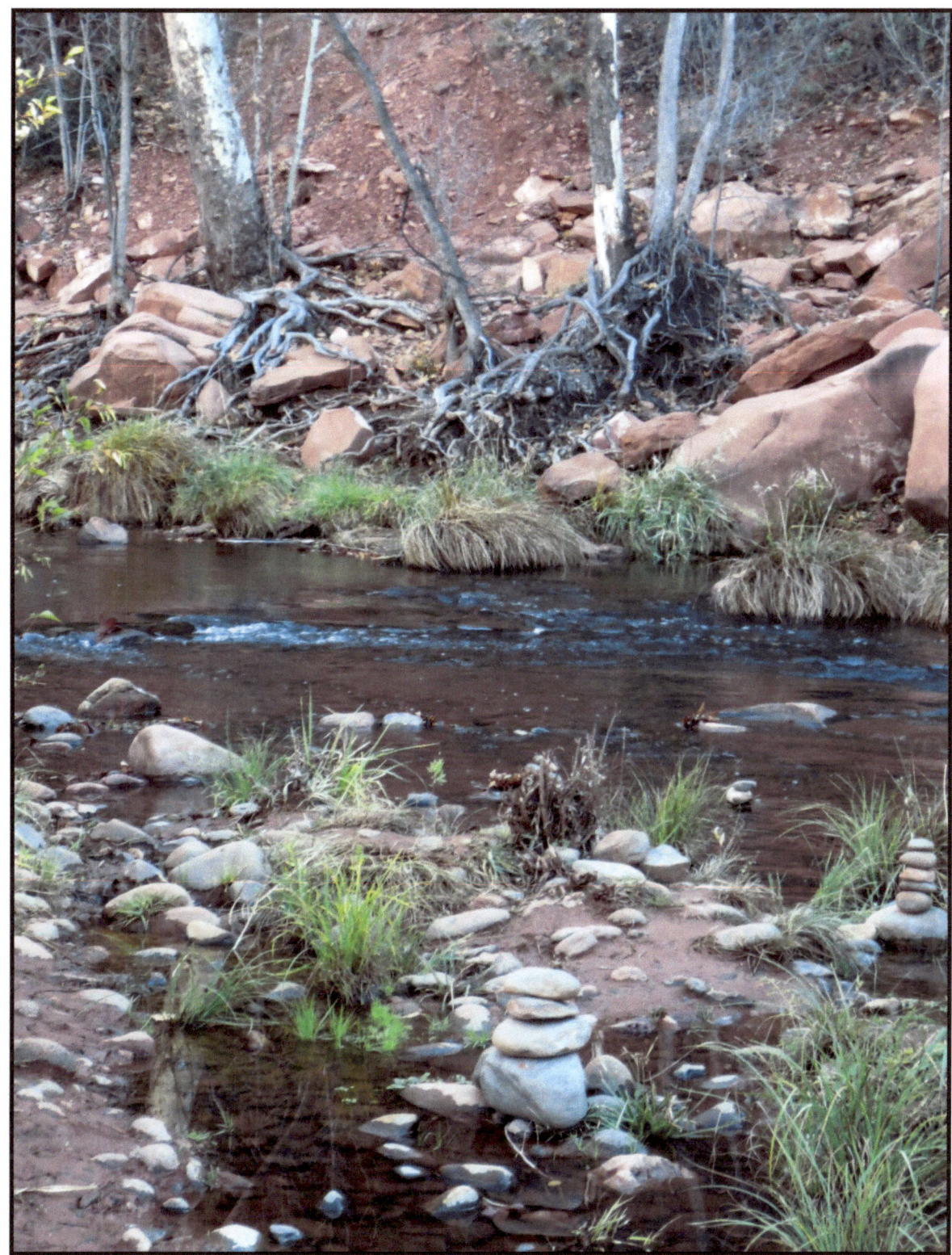

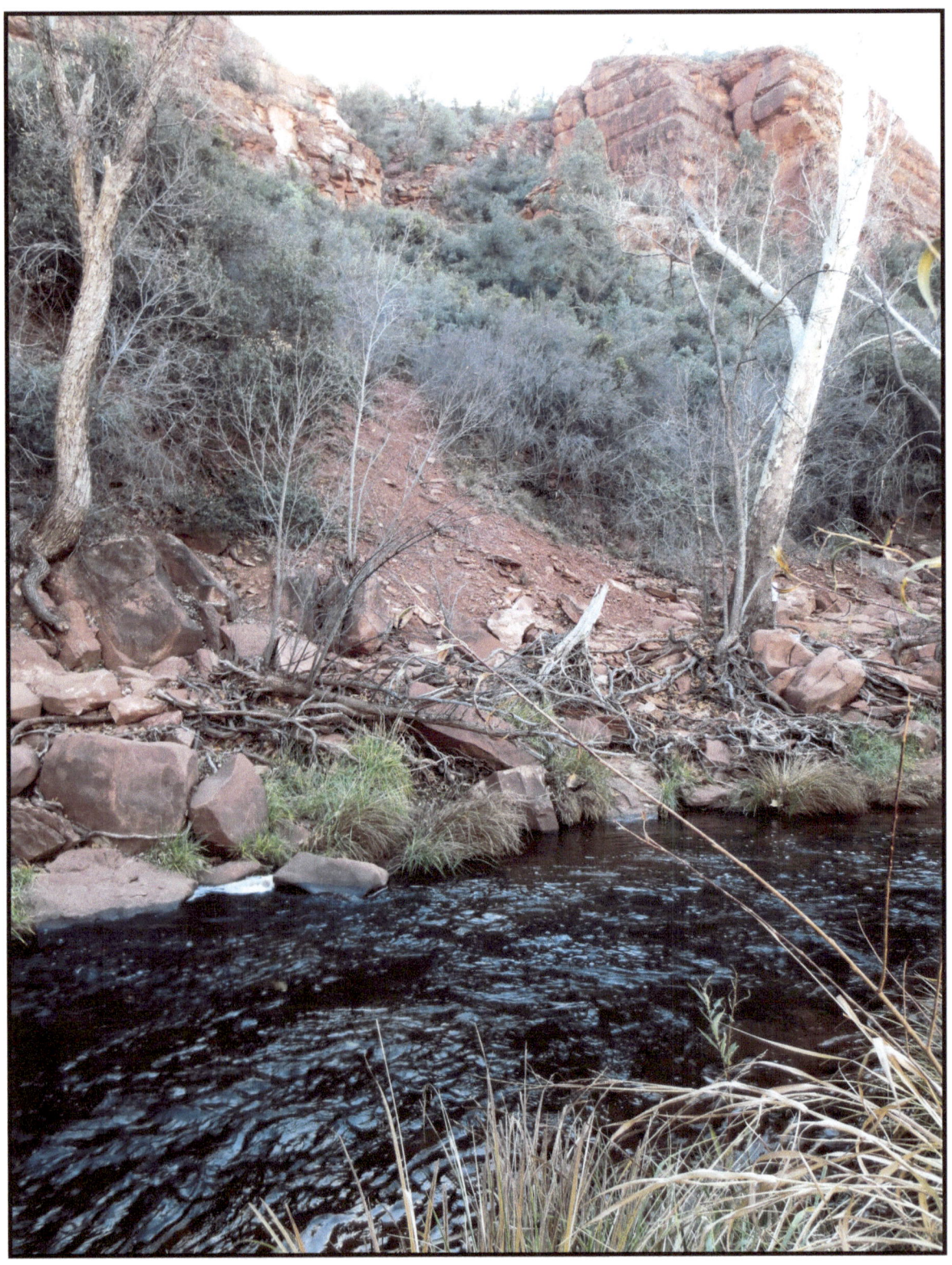

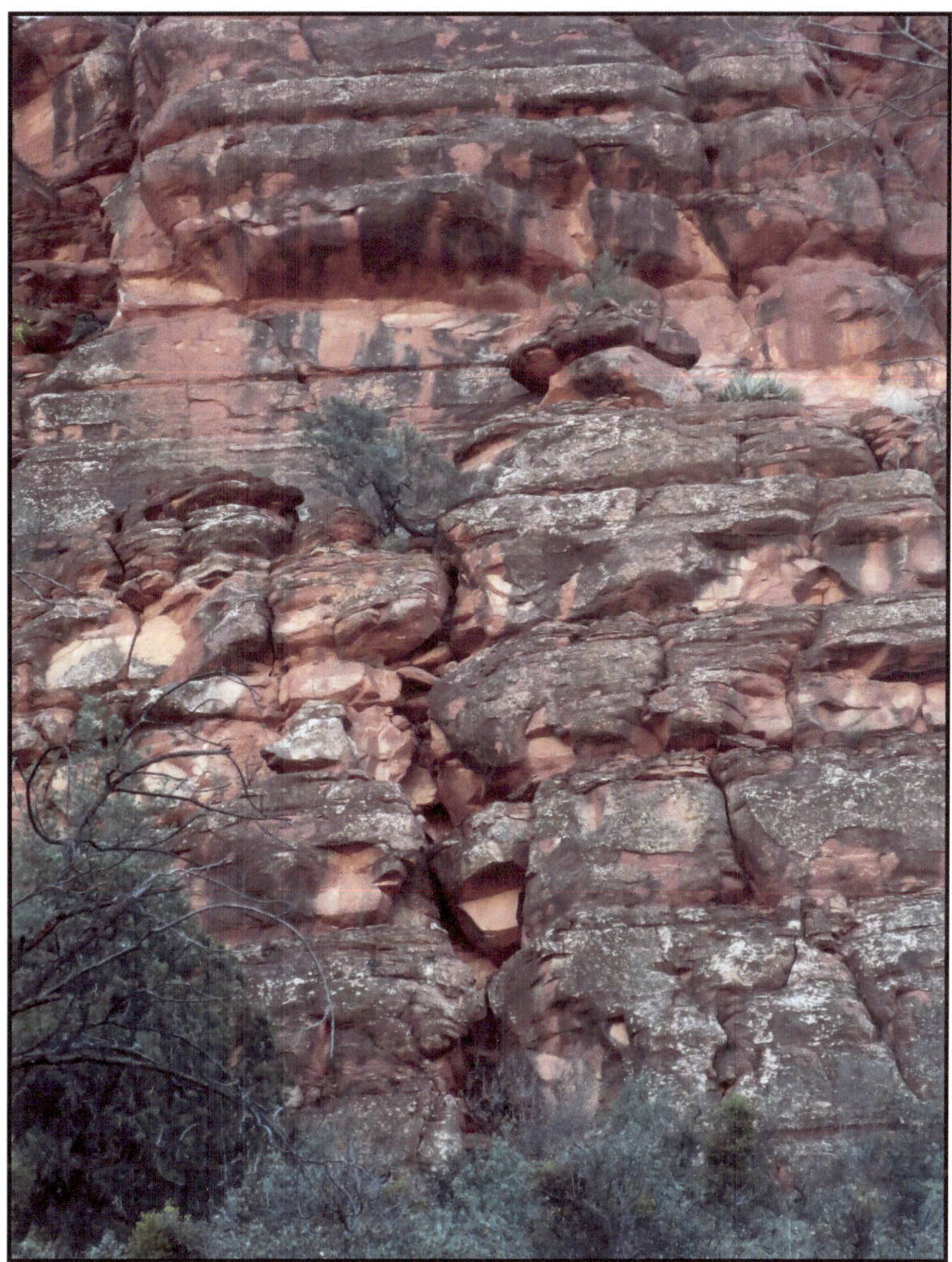

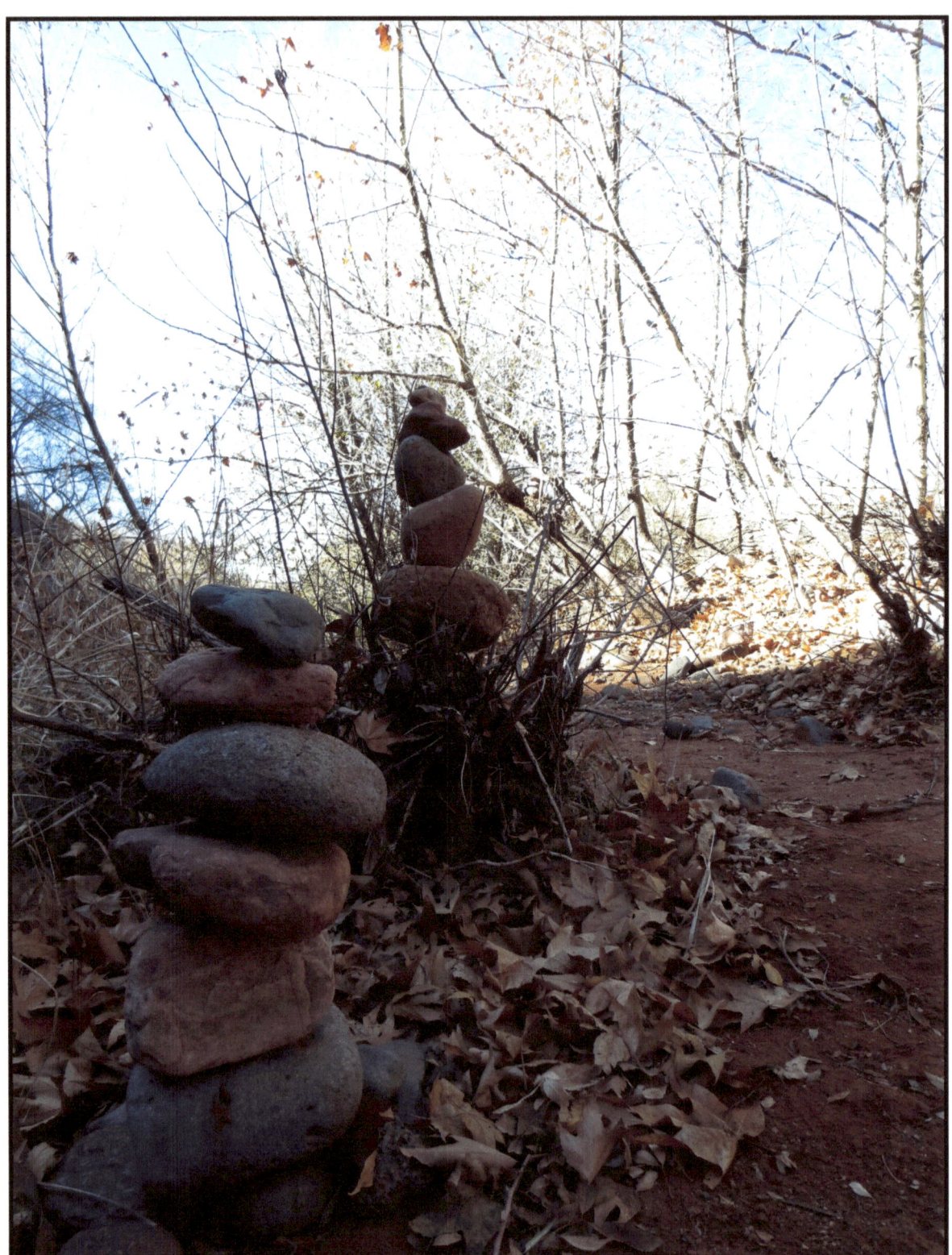

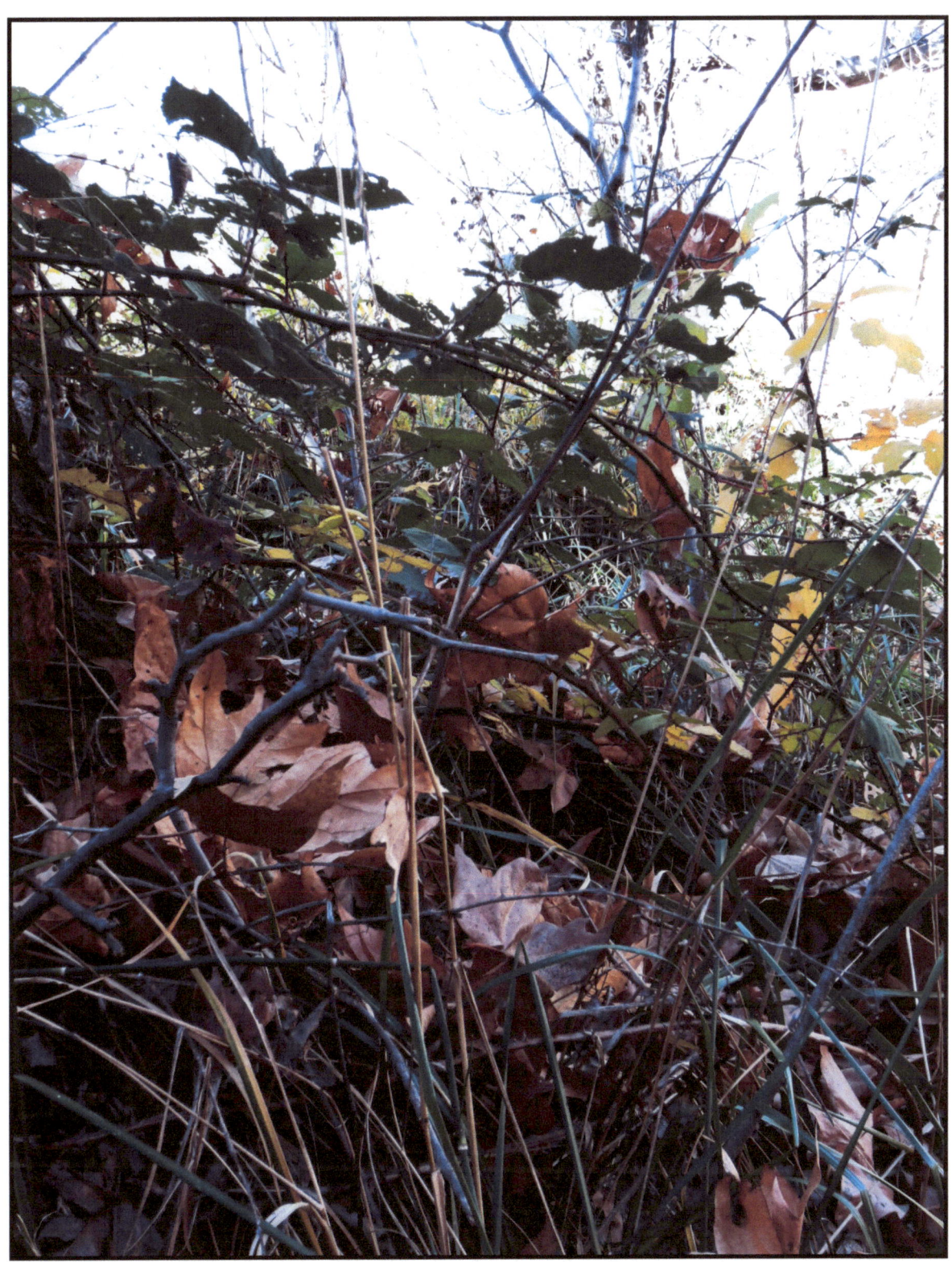

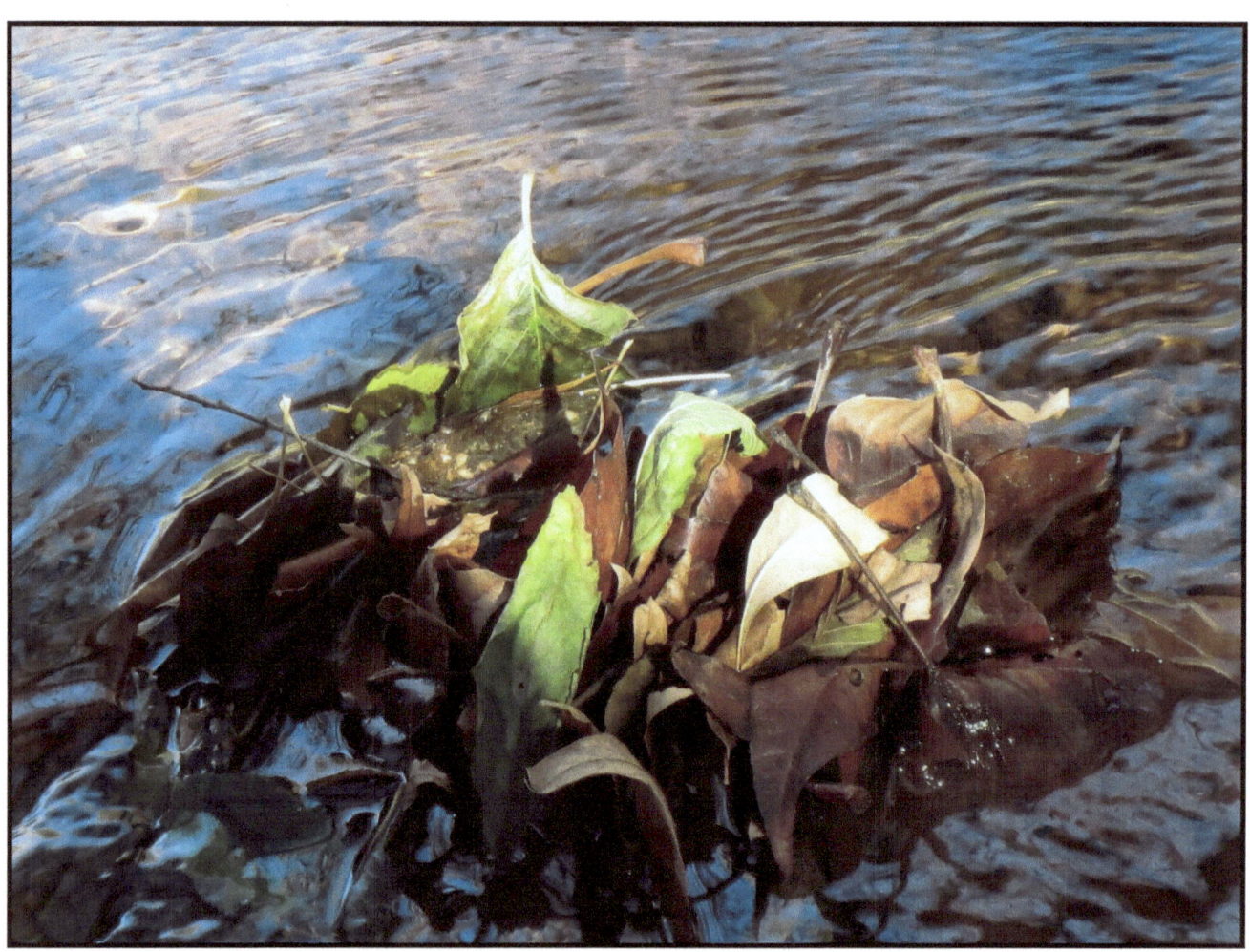

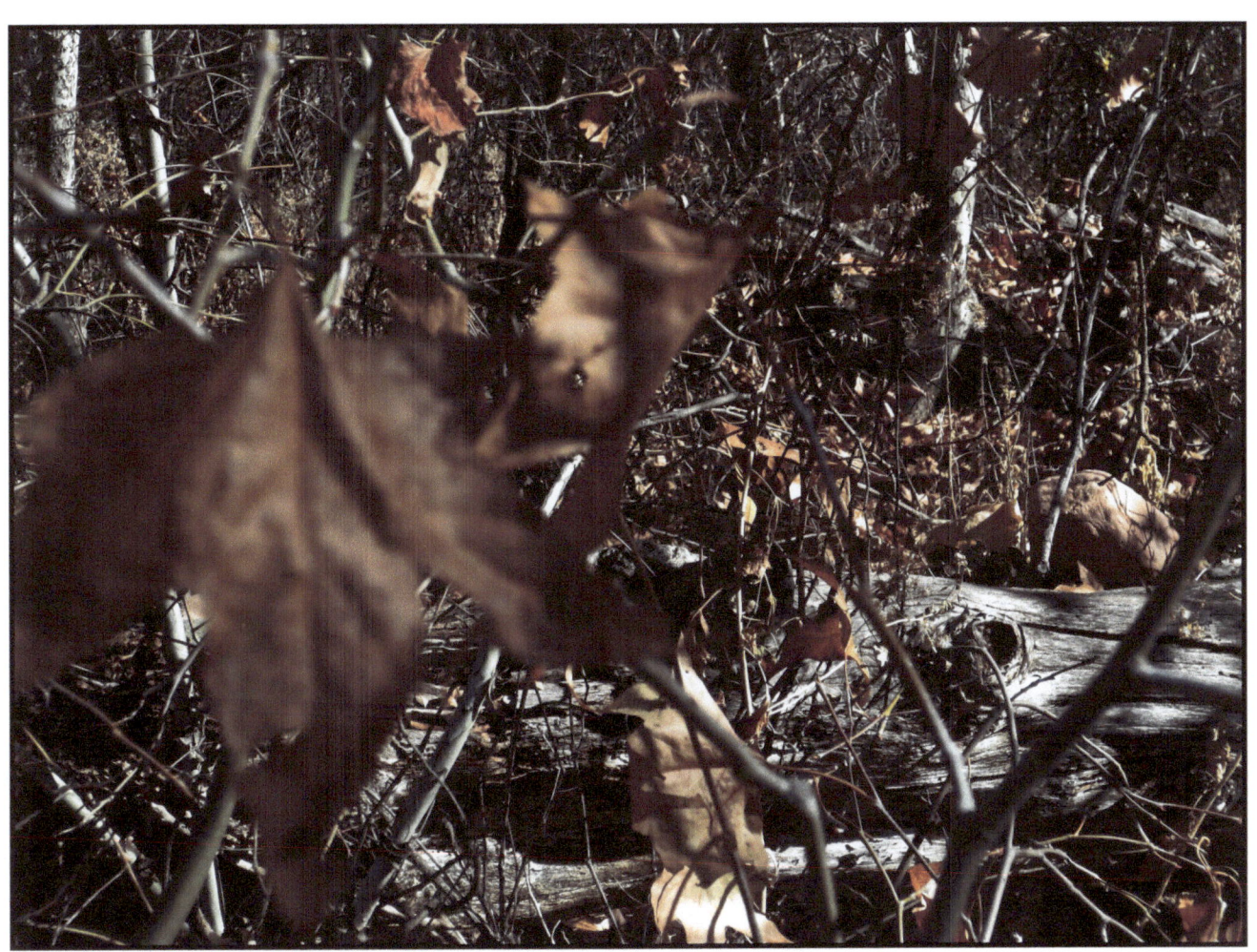

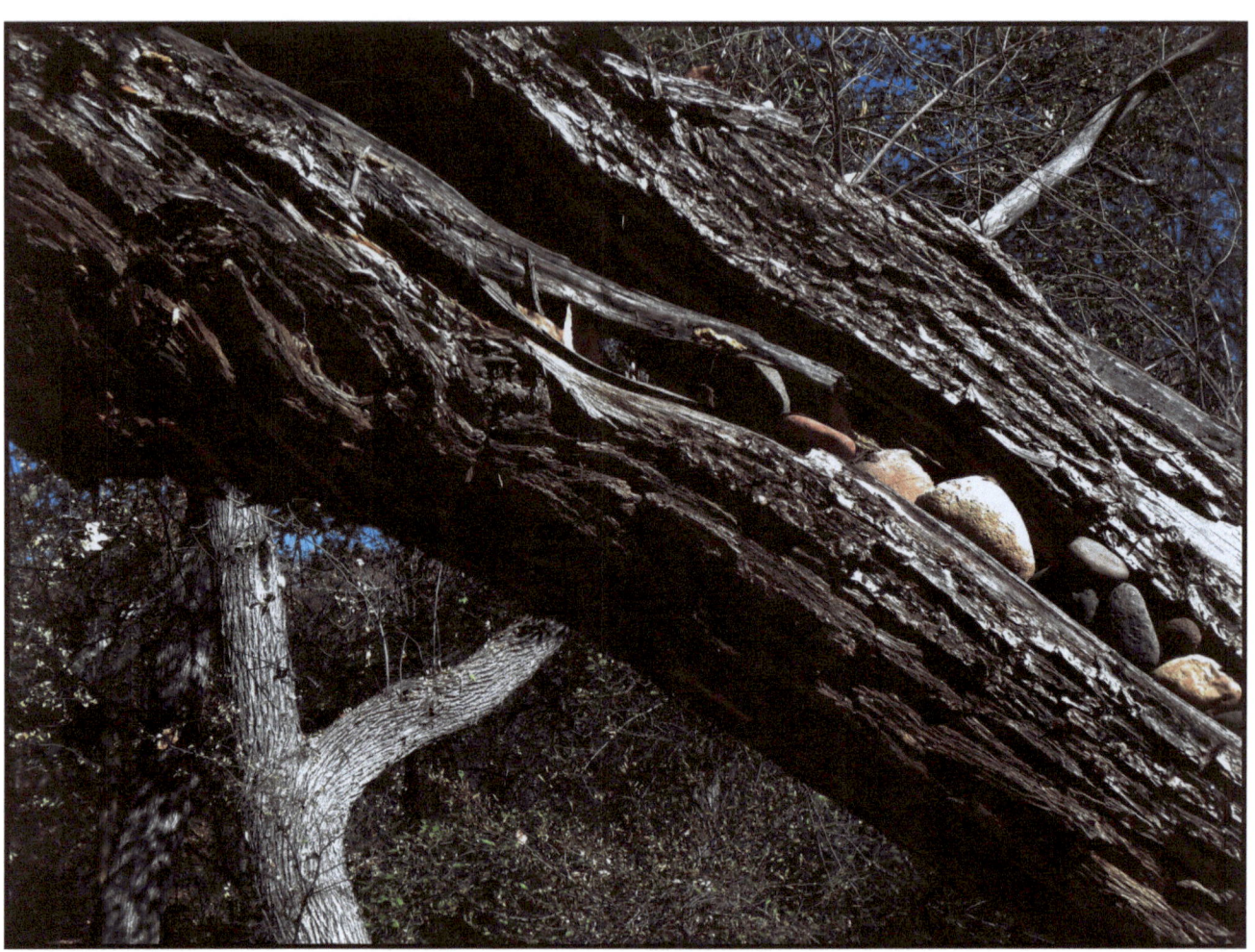

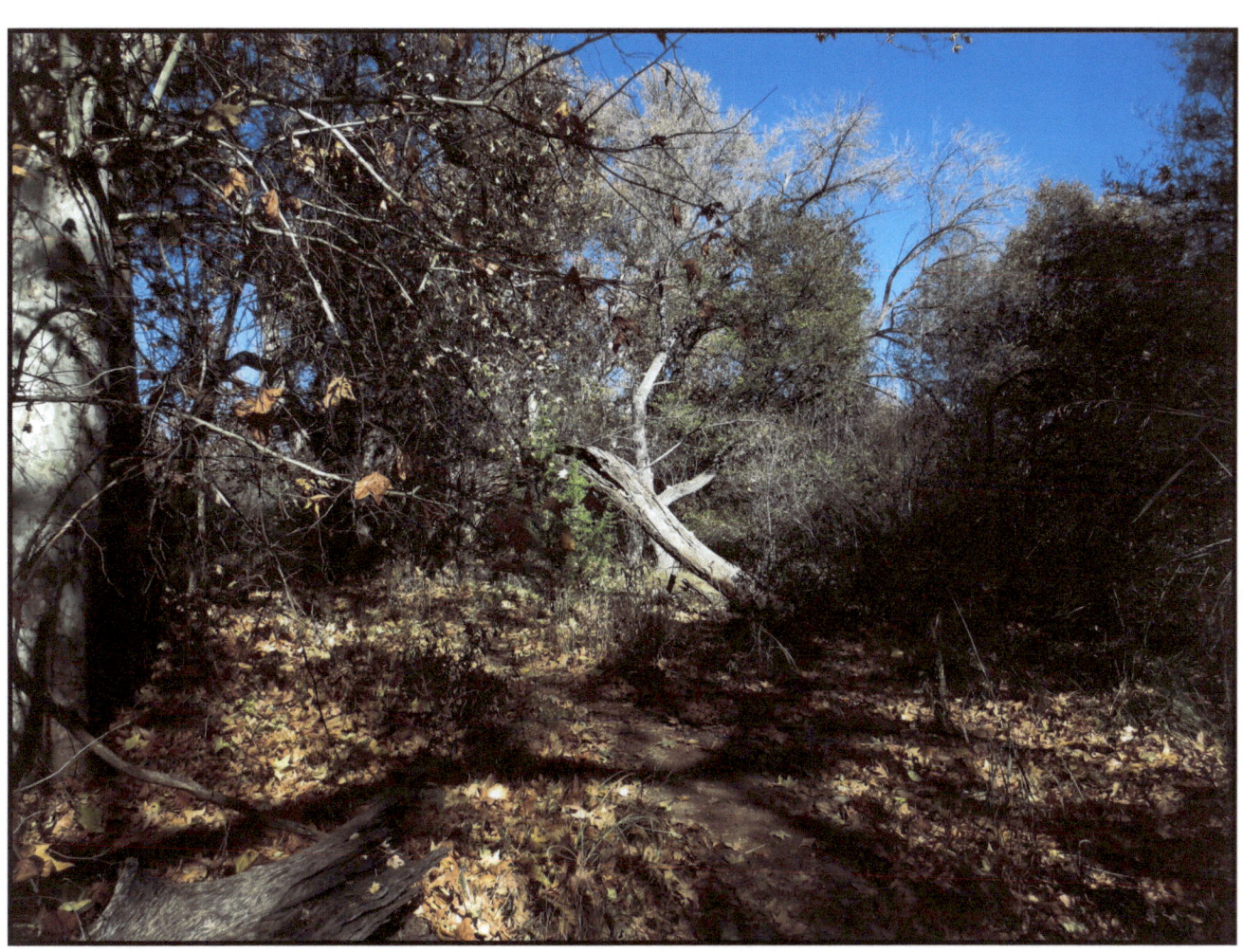

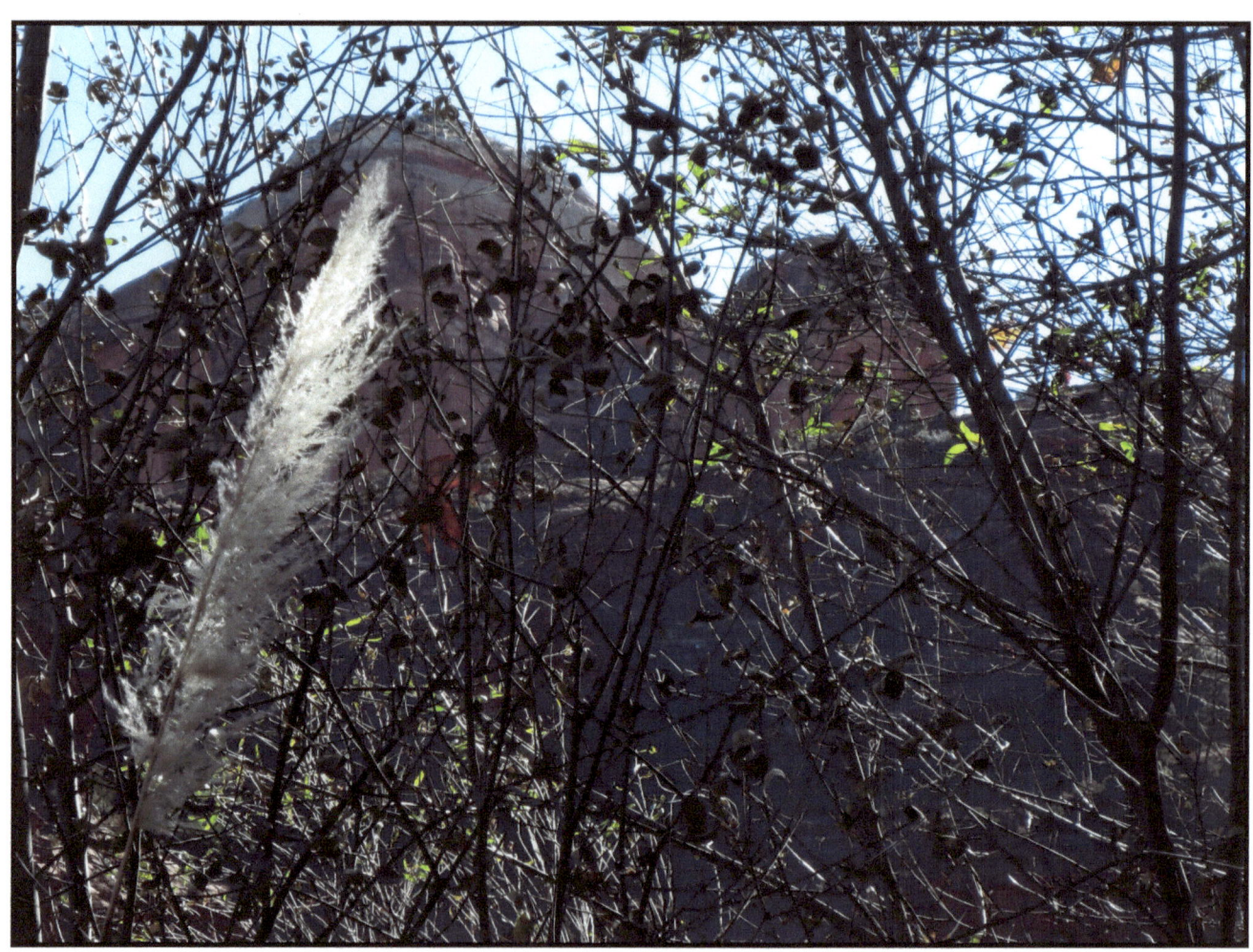

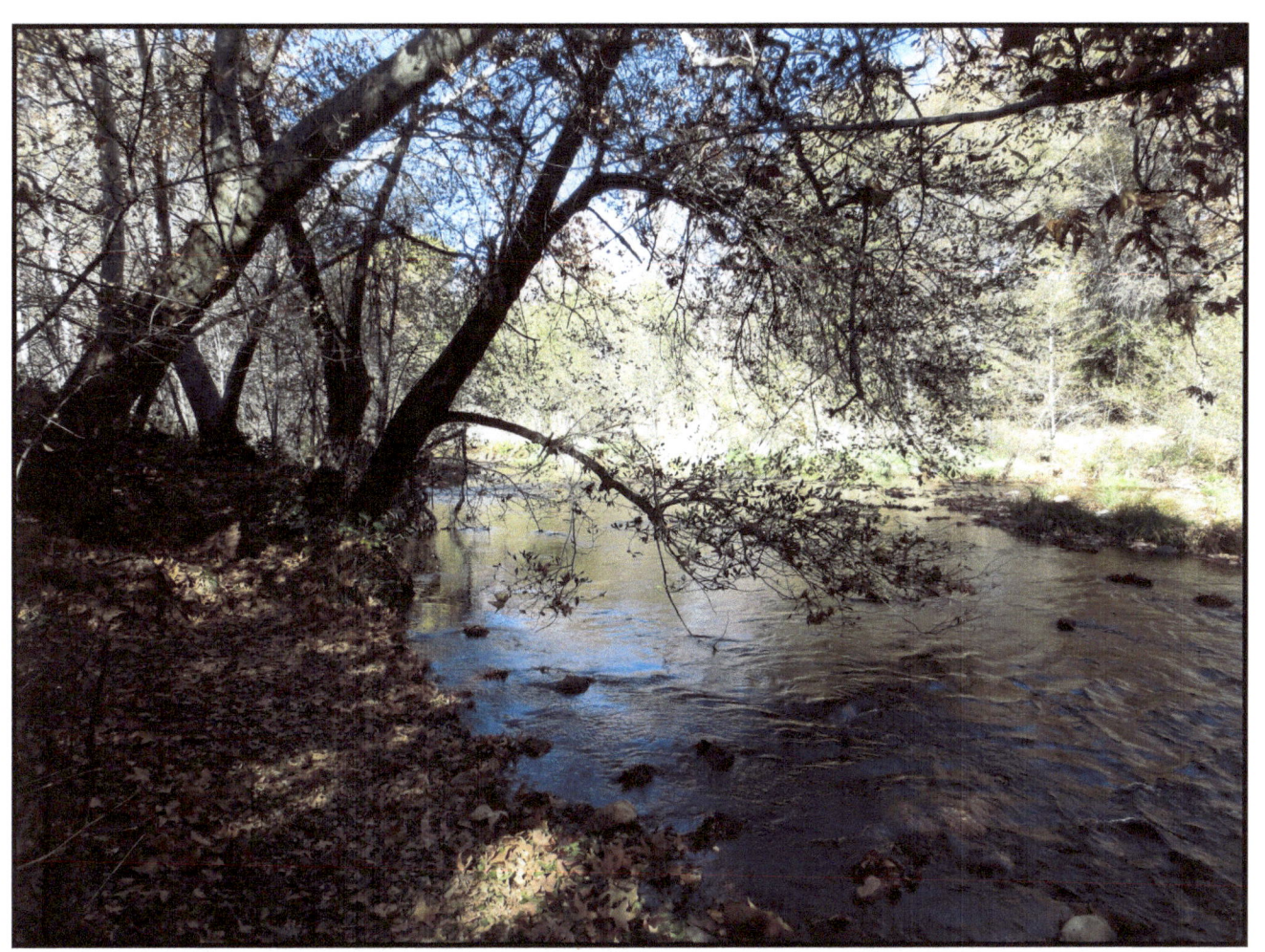

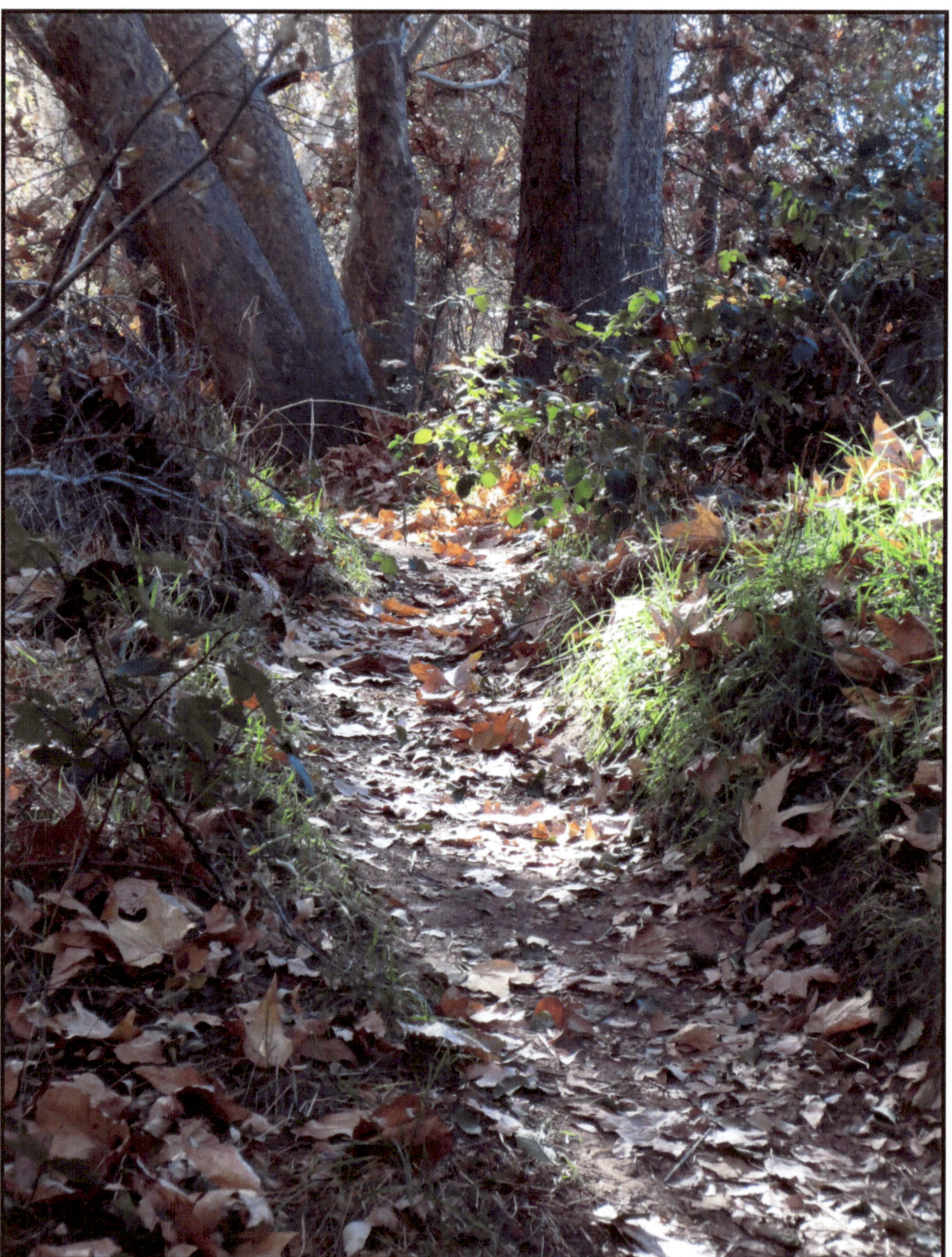

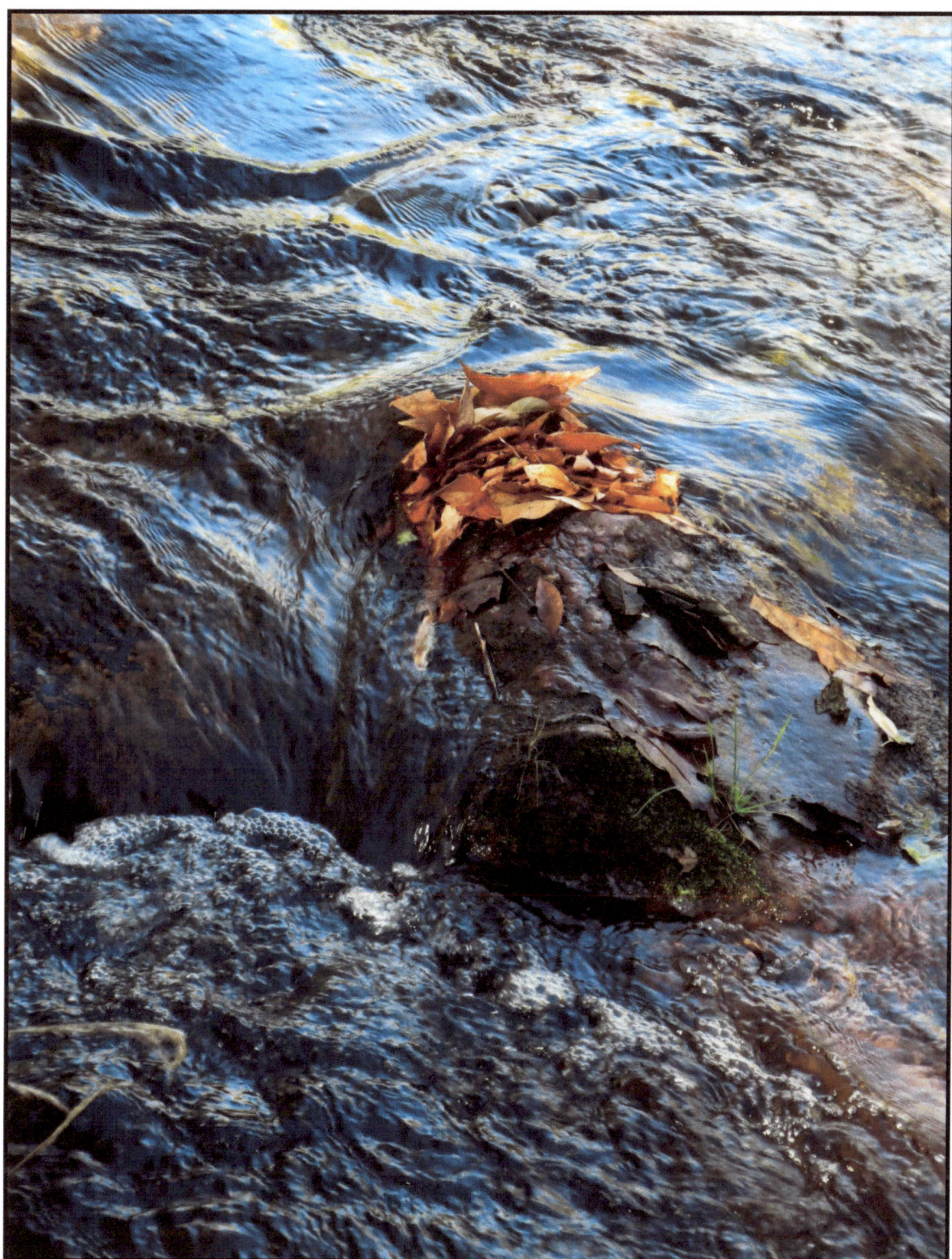

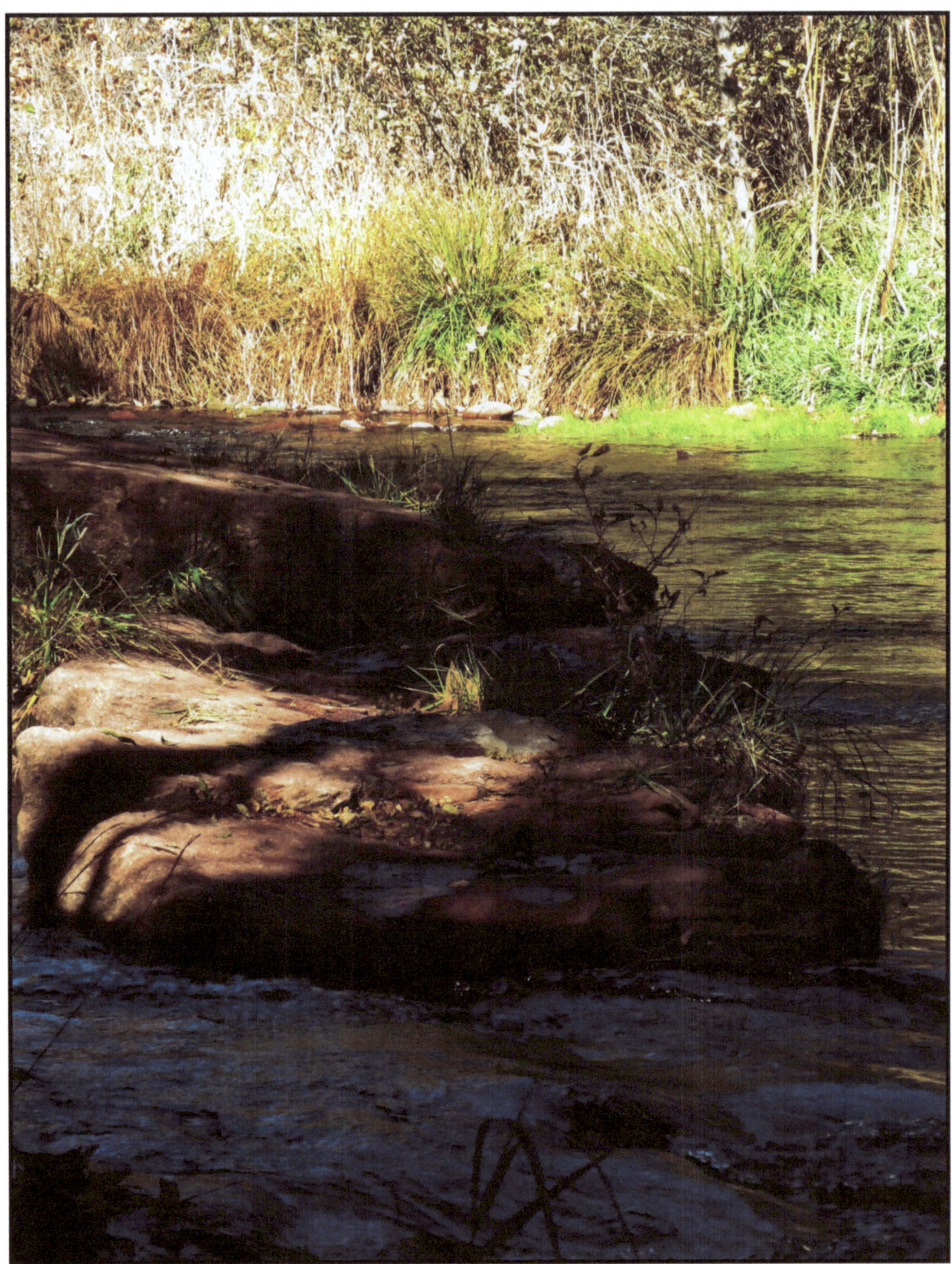

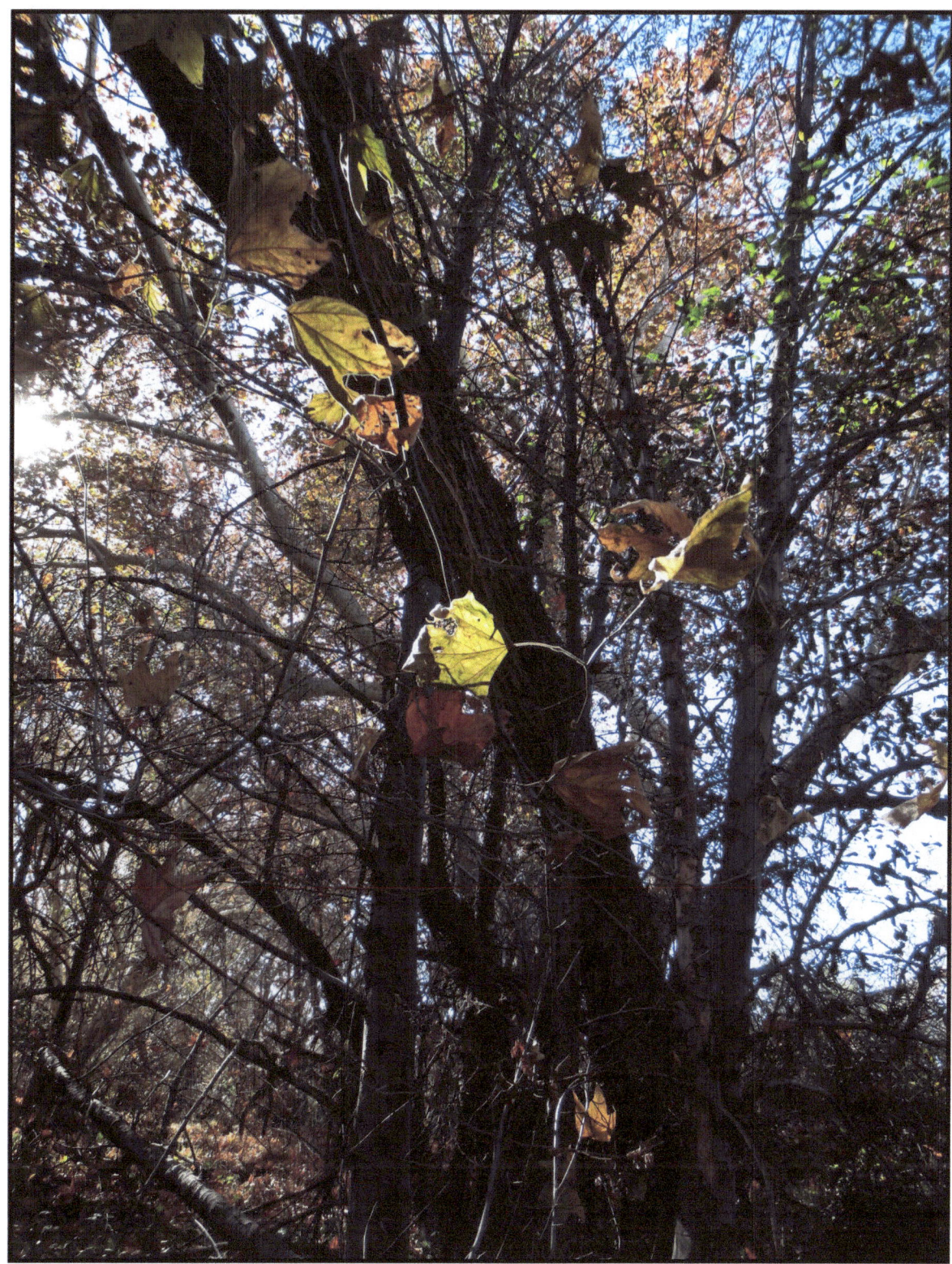

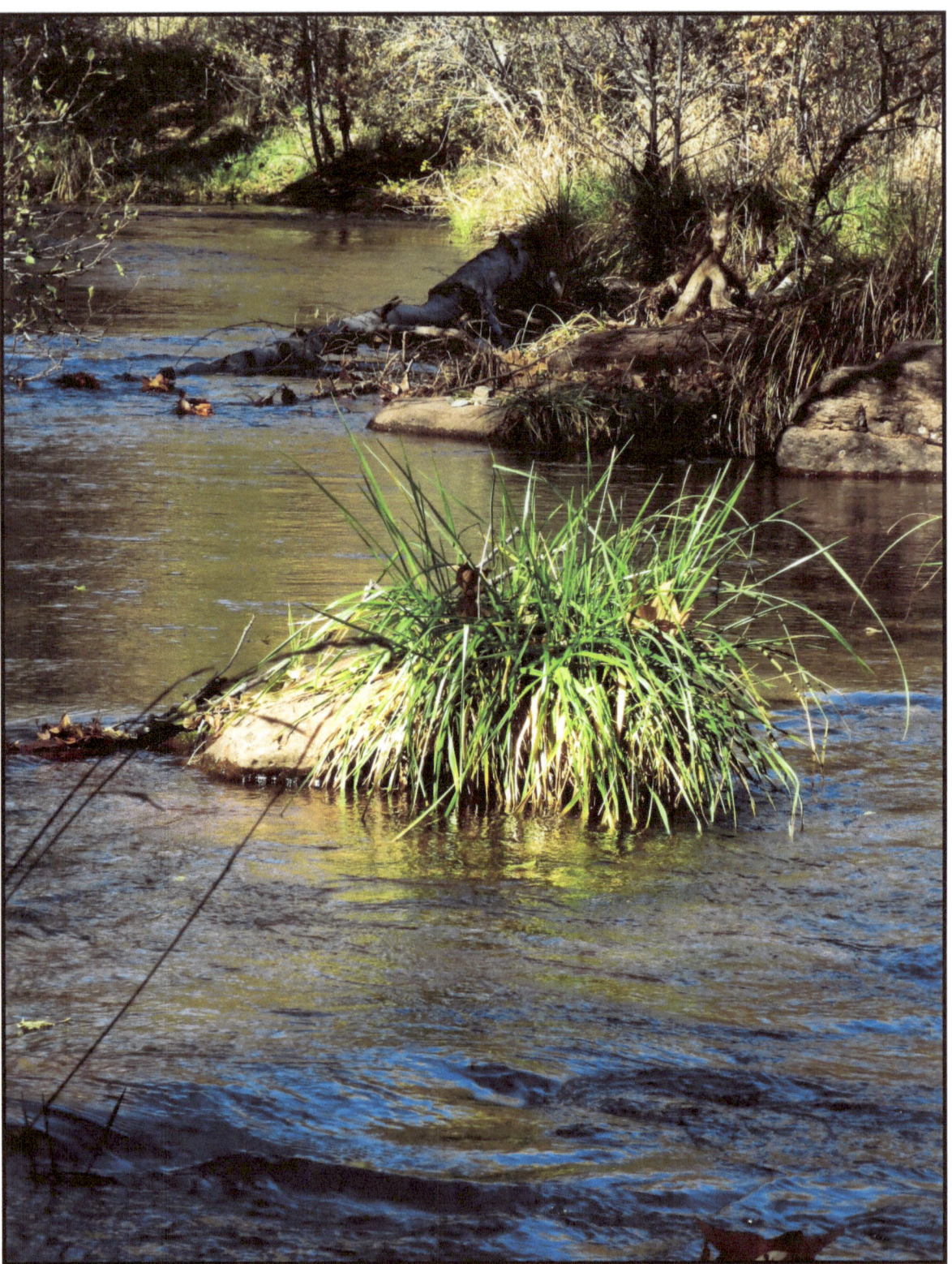

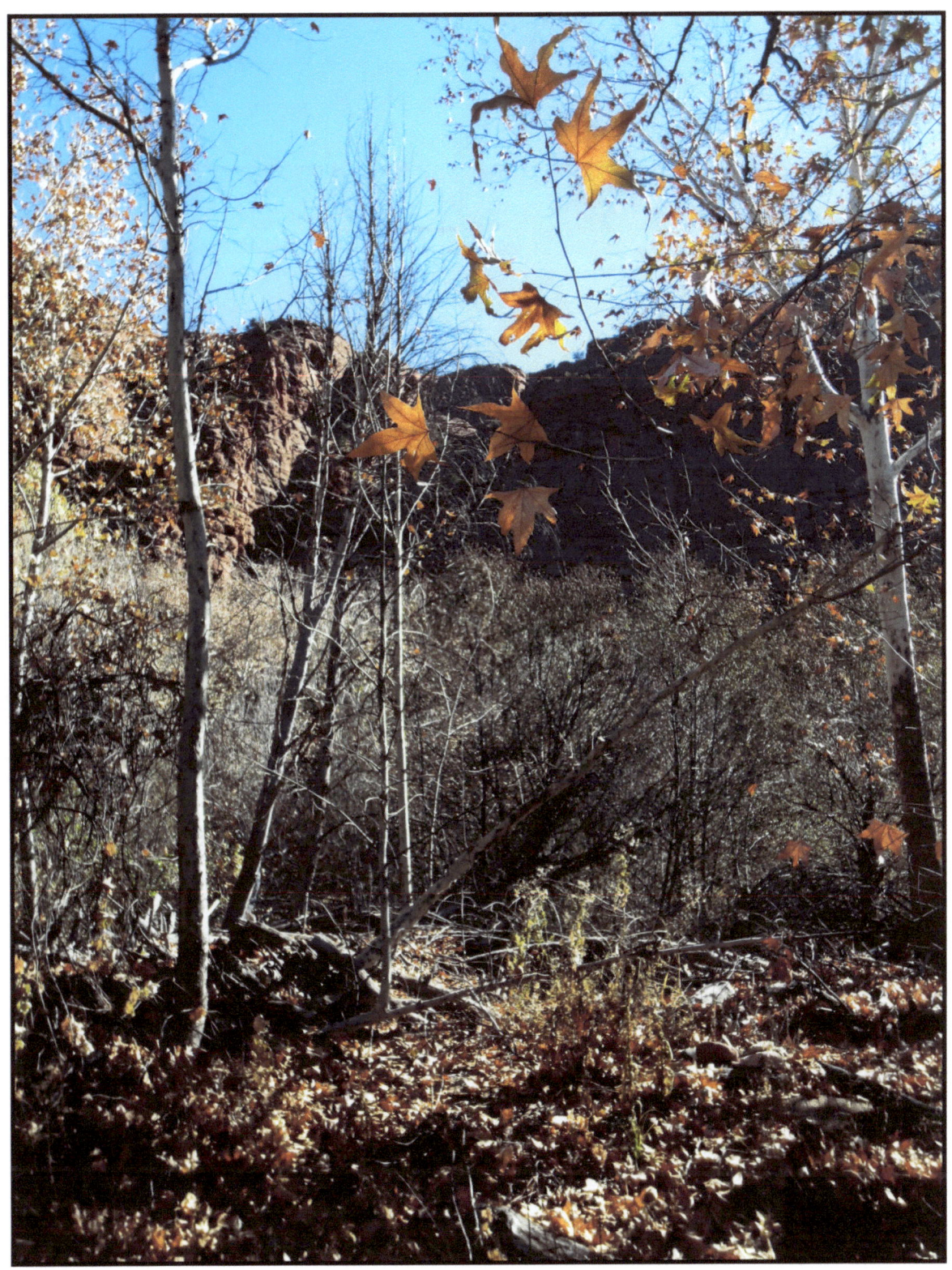

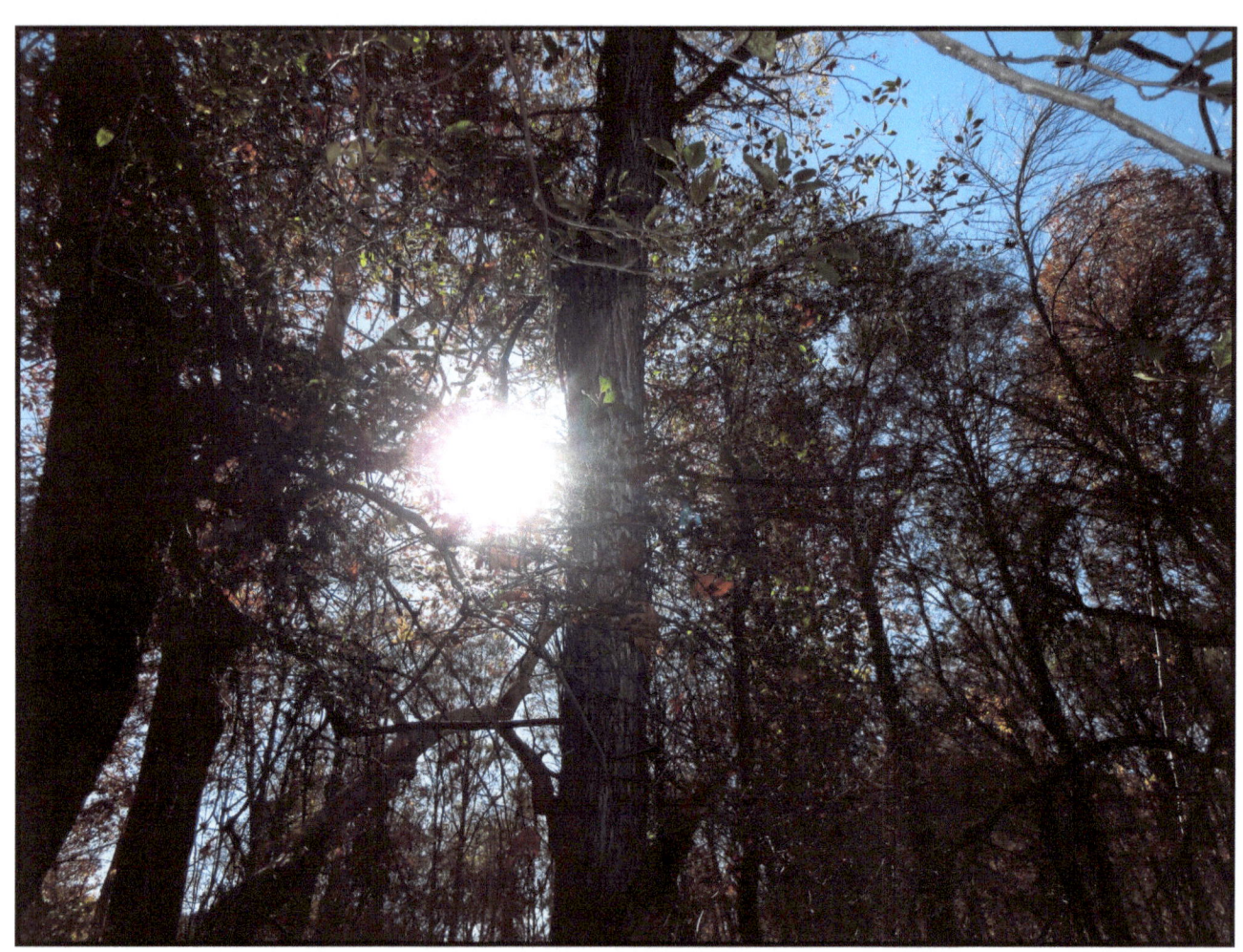

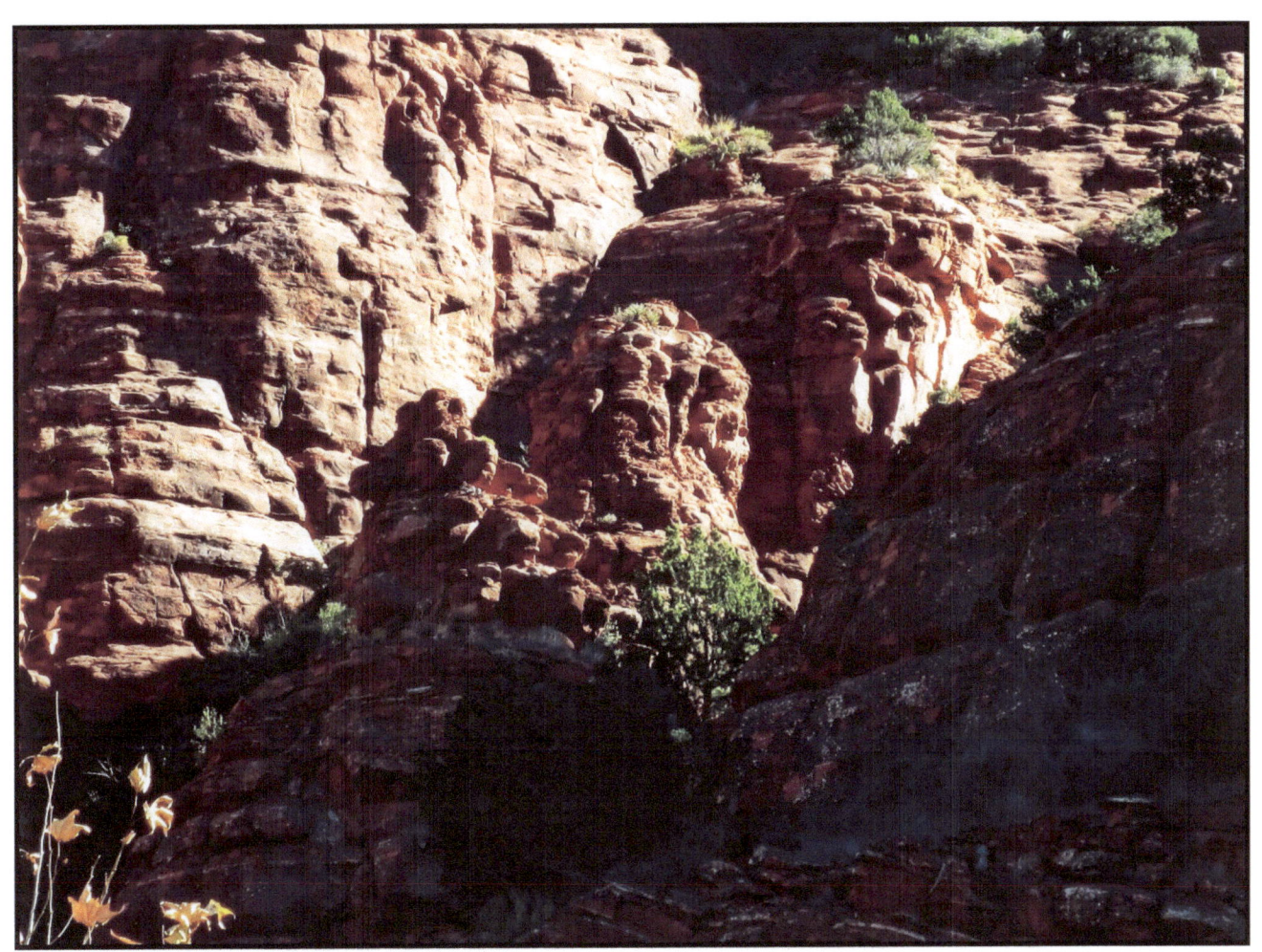

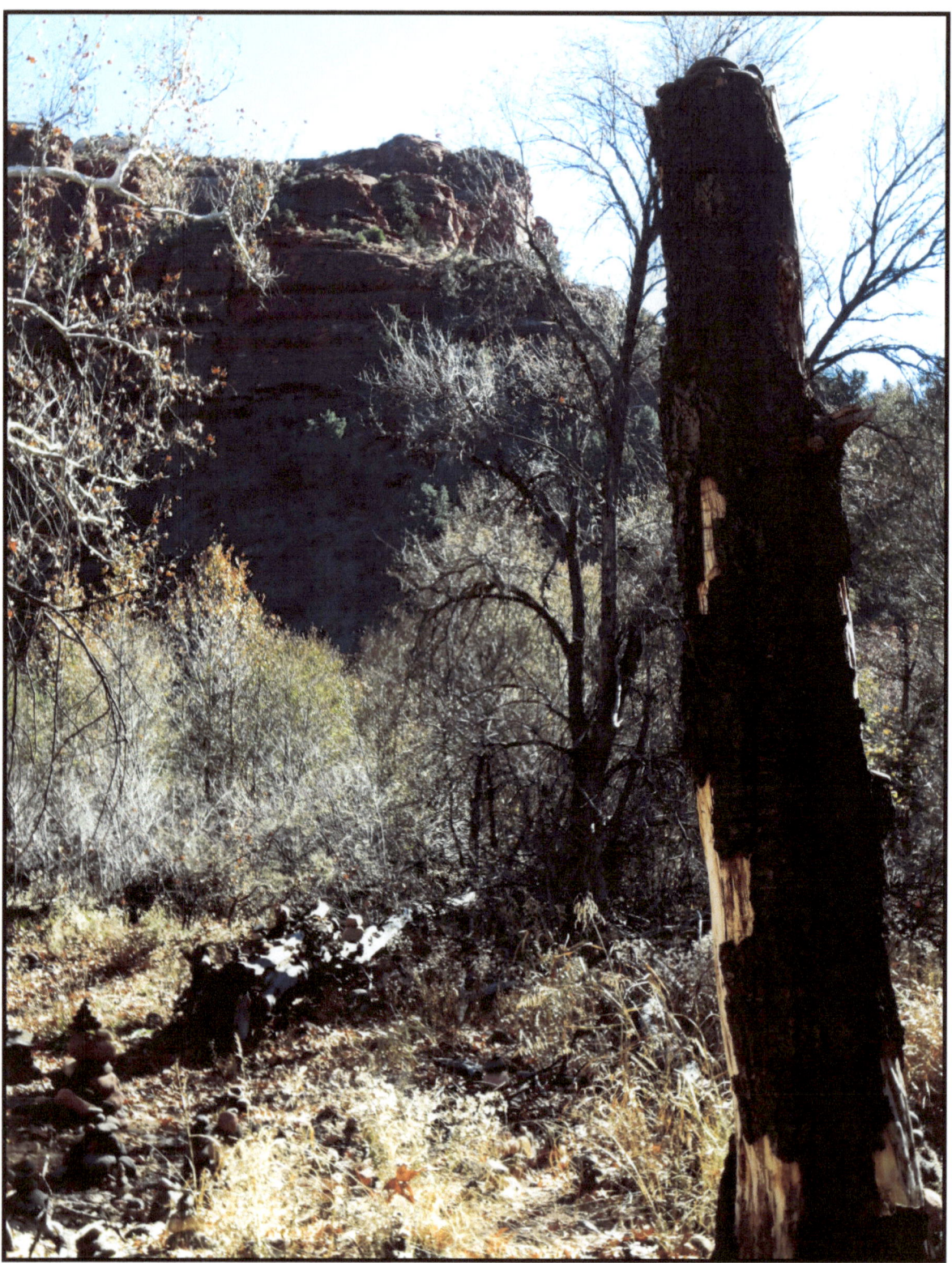

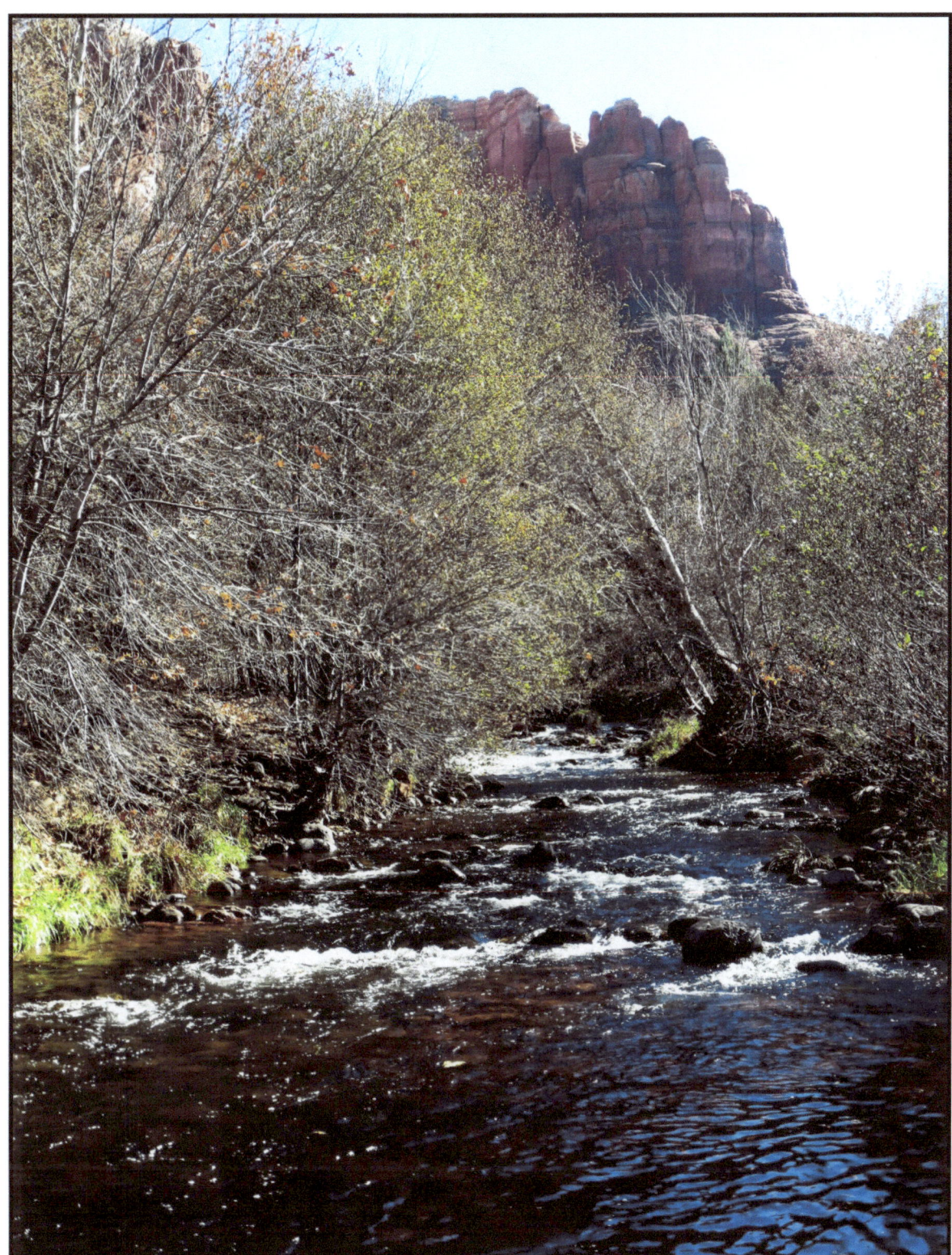

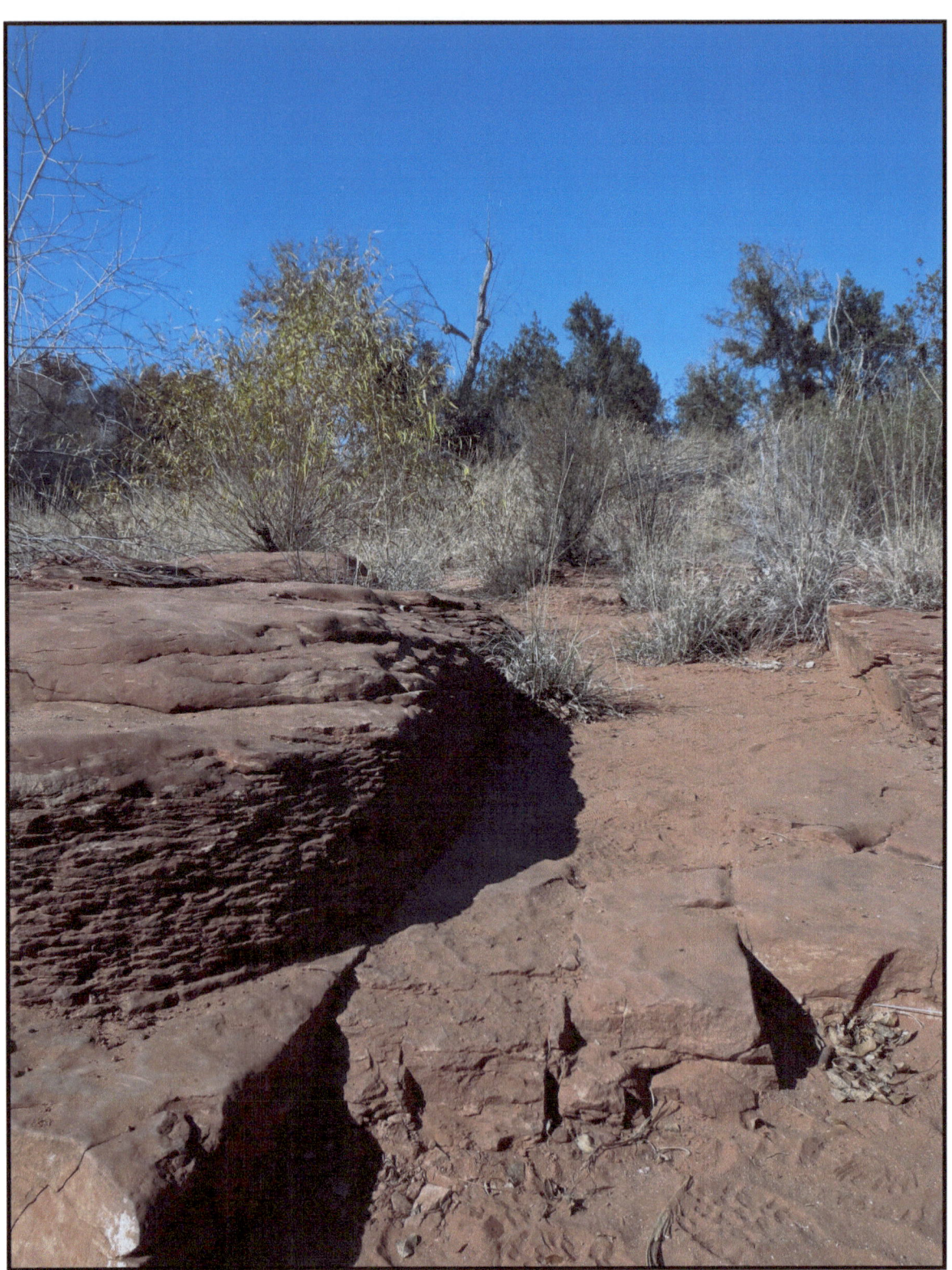

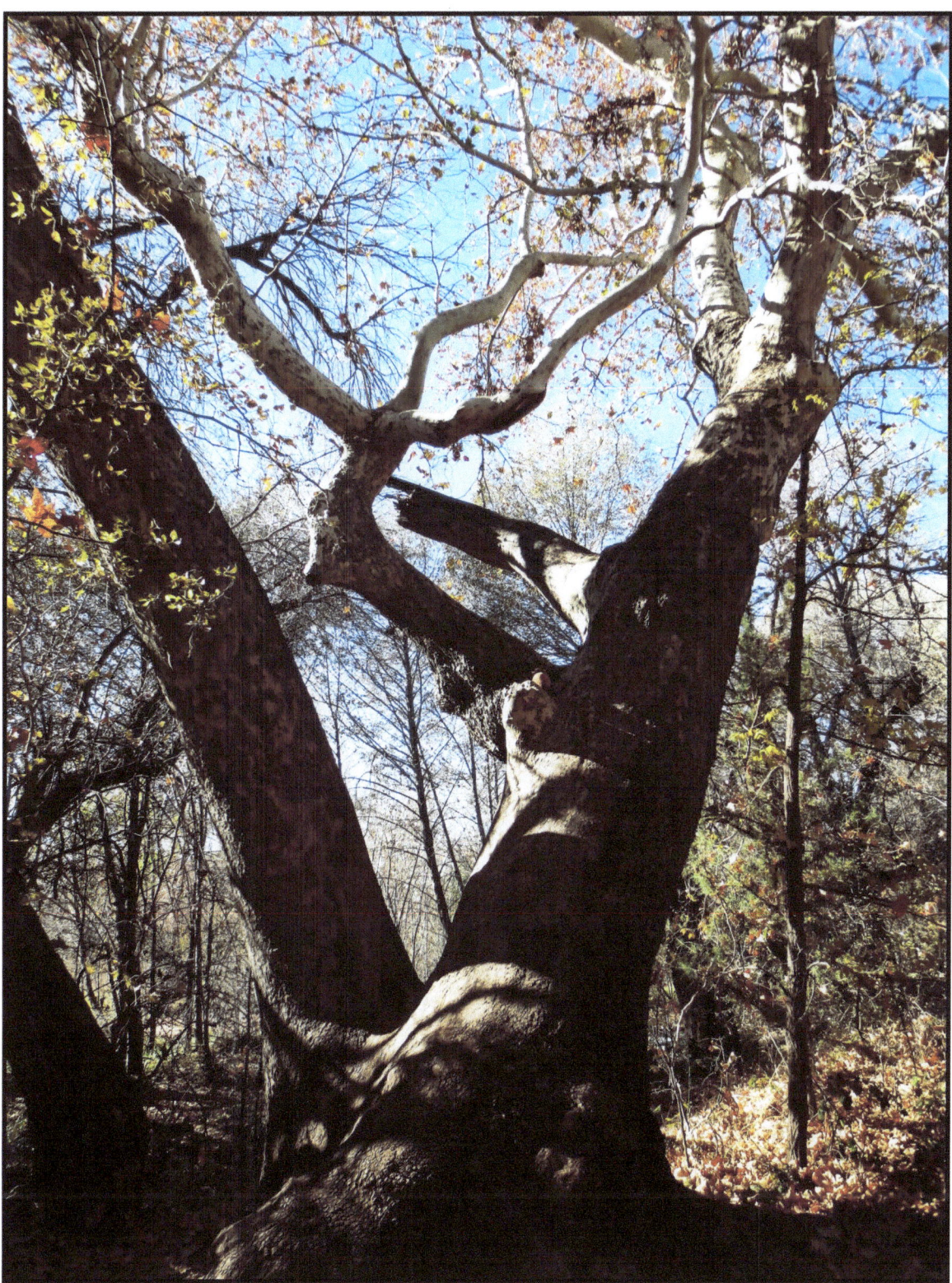

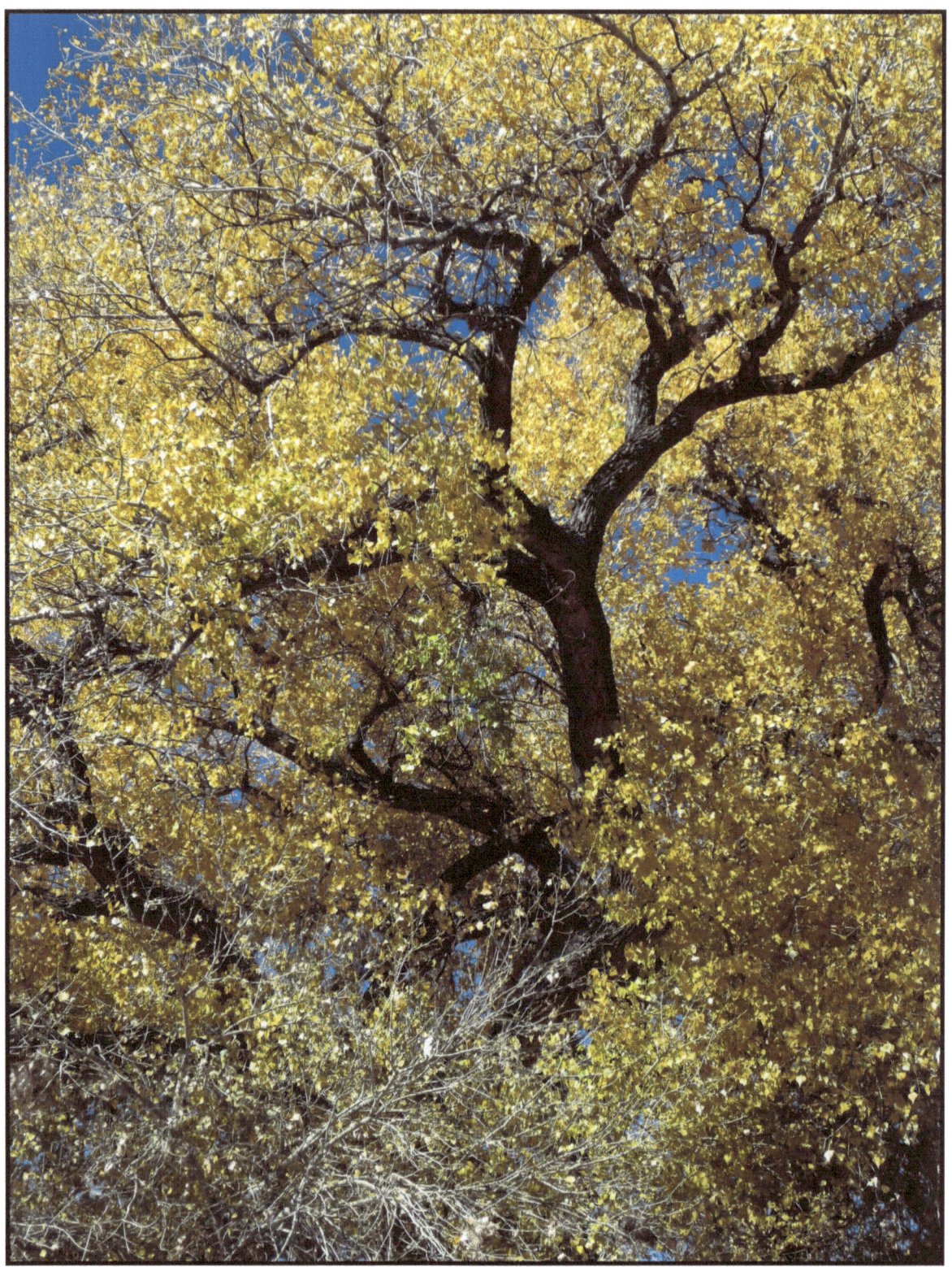

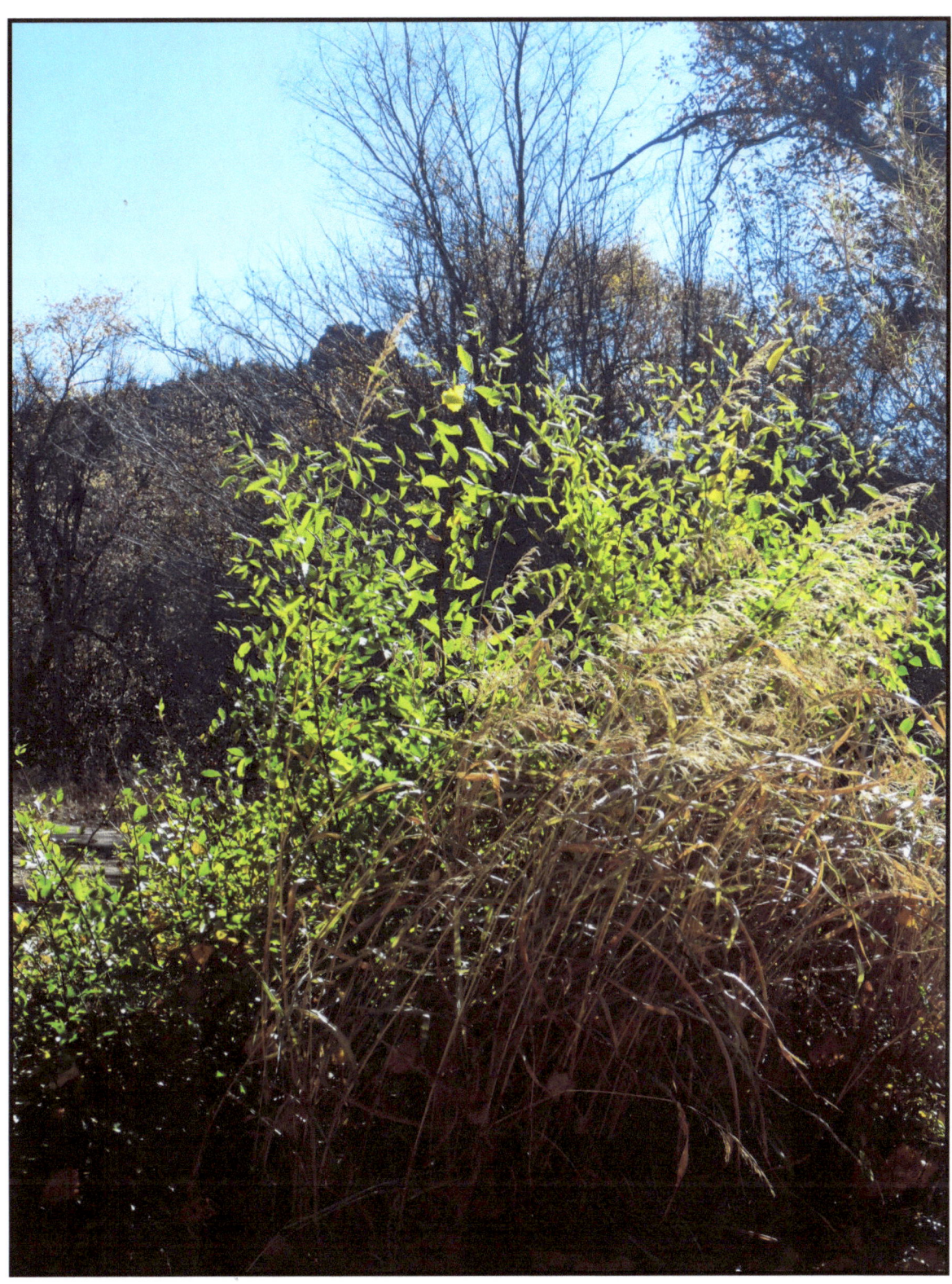

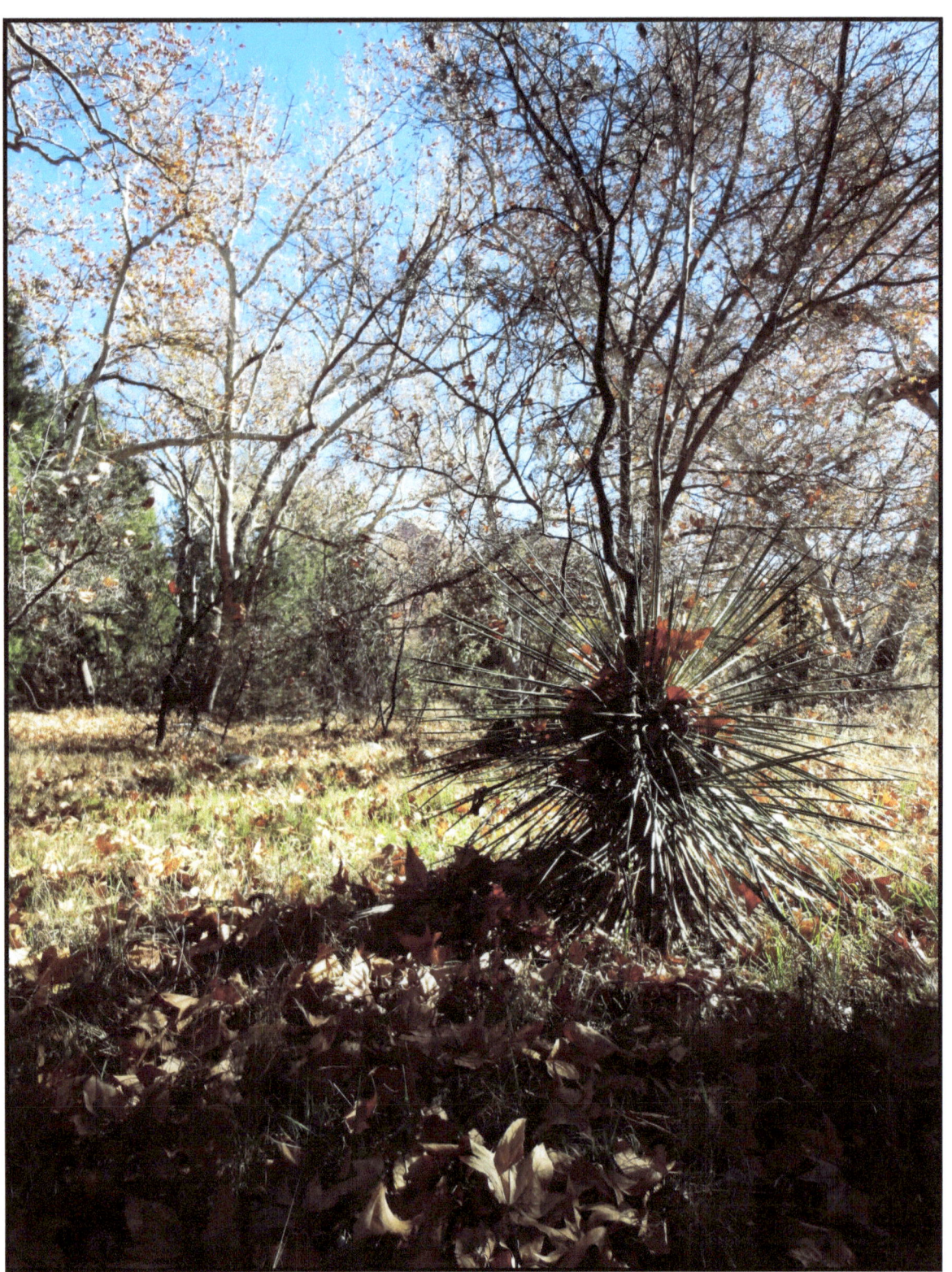

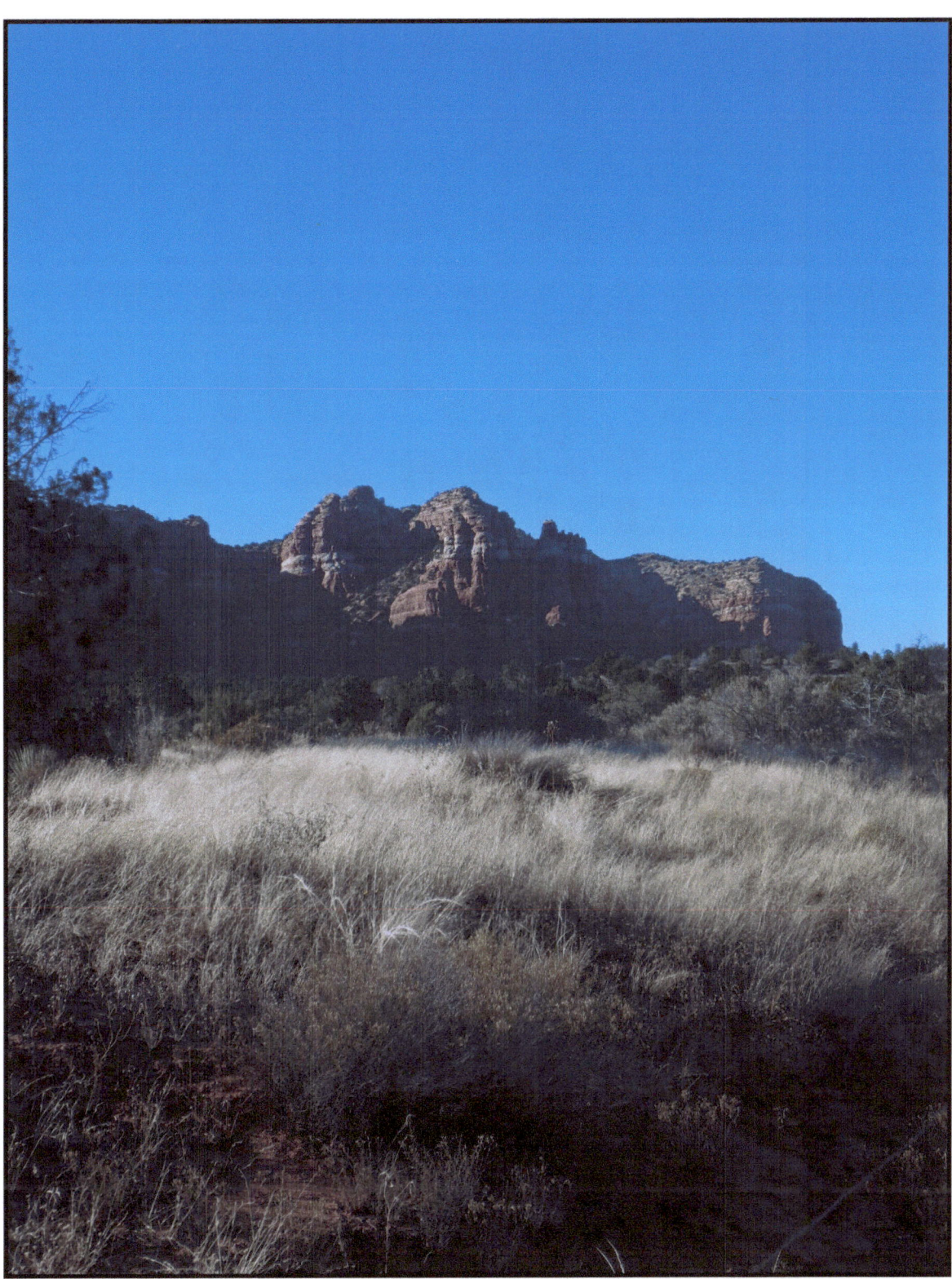

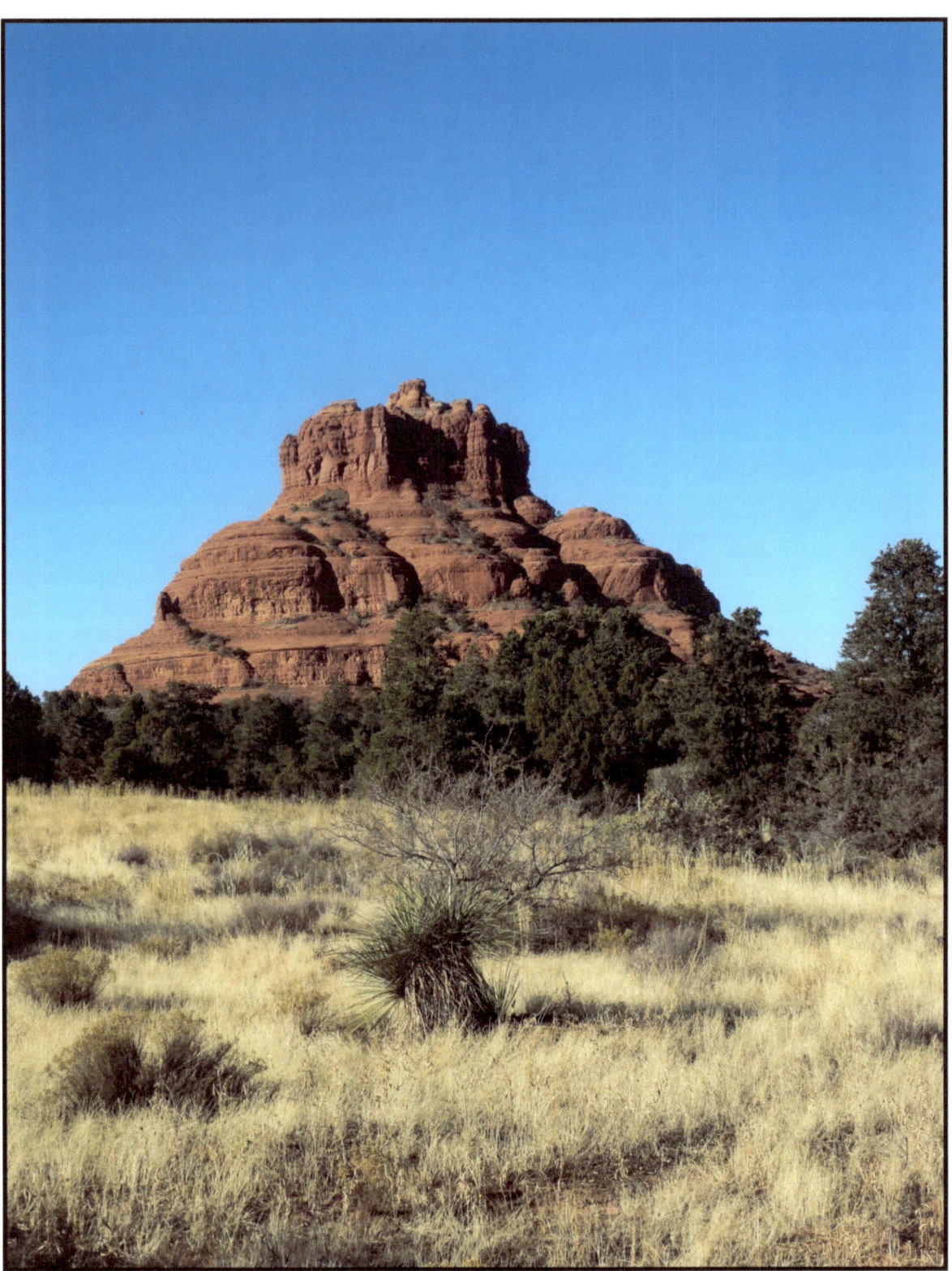

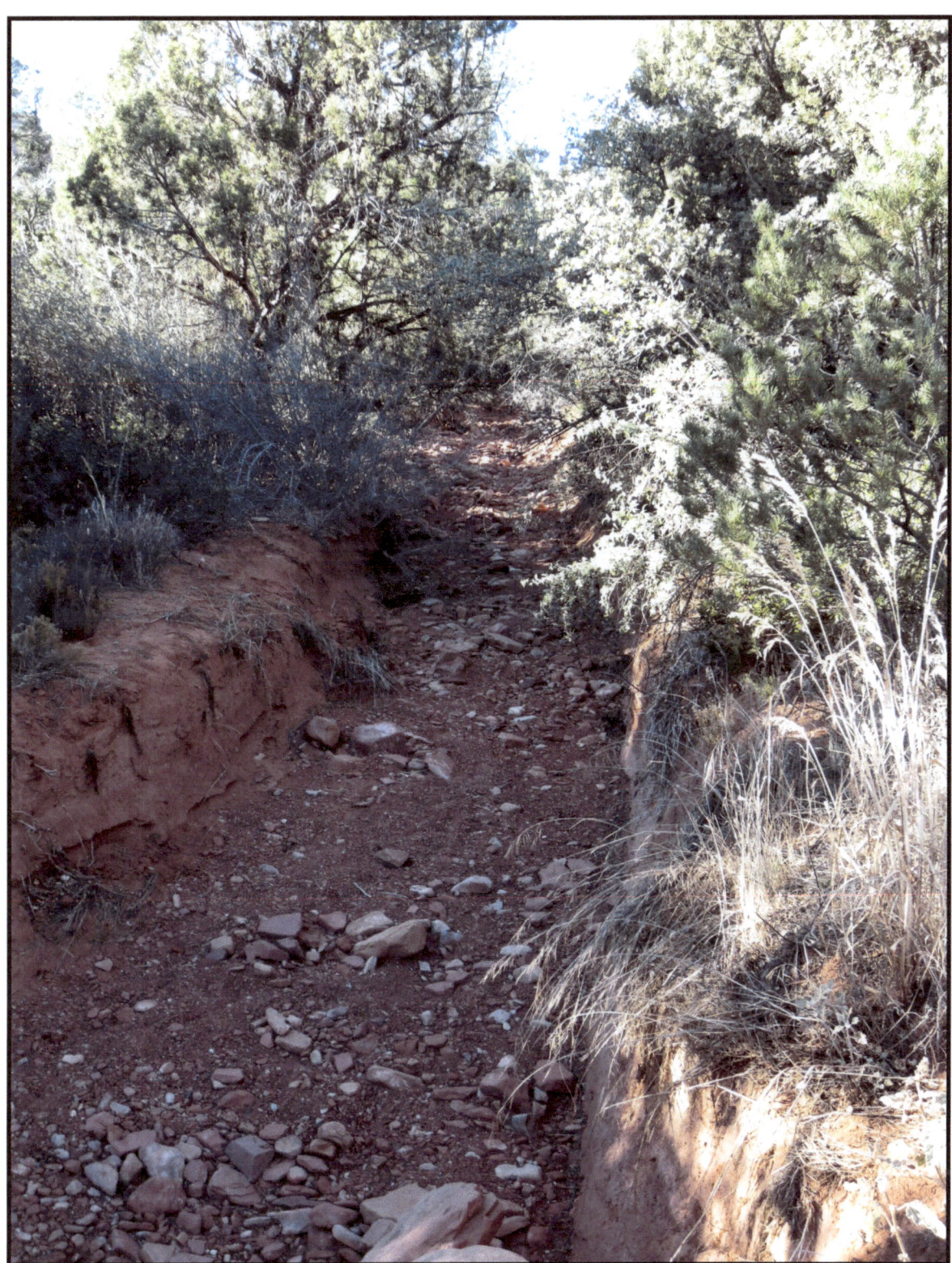

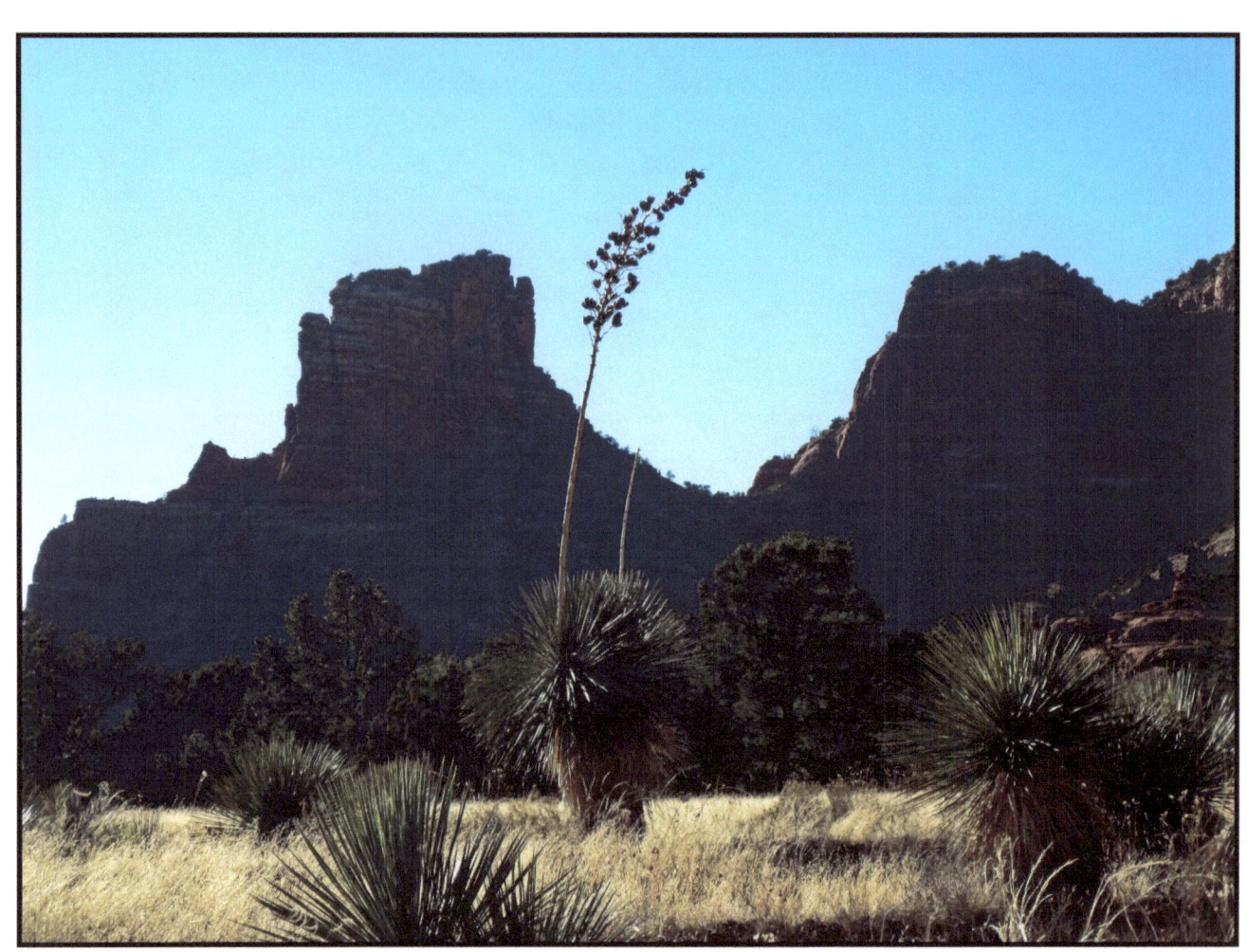

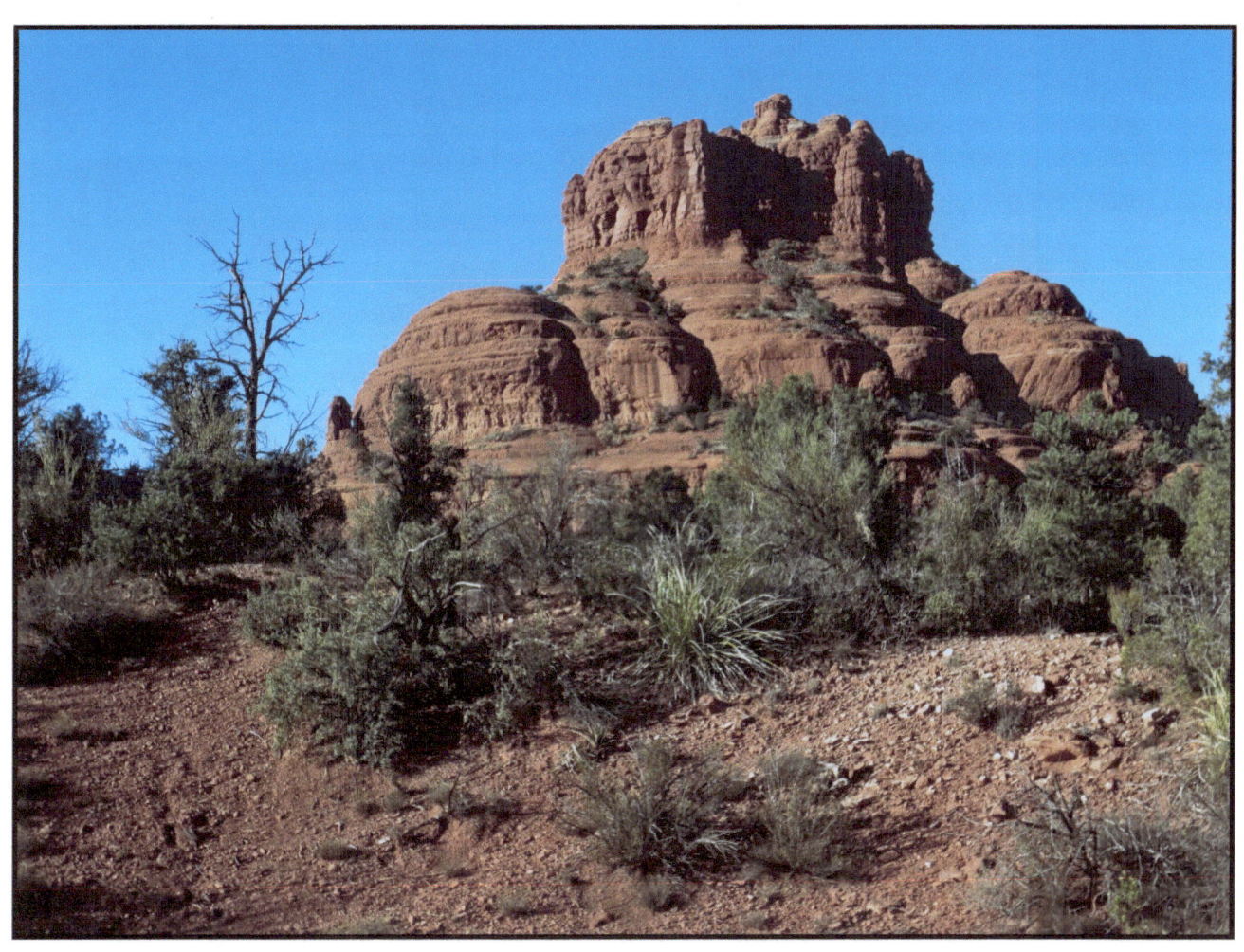

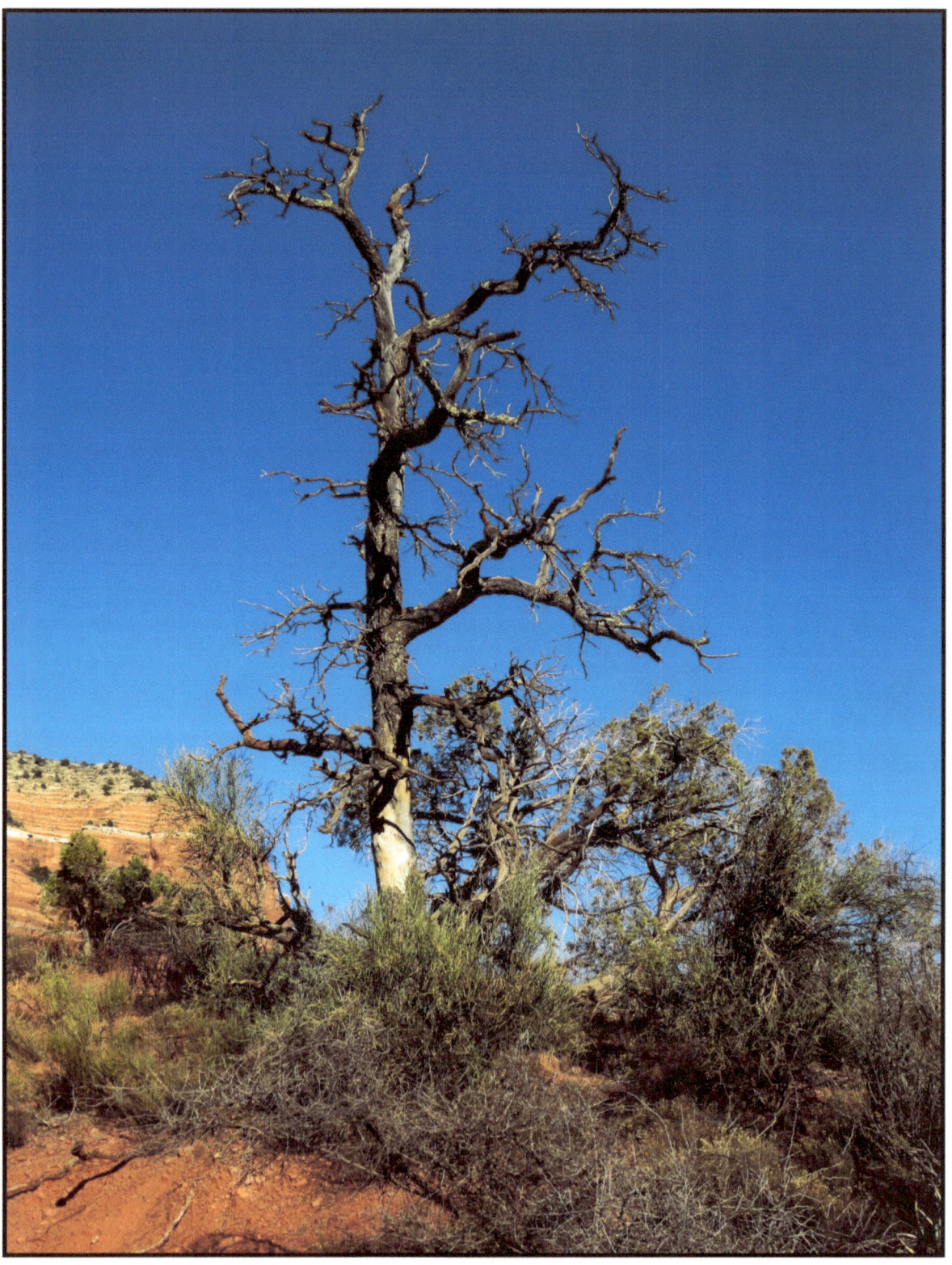

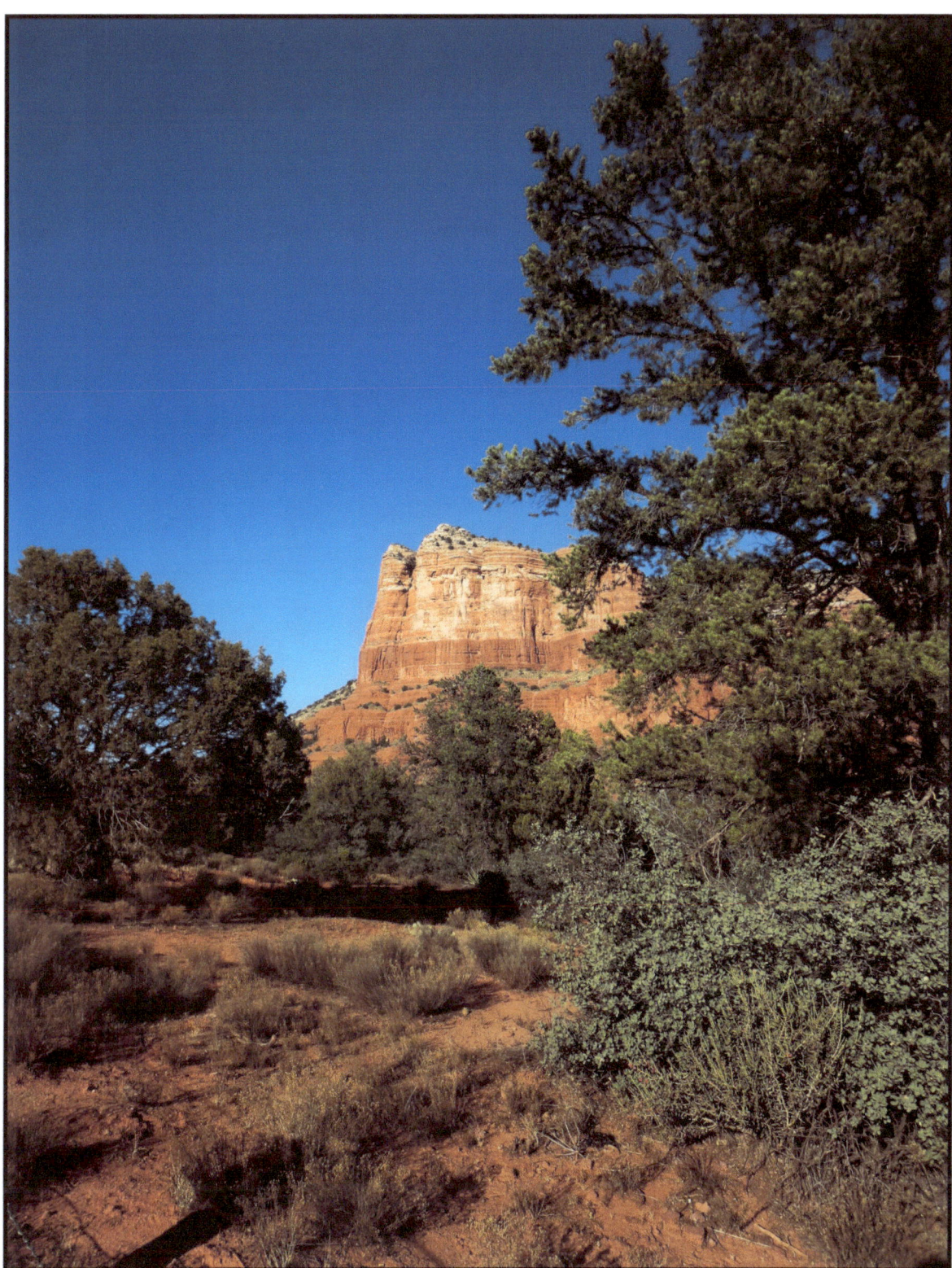

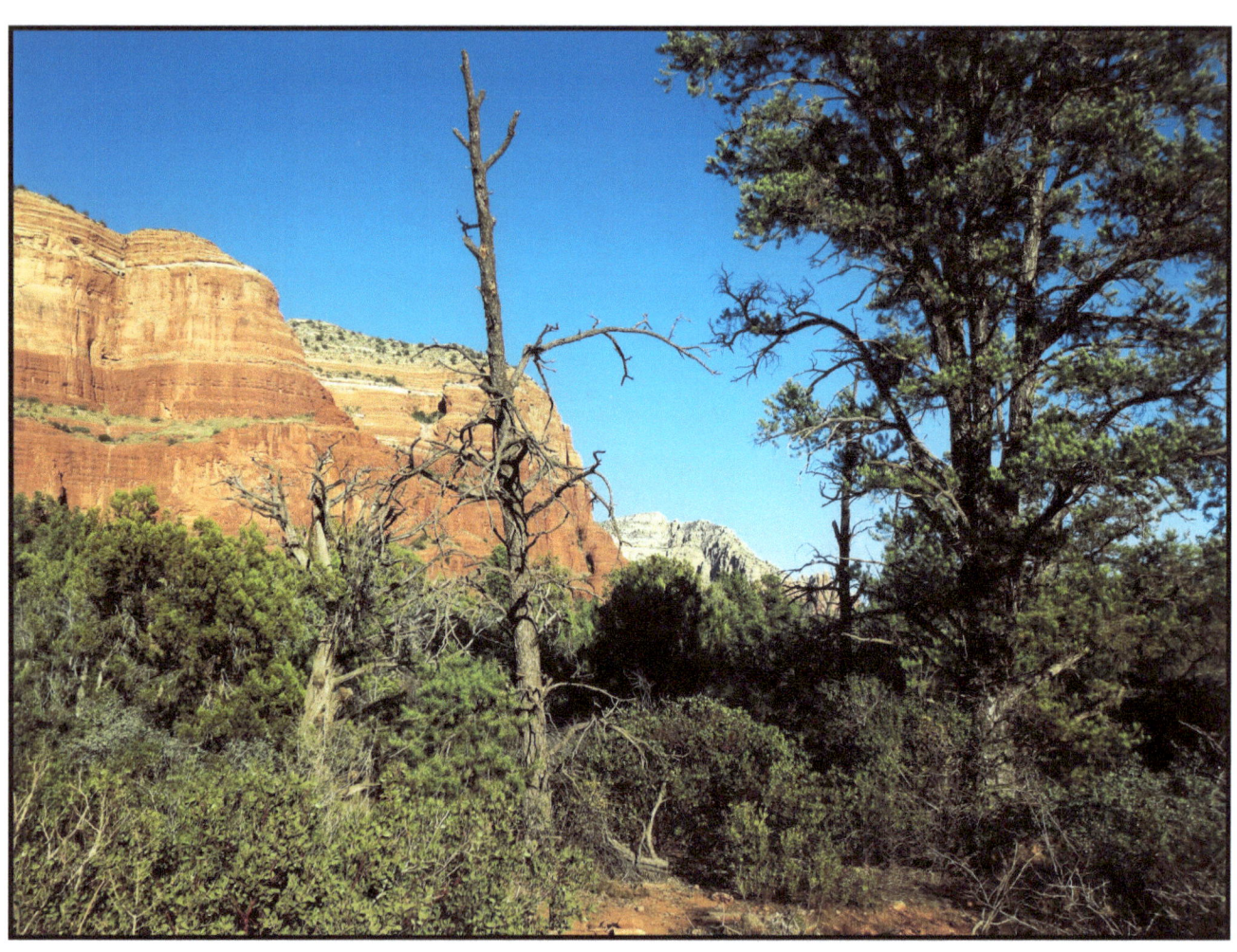

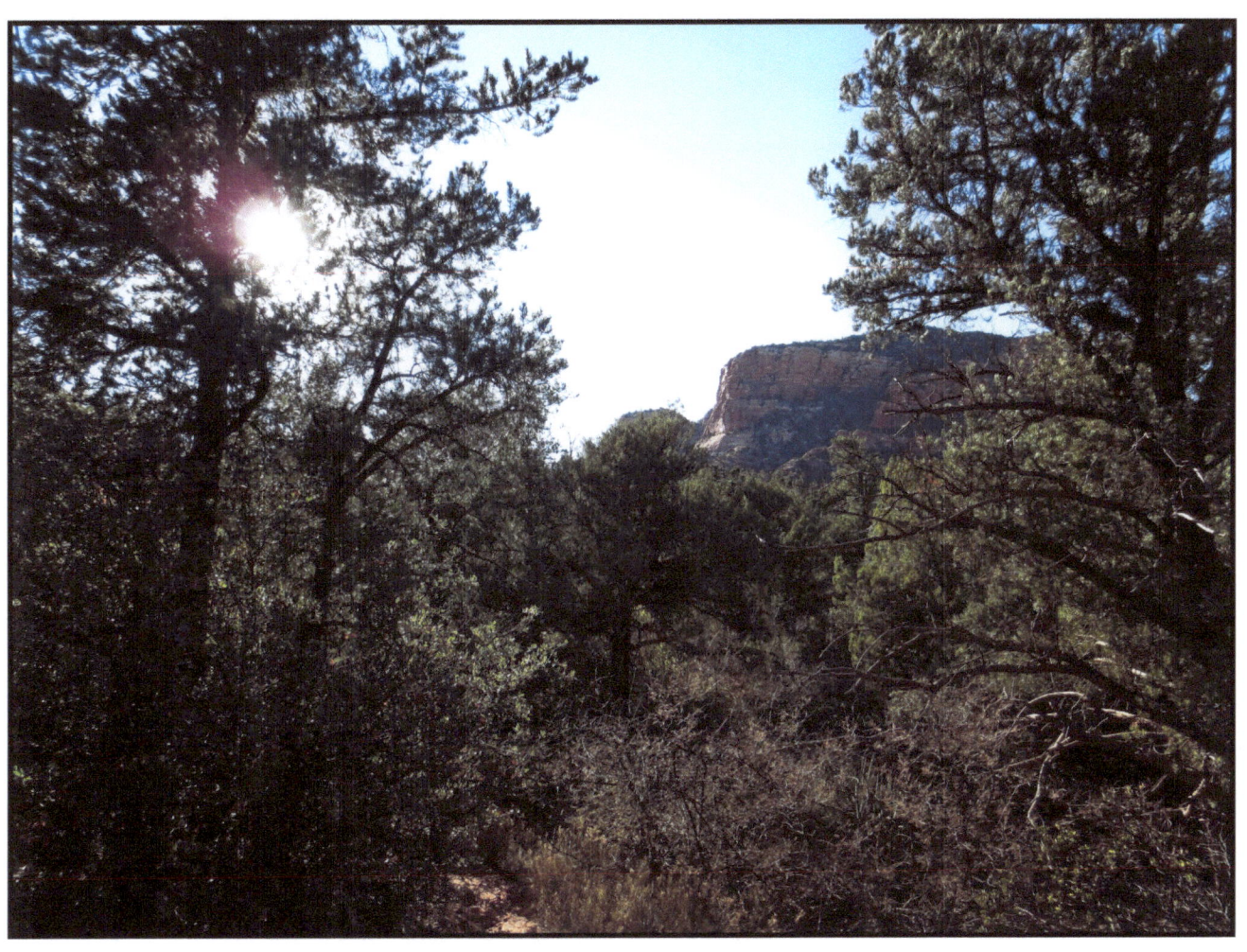

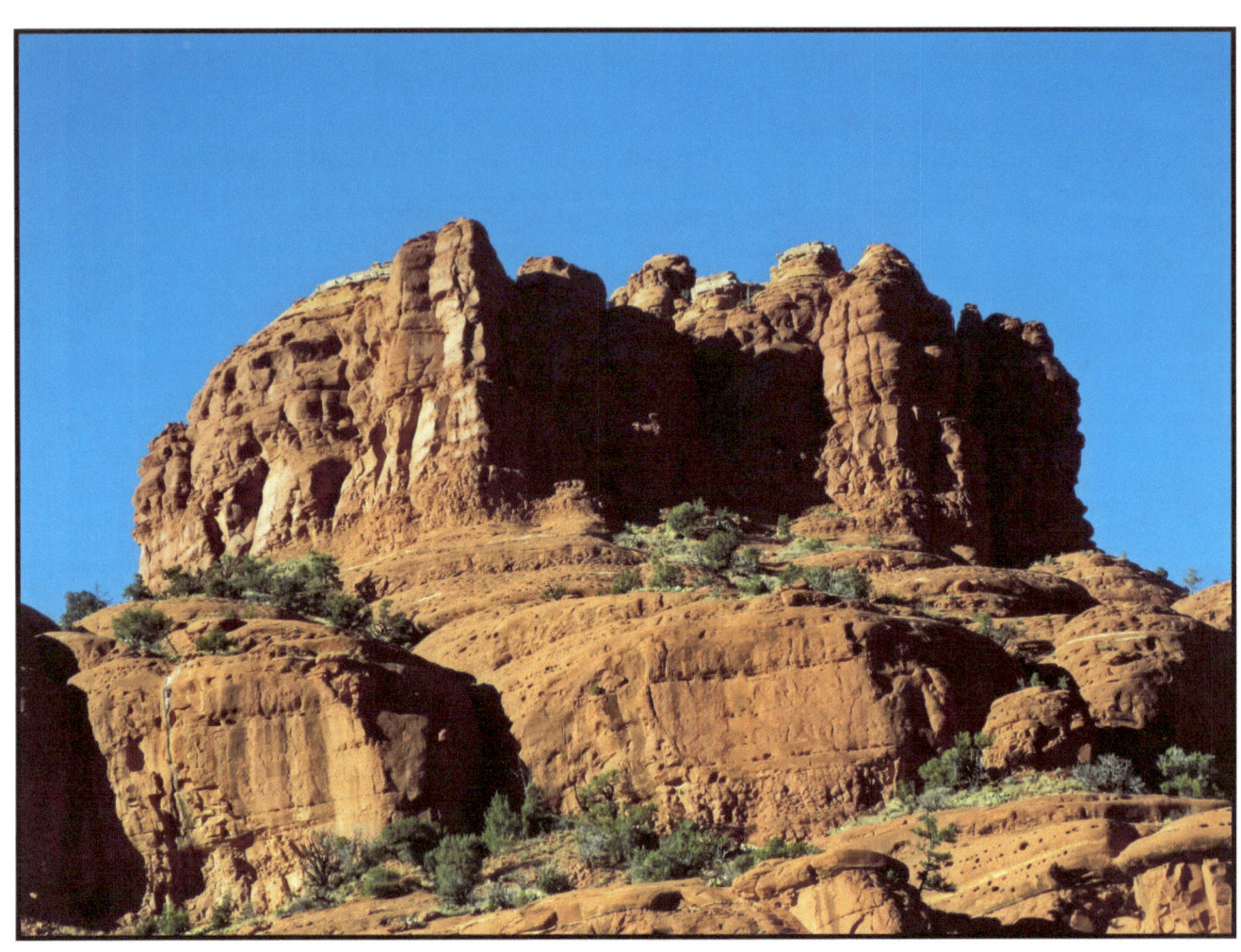

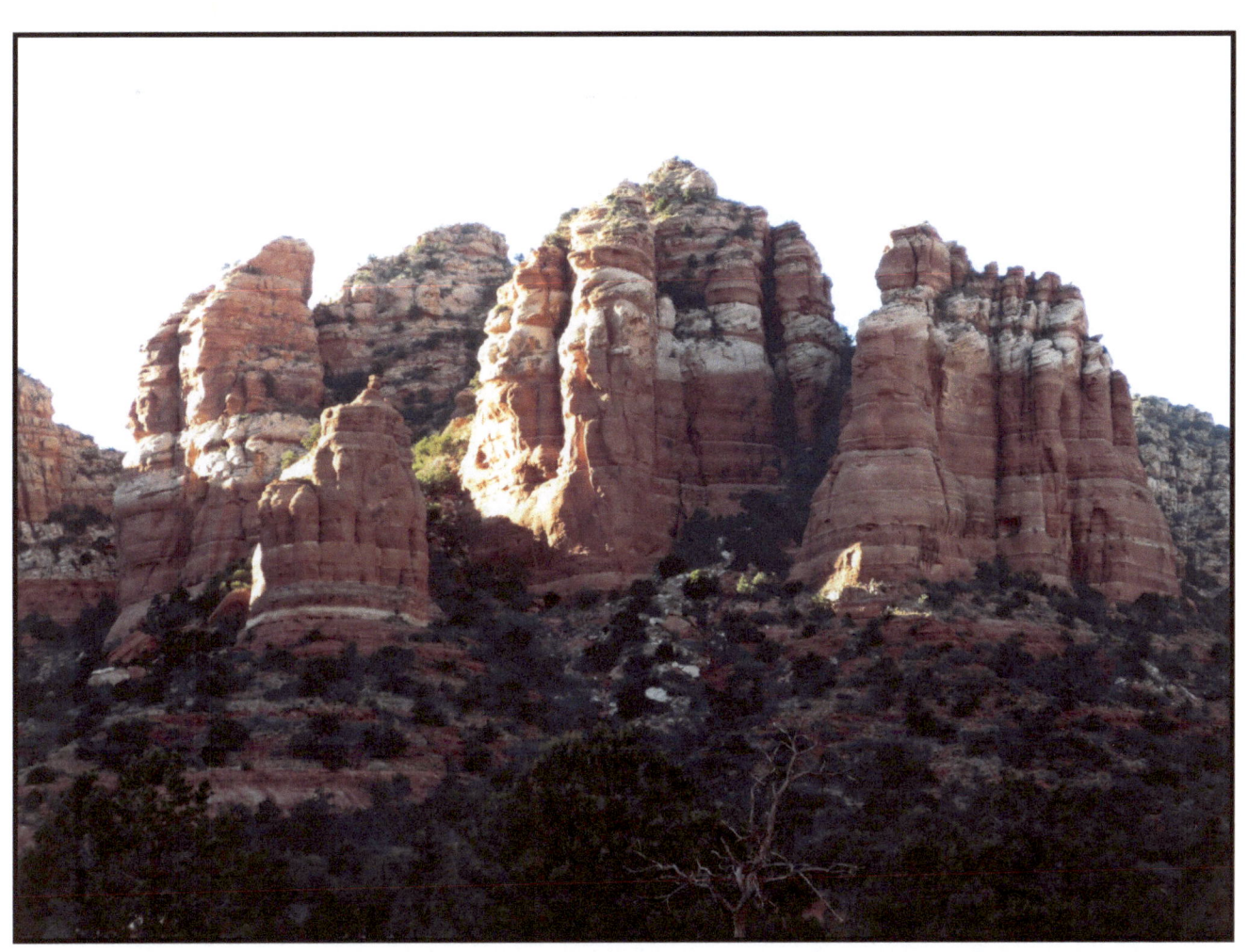

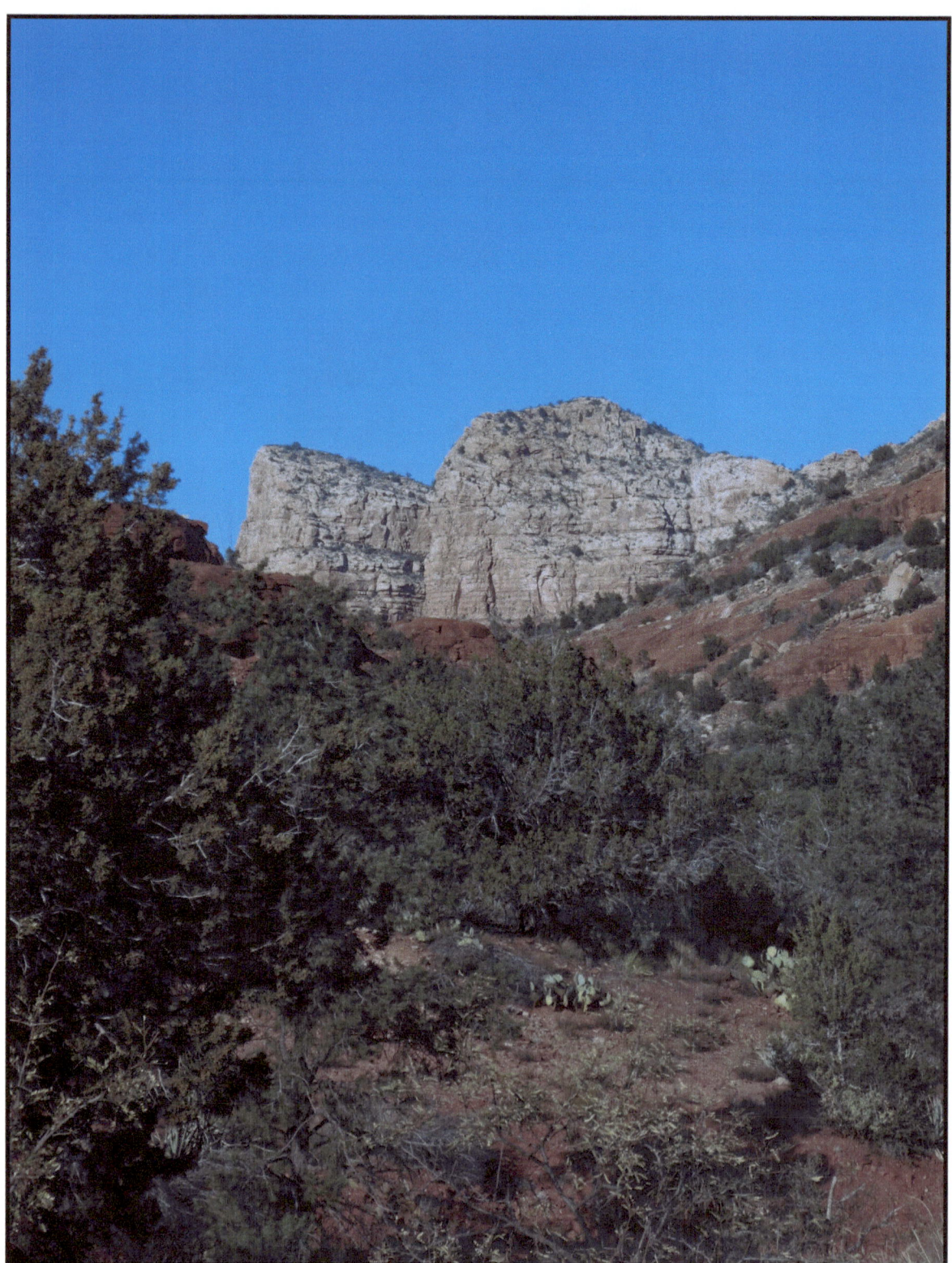

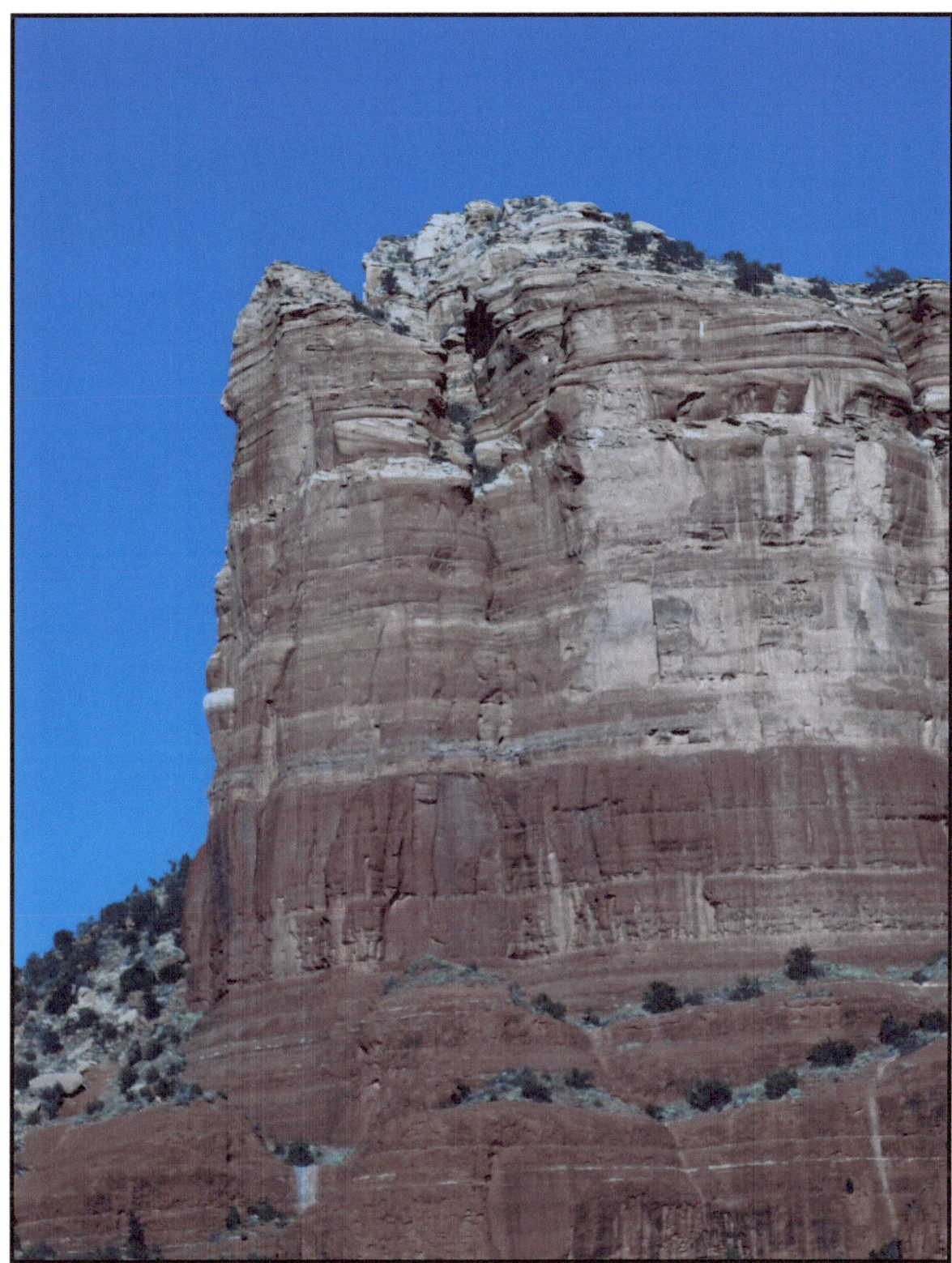

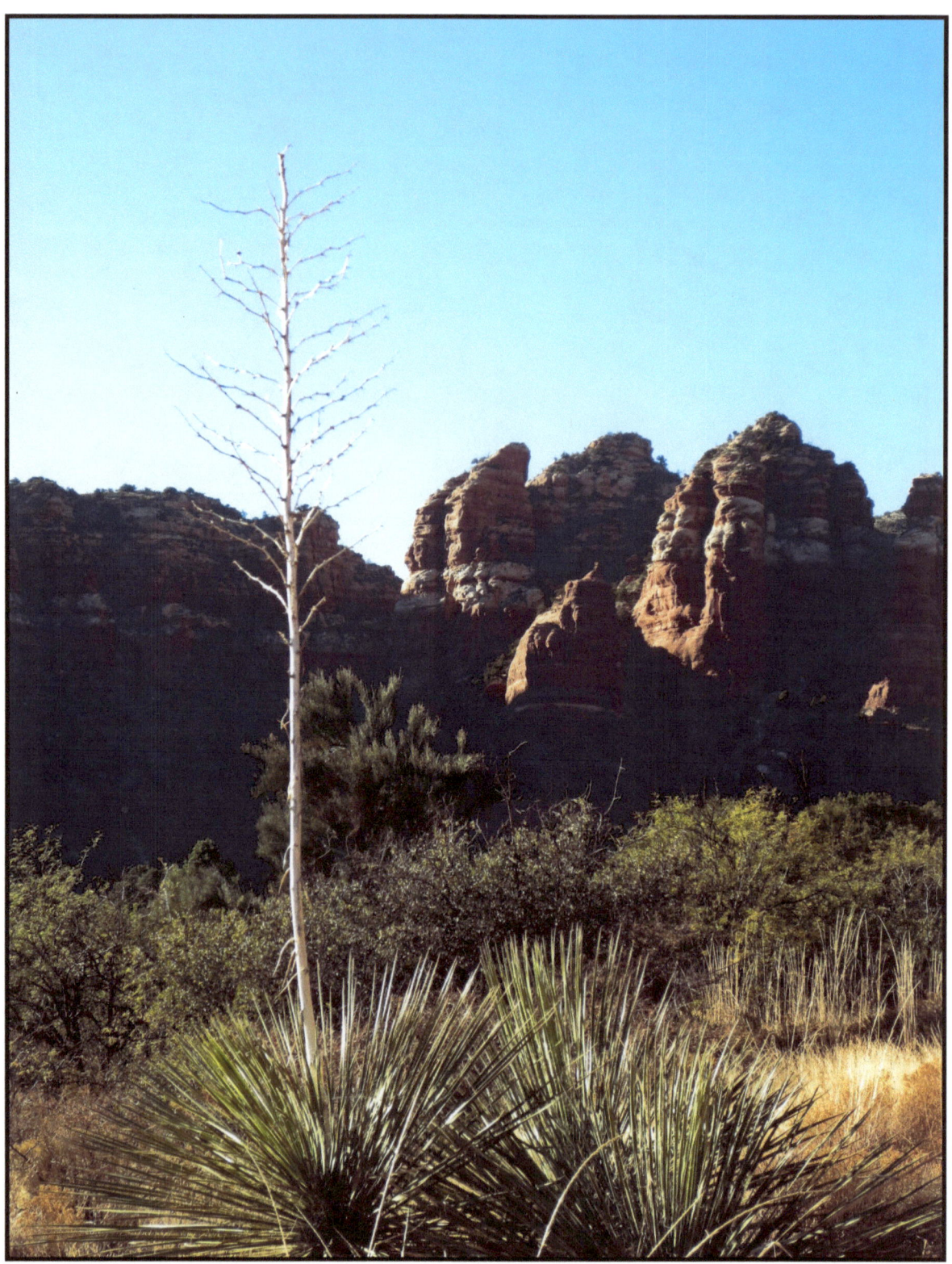

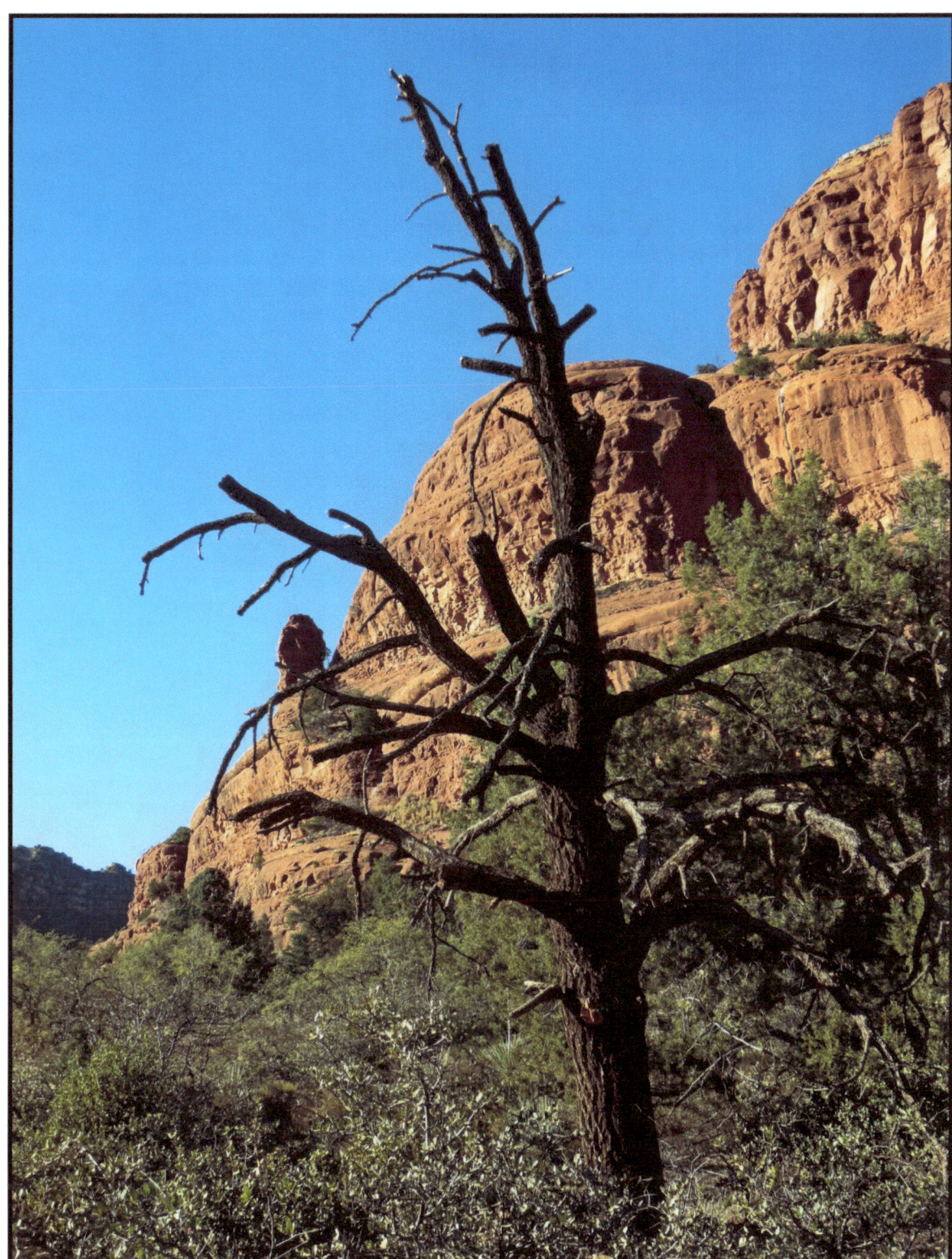

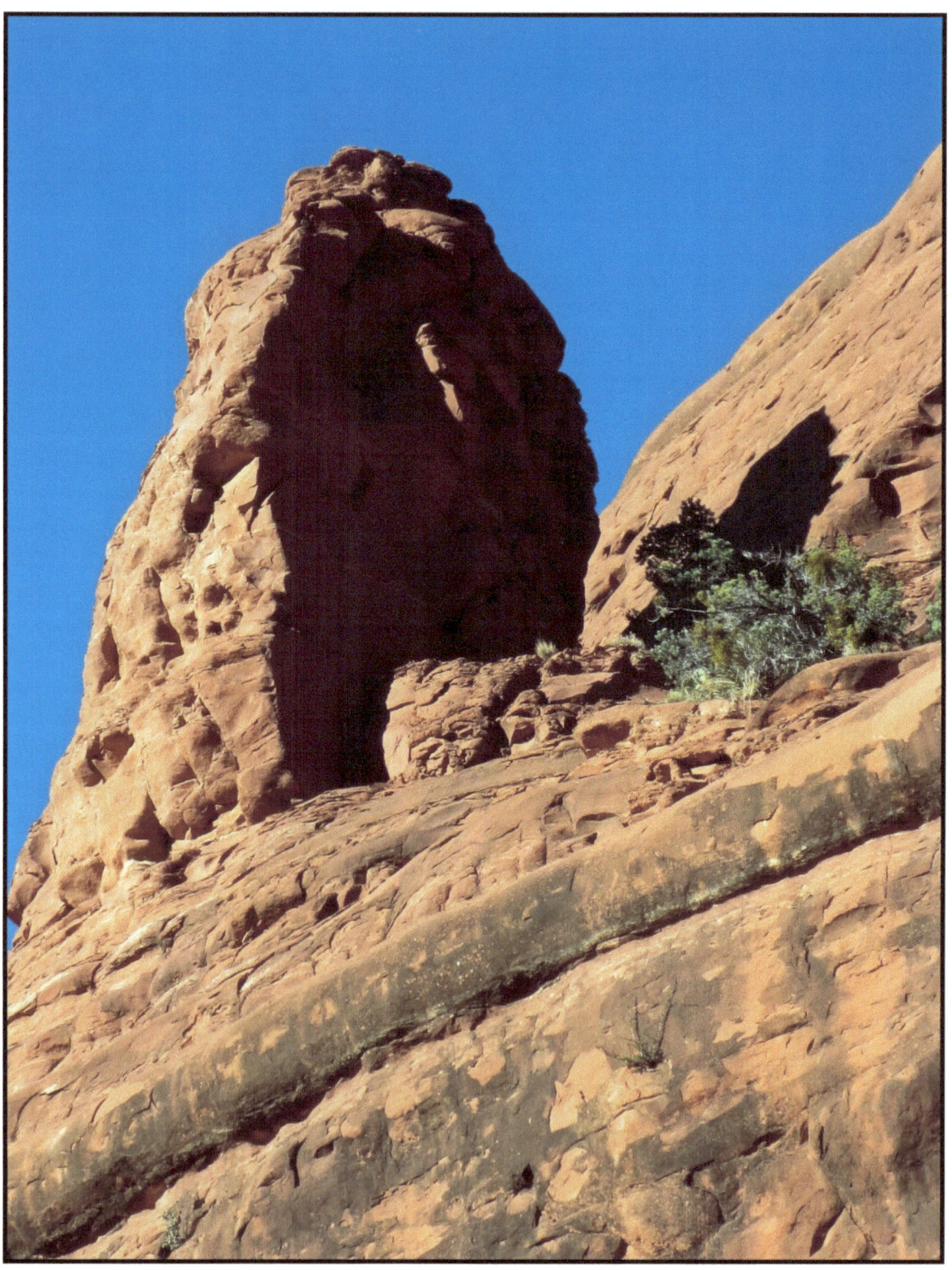

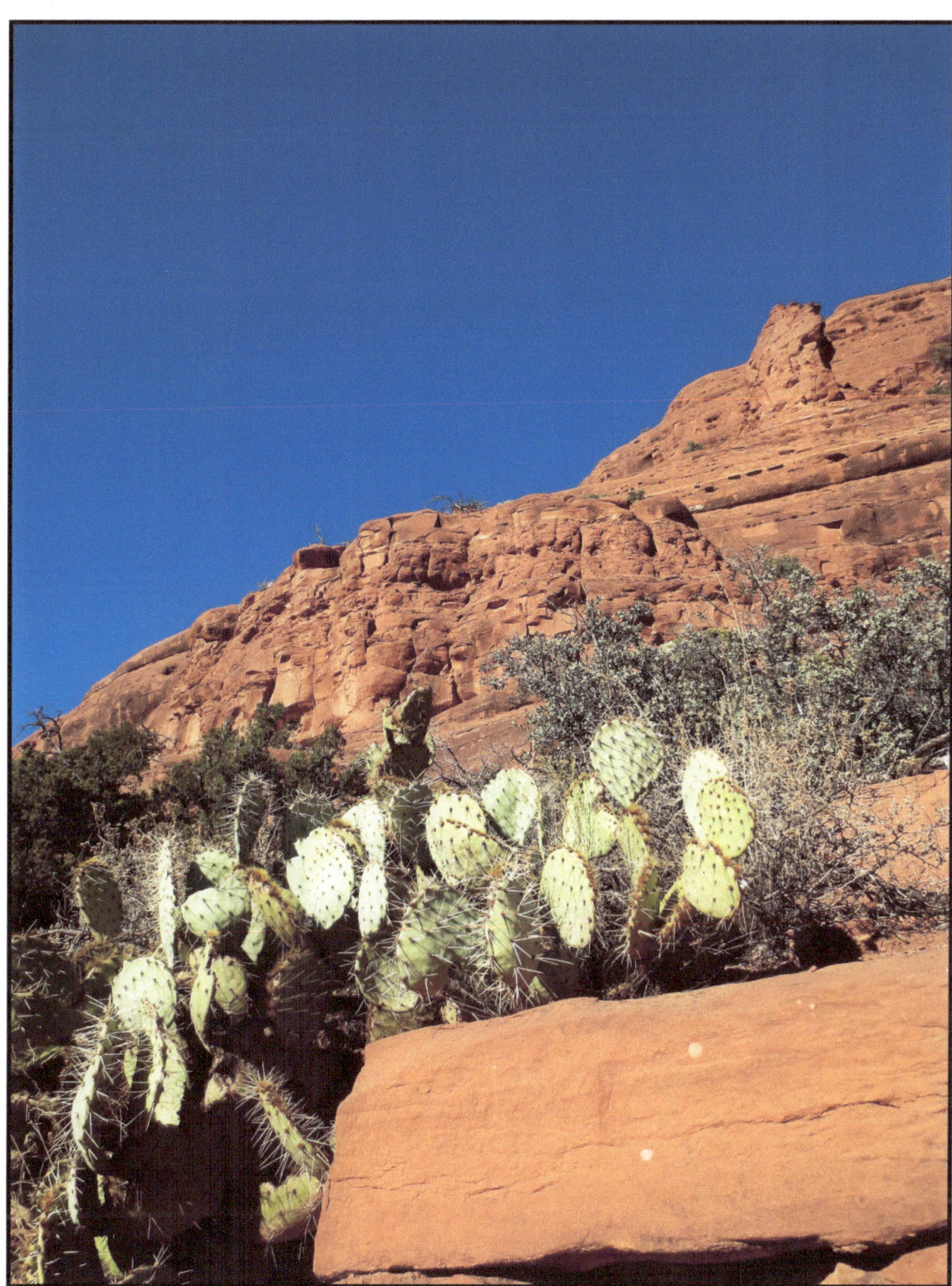

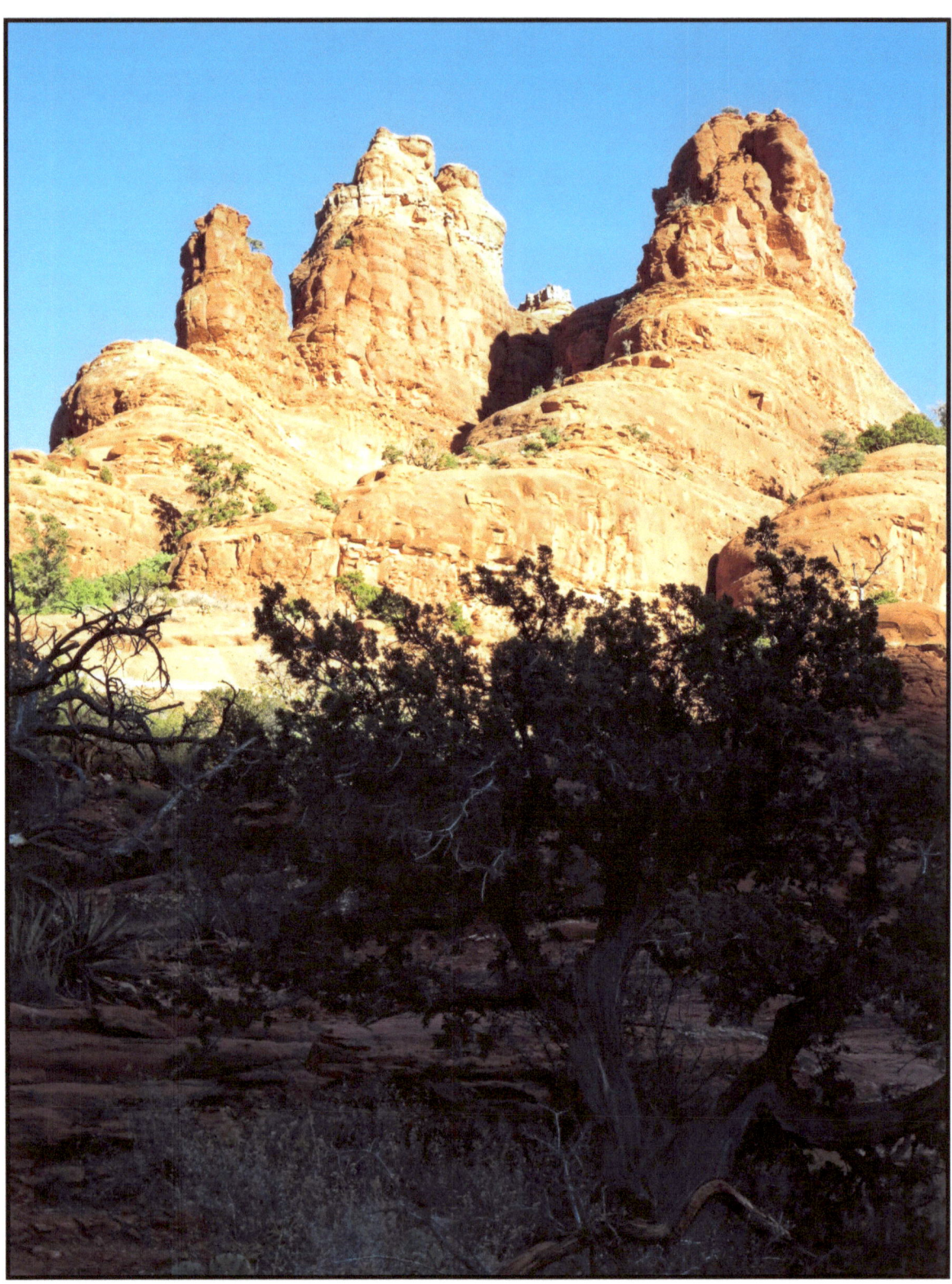

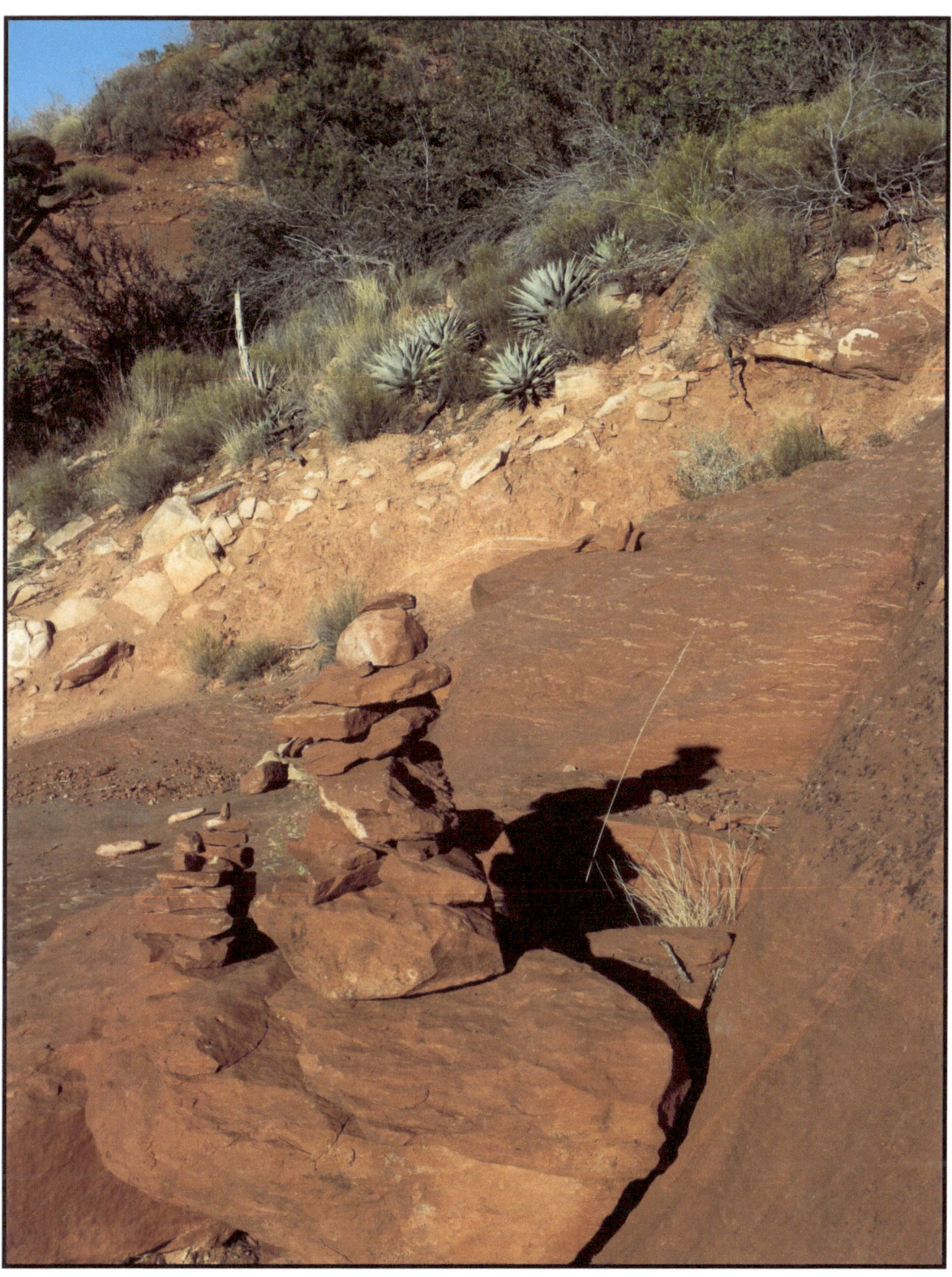

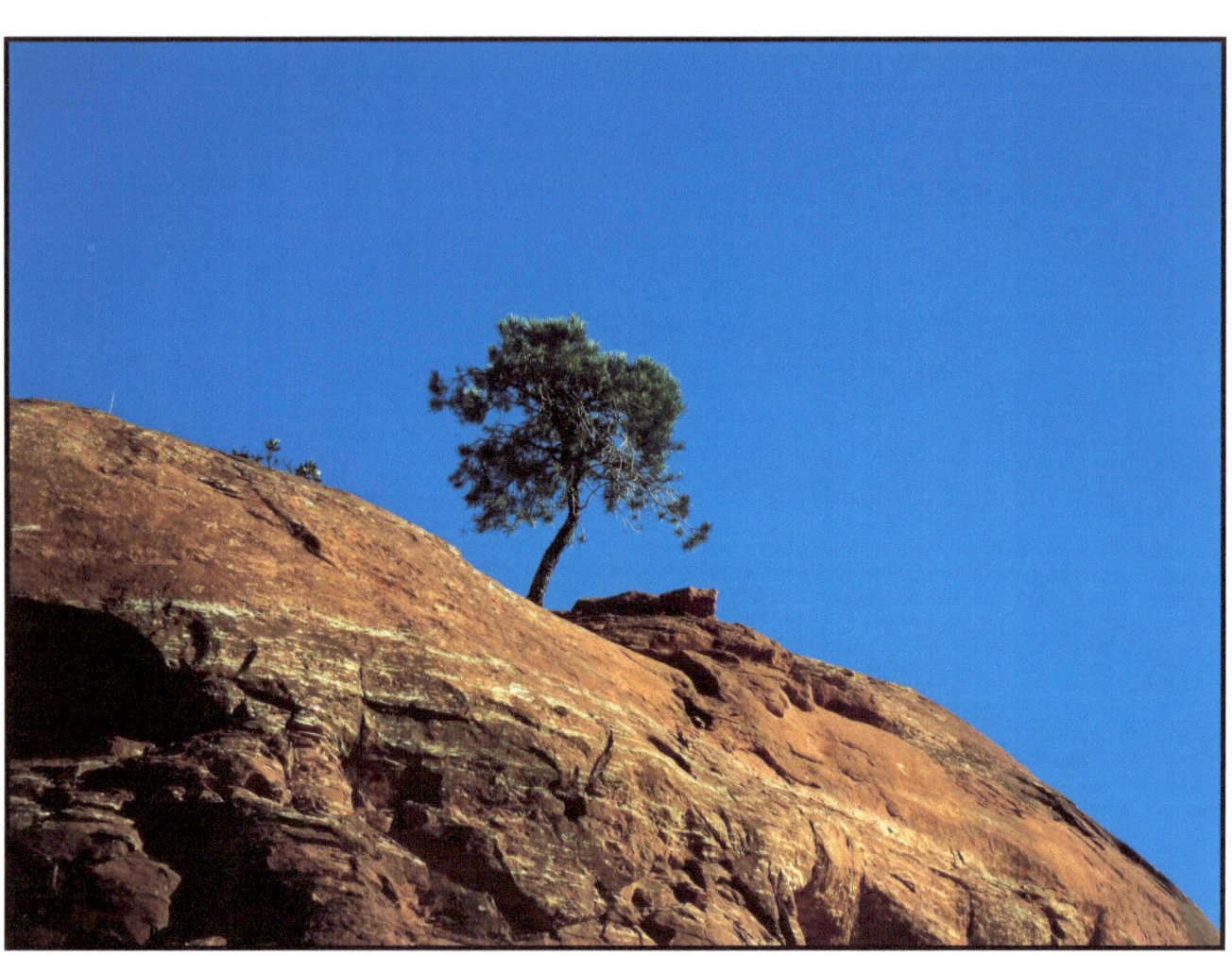

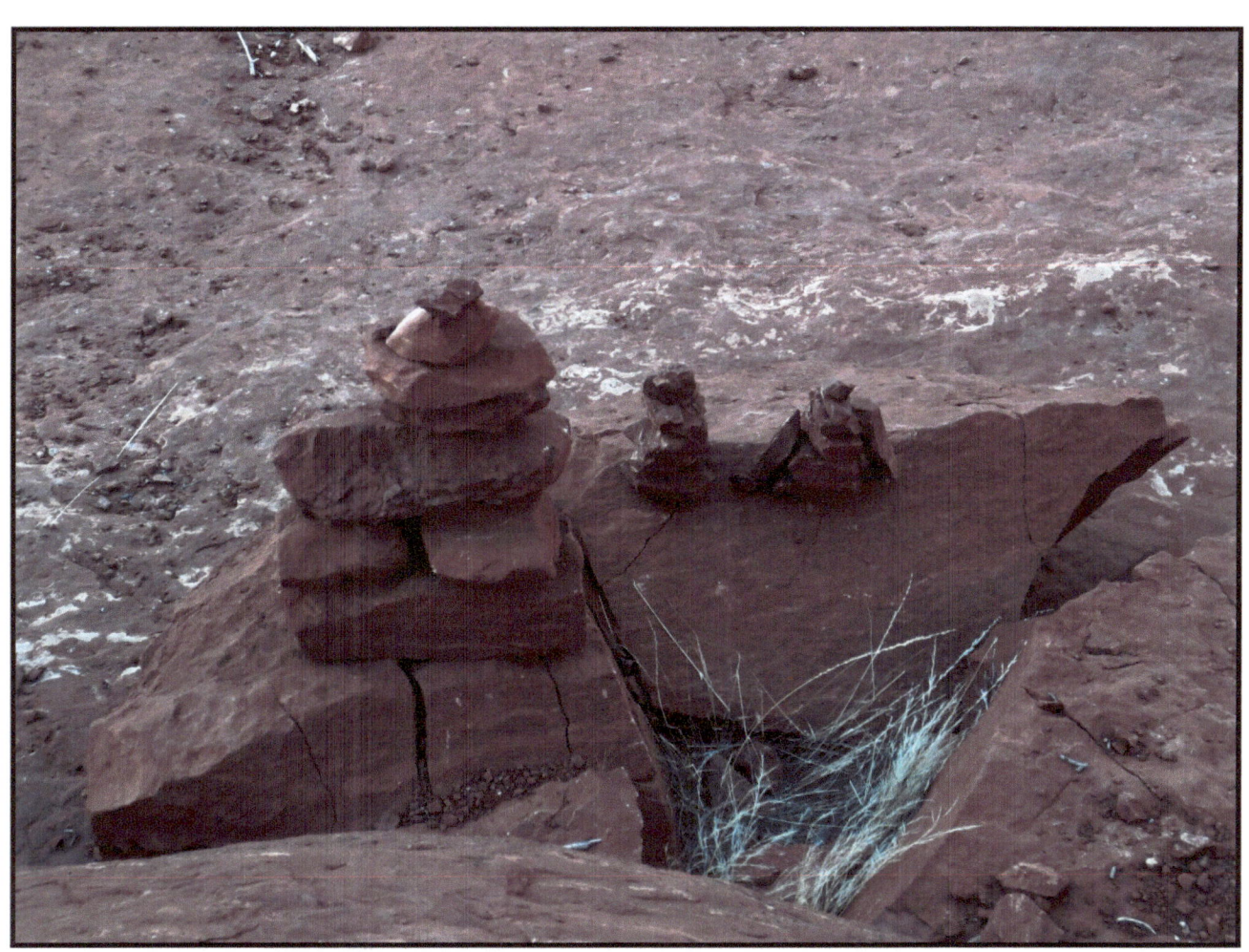

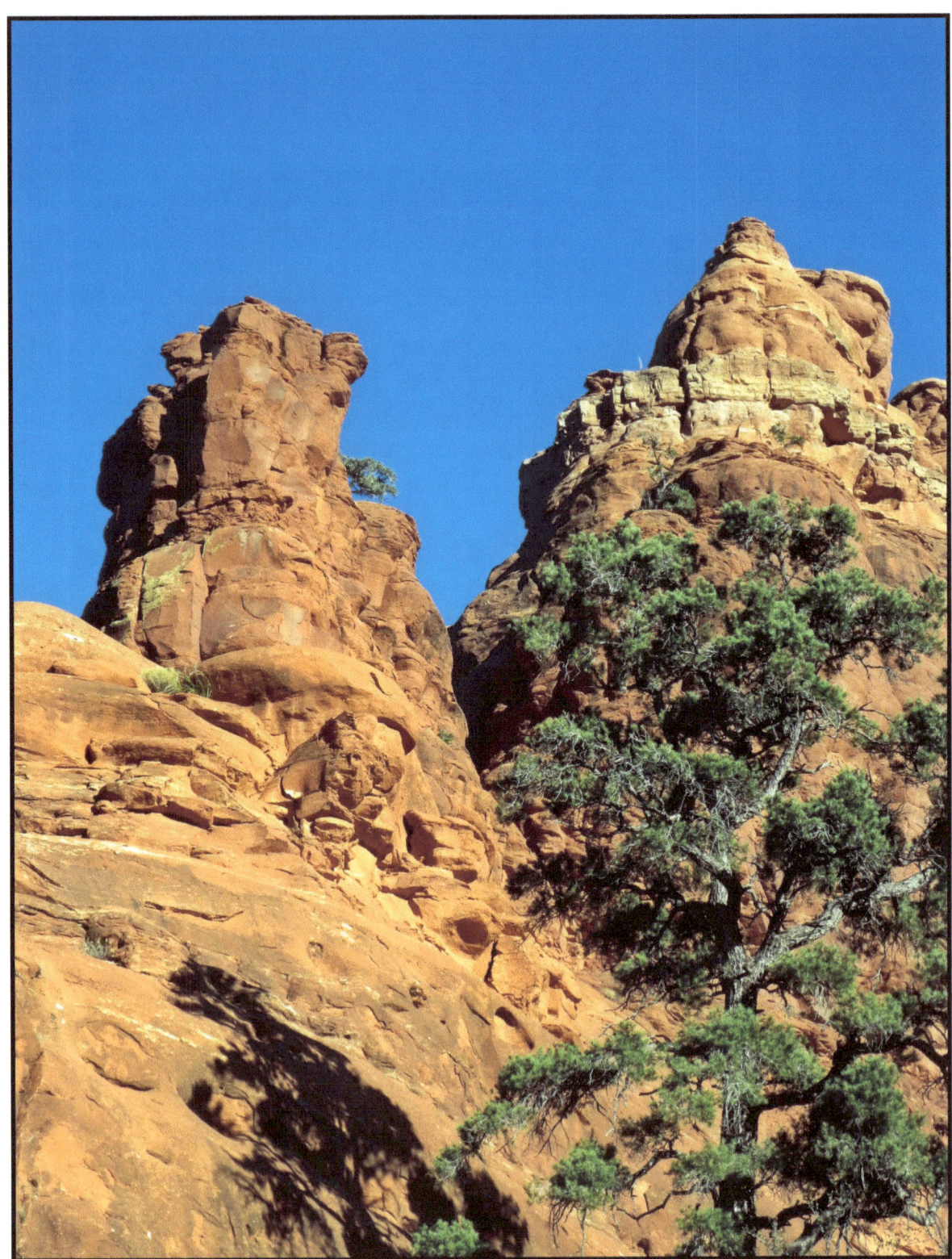

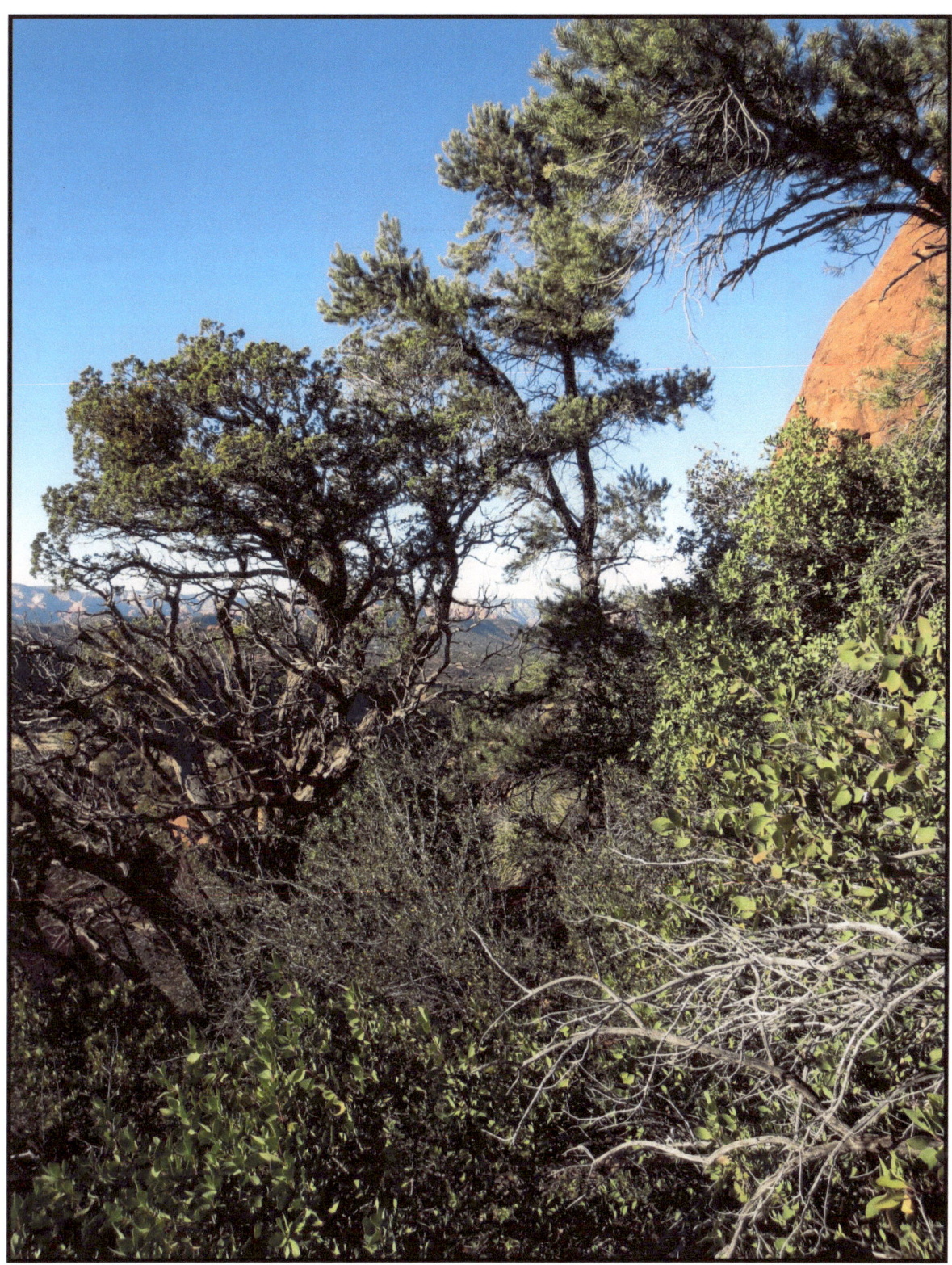

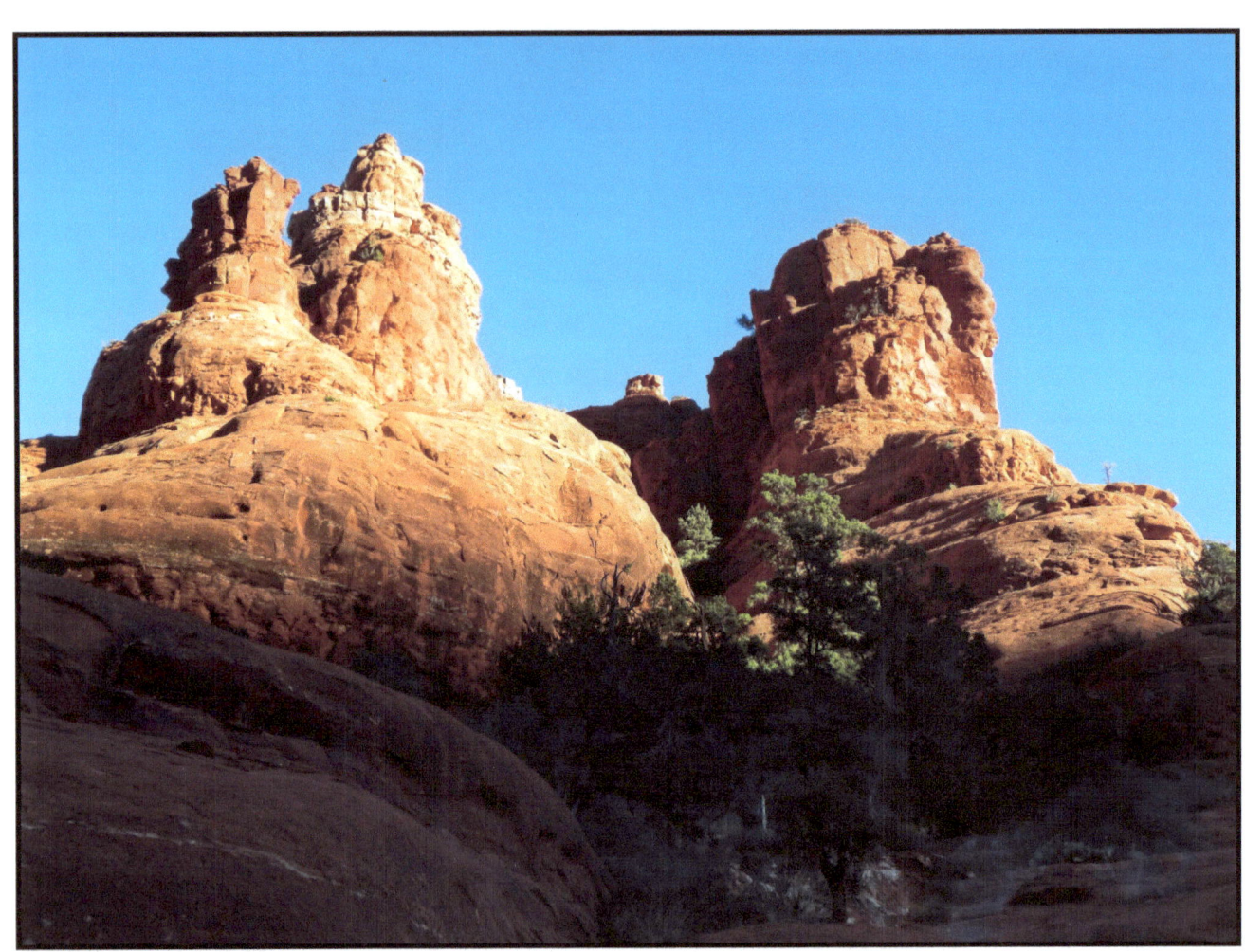

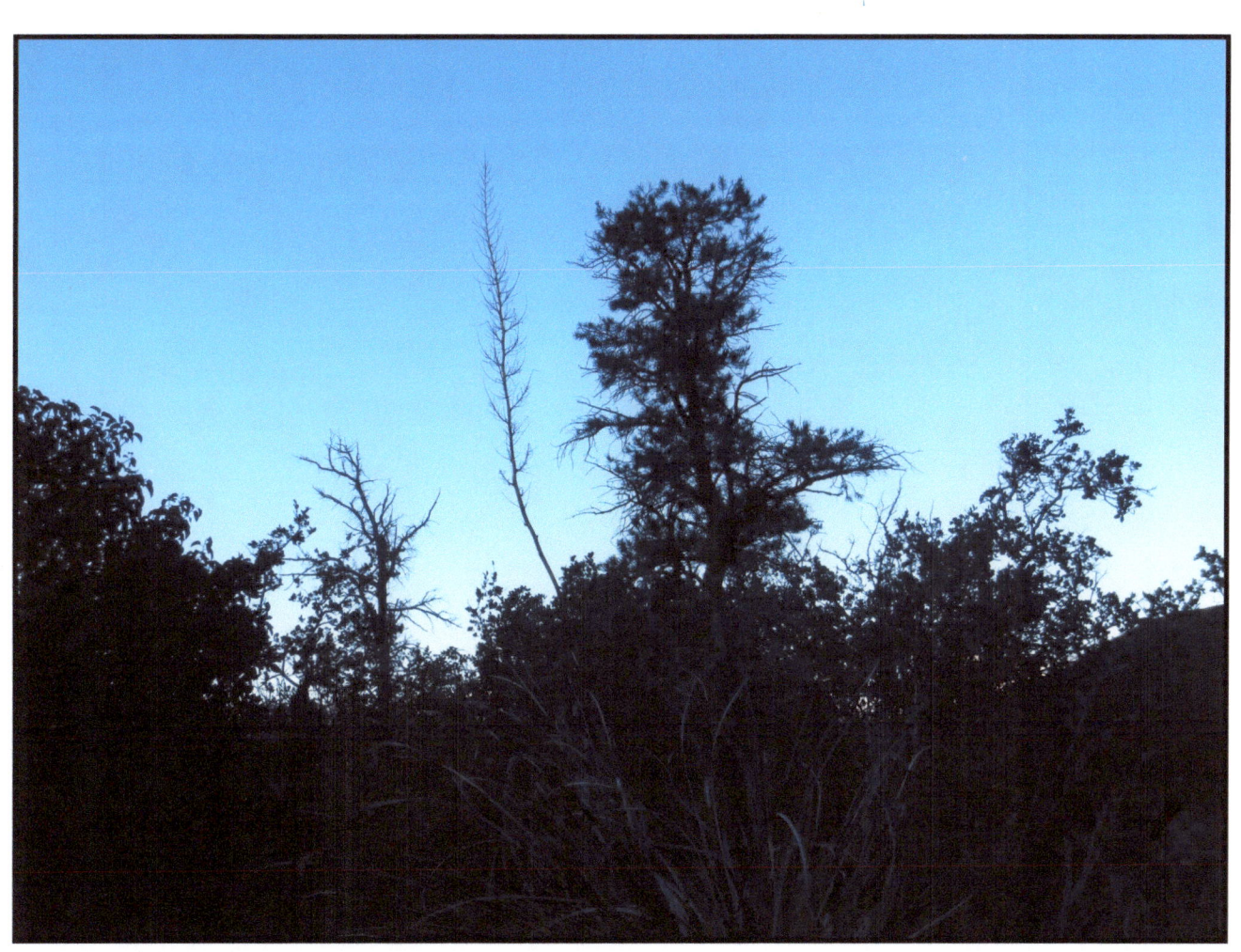

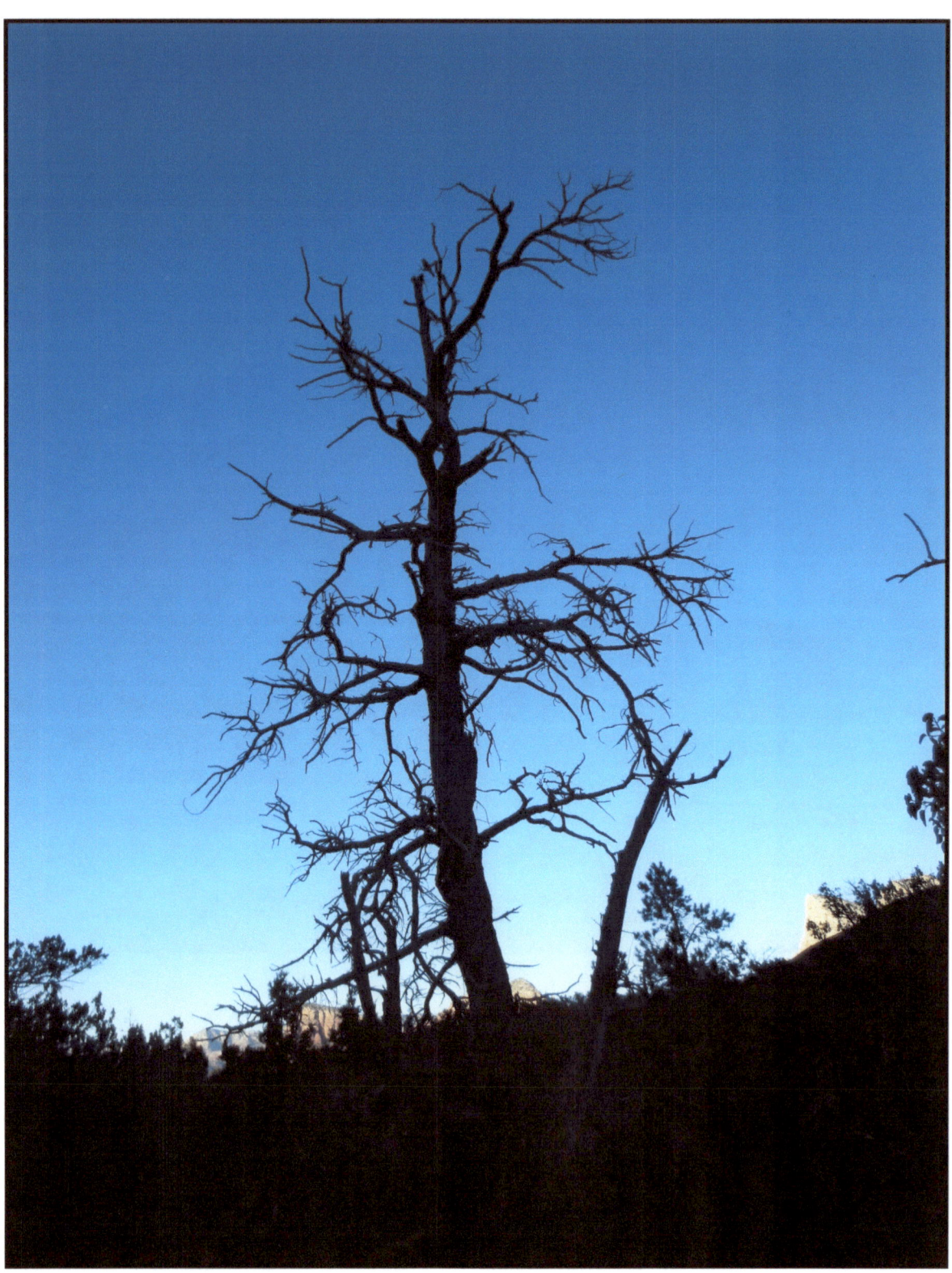

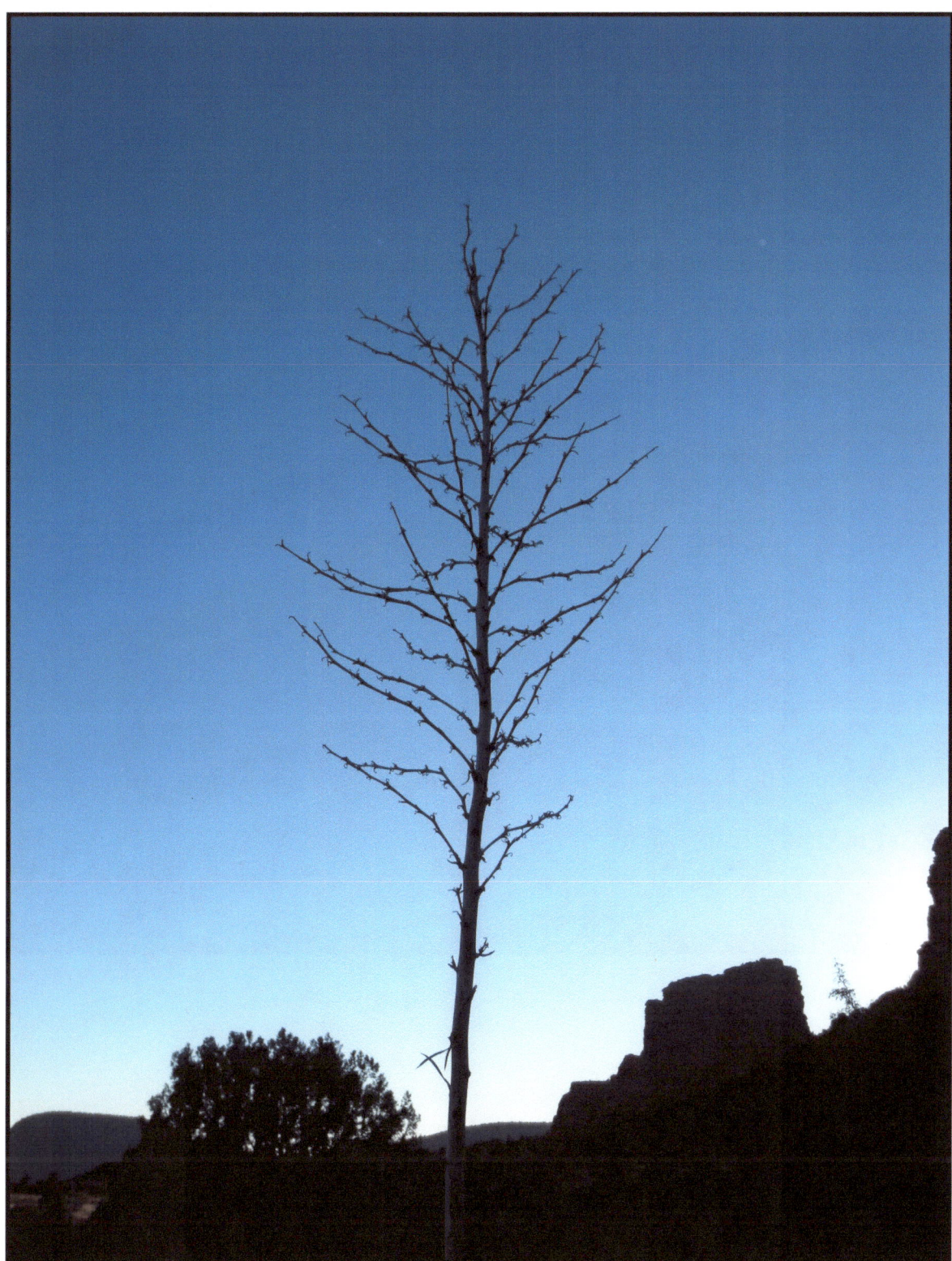

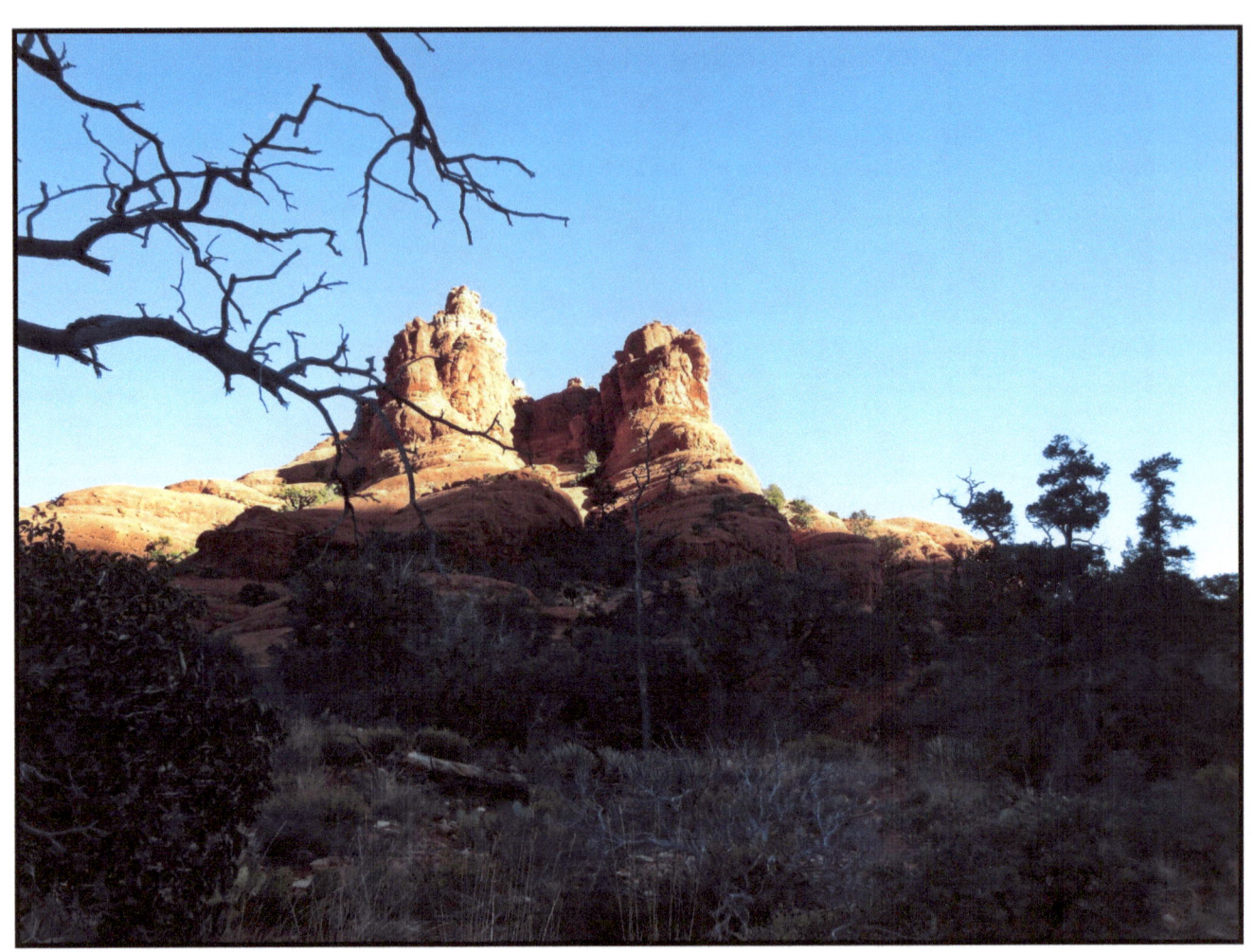

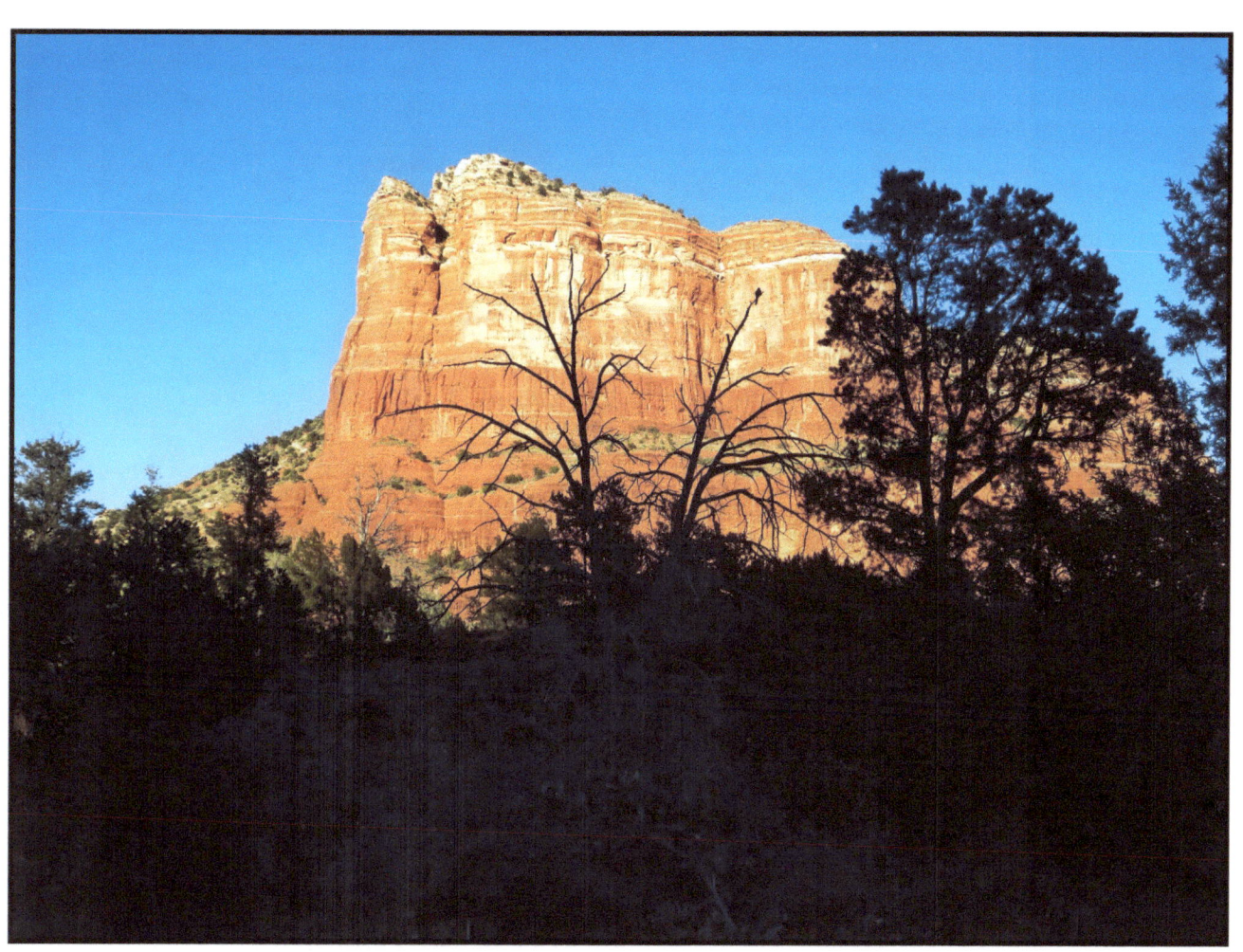

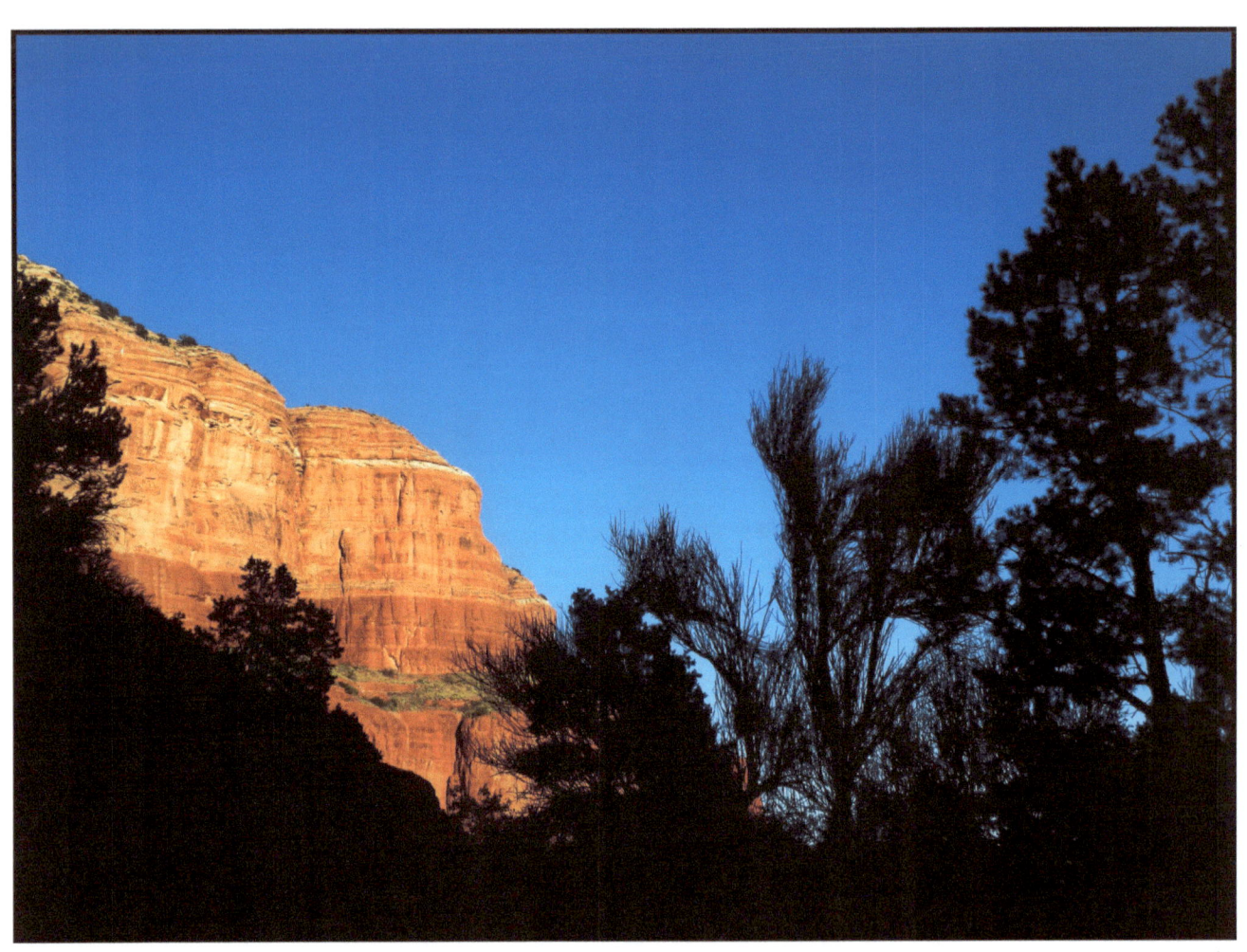

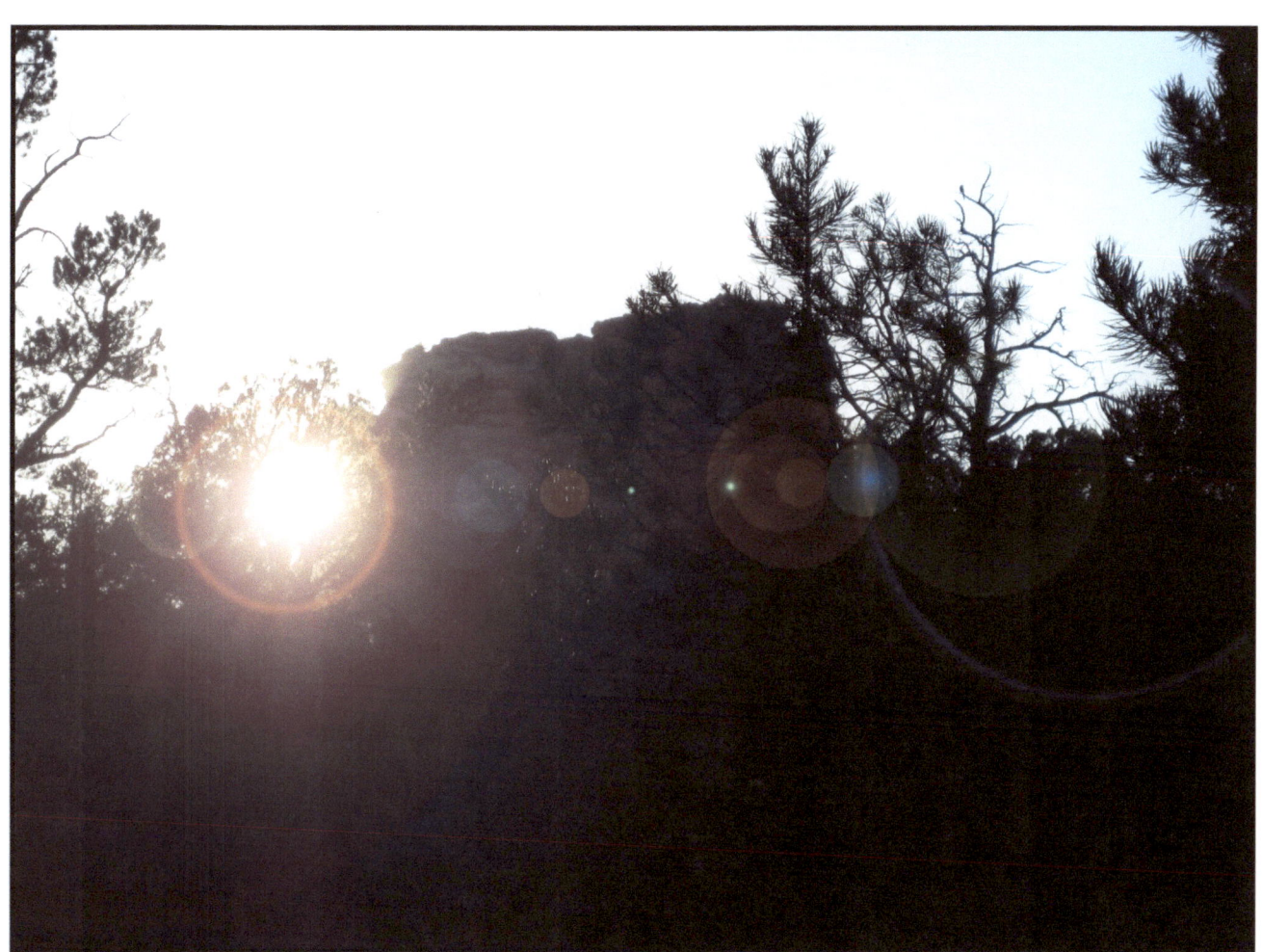

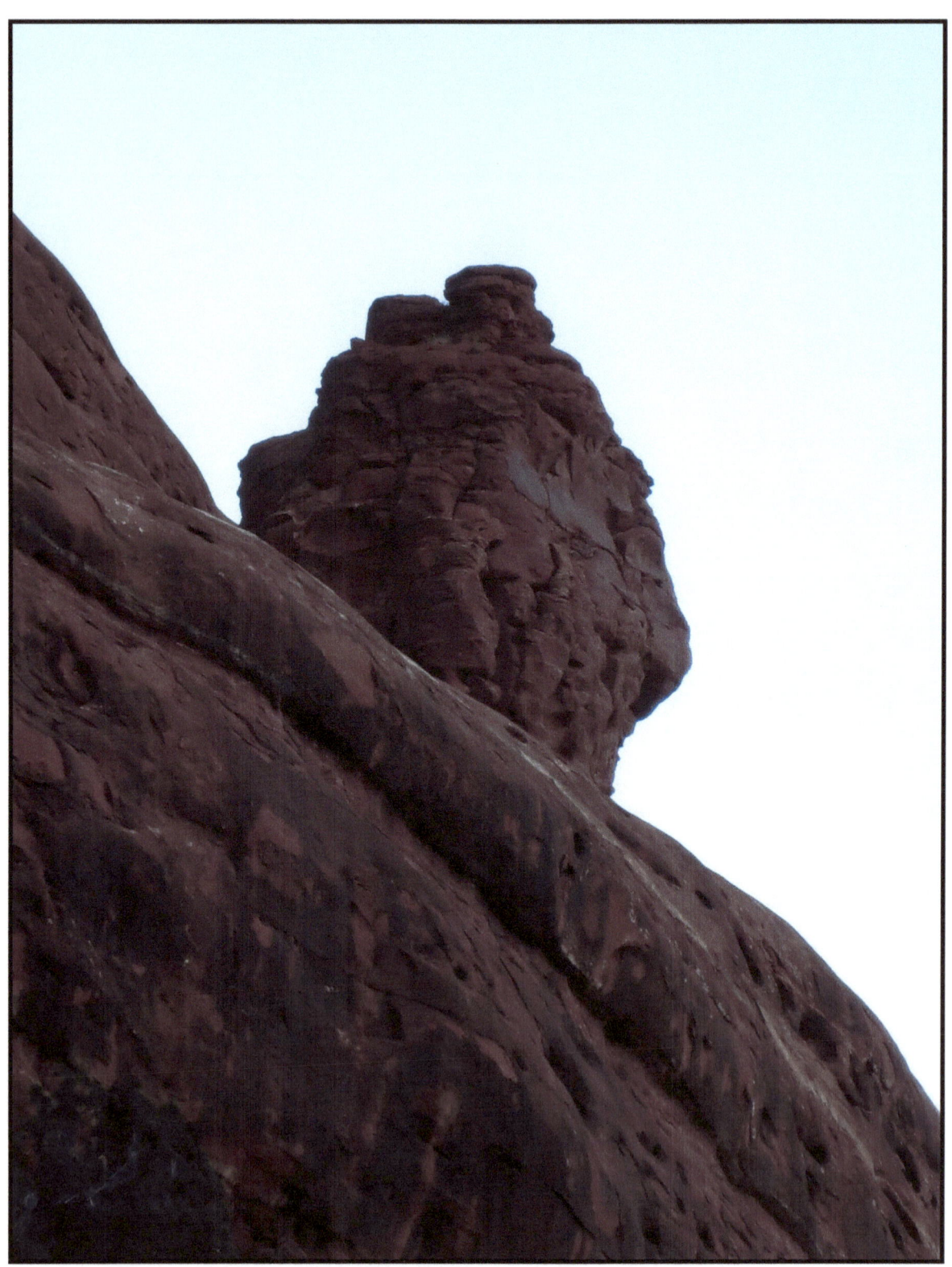

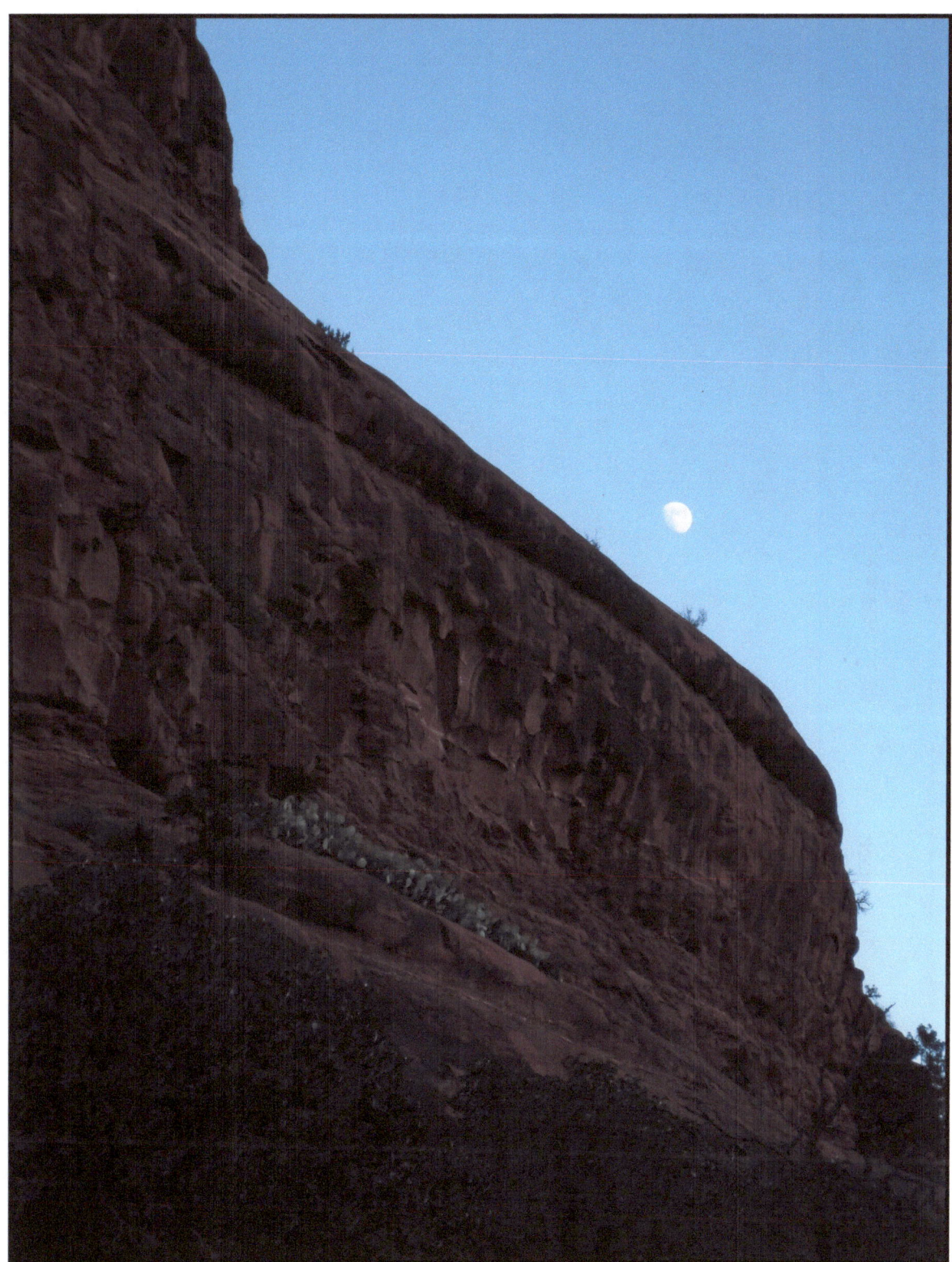

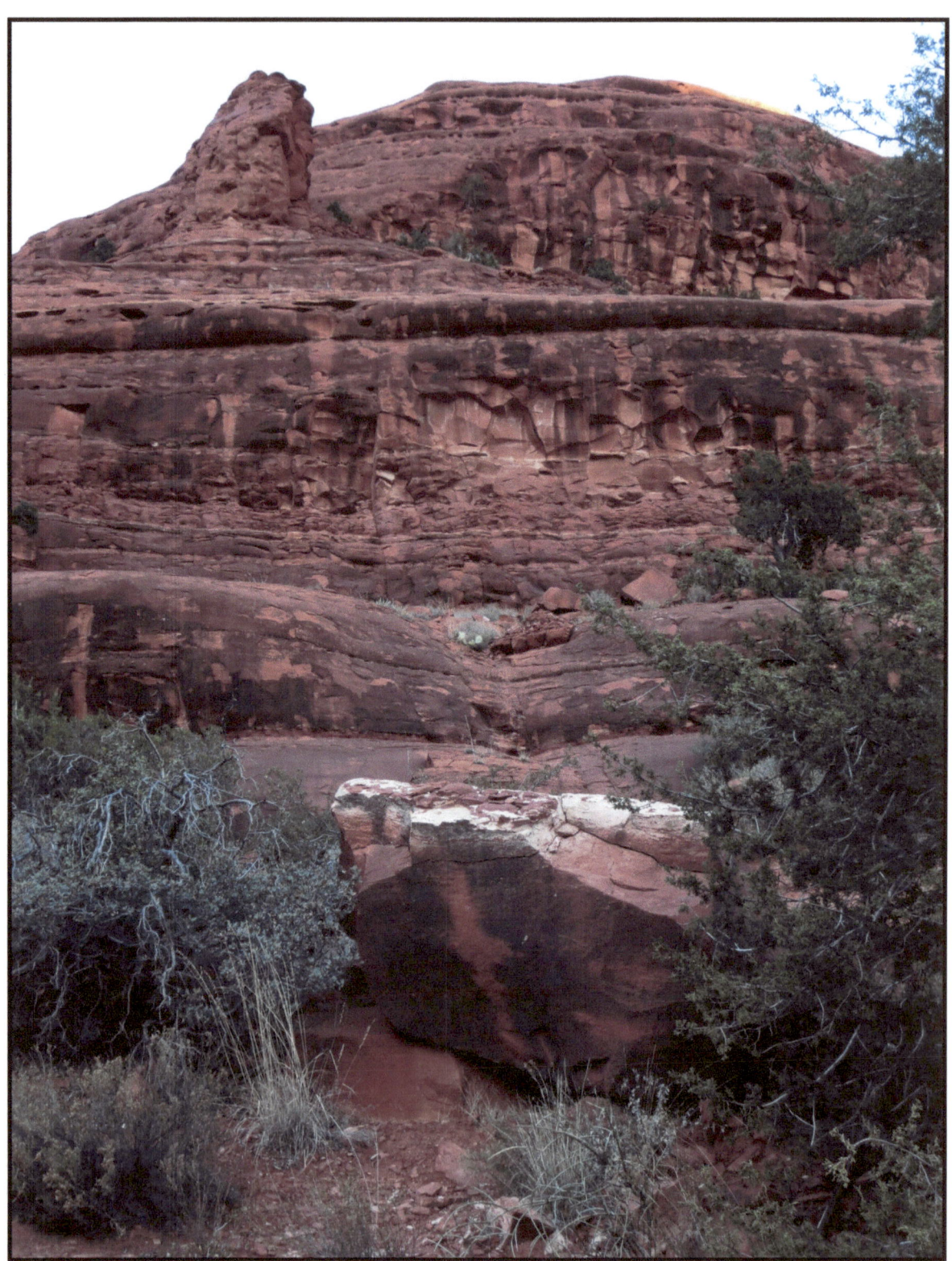

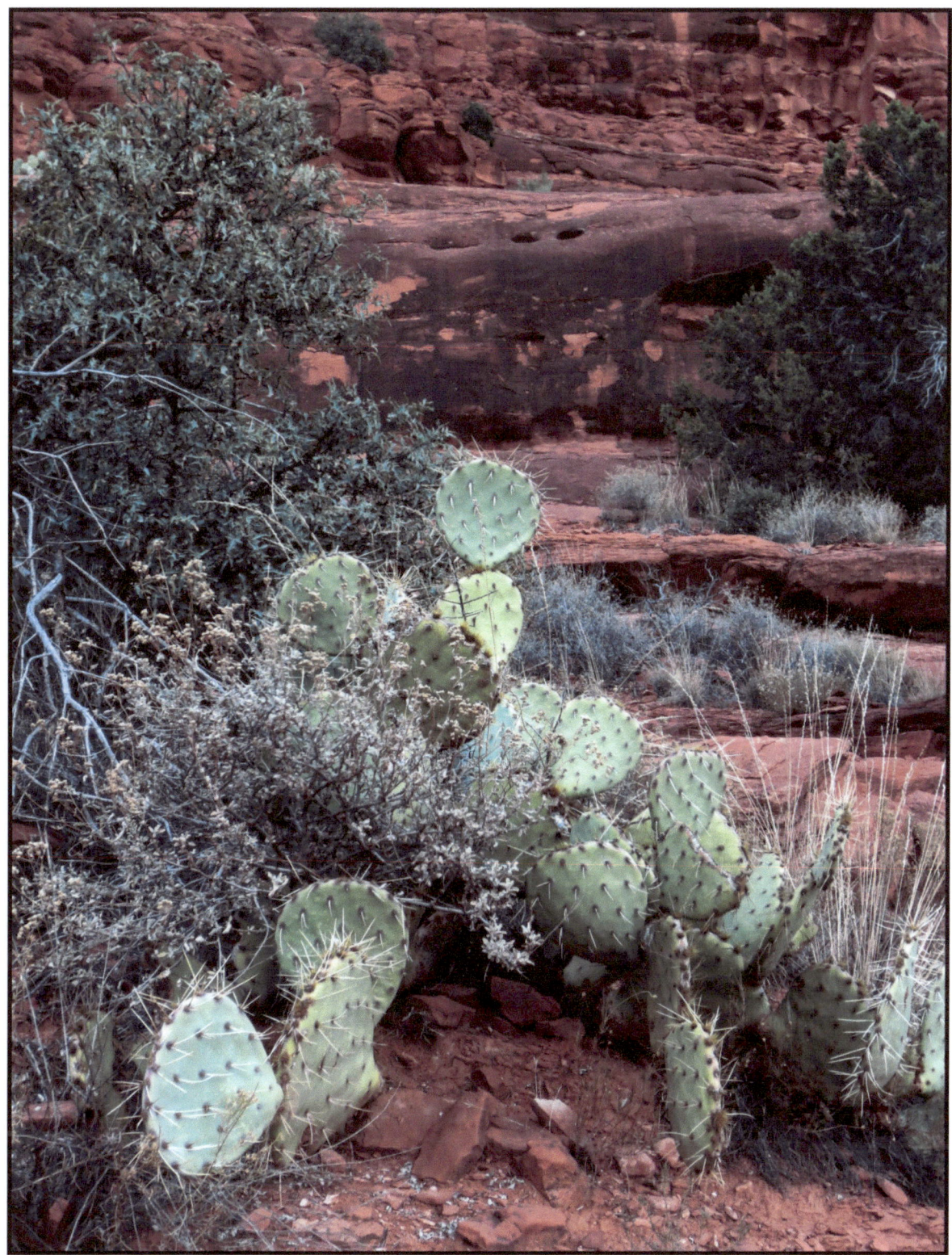

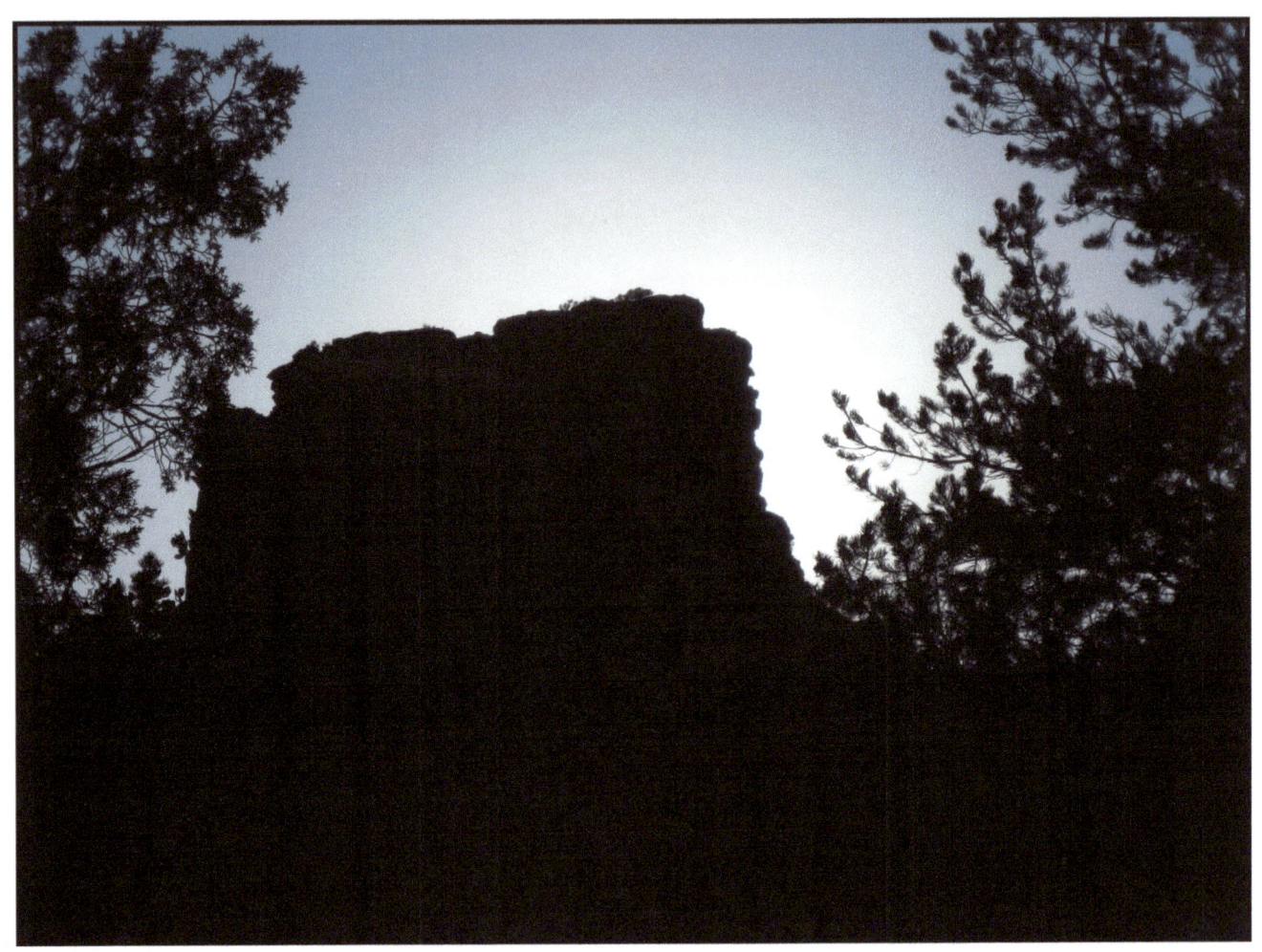

www.ingramcontent.com/pod-product-compliance
Lightning Source LLC
Chambersburg PA
CBHW051146220526
45473CB00003B/671